THE FATHERS OF THE WESTERN CHURCH

The FATHERS *of the* WESTERN CHURCH

by
ROBERT PAYNE

Dorset Press
New York

This edition published by Dorset Press,
a division of Marboro Books Corporation,
by arrangement with Sheila Lalwani Payne
1989 Dorset Press

ISBN 0-88029-403-5

Printed in the United States of America
M 9 8 7 6 5 4 3 2 1

For Dorothea
with love

❧ CONTENTS

I. ❧ INTRODUCTION

To our modern eyes the church fathers seem to belong to a time of darkness. Except for Augustine, who dazzles with his peculiar modernity, the Fathers remain shadowy and ghostly, unread and unsought, though the difficulties they faced were very similar to our own and they fought their battles against the barbarians with a courage we might envy. We forget Gregory's *Moralia*, which is still one of the most exciting commonplace books ever written, and the subtle discourses on the nature of love that Bernard wrote in old age. Though we read the *Confessions* and sometimes dip into *The City of God*, we forget the earlier Fathers, who were martyrs. Thomas Aquinas we know, for the Catholic Church reposes solidly on the dogmas he enunciated, but we forget that he could also write passionately and even wittily on subjects which concern even the least religious of us. There was Tertullian, who roared against the evils of the Empire, and Jerome who described Roman women with a tart cunning that suggests Balzac describing the women of Paris.

We forget that there were great philosophers, great psychologists, even great poets among the Church Fathers, and that they sometimes understood better than we do the complexities of the human soul. We forget they are a part, perhaps the greater part, of all that we mean by Western civilization, for they laid the foundations. They were the mediators between the Renaissance and the civilizations of Greece and Rome, and they were perfectly conscious of their high role in history as they called upon people to live dangerously. They kept the flame burning; and if sometimes it seems to die out in their shielding hands, how eagerly they blow upon it, with what delight they greet its awakening and with what an uproar of praise they greet the upright flame. The Church Fathers were very human, and they adored the warmth of the flame which had traveled so far and through so many hands until it reached their own hearths.

As we see them now, through dark mists, they are larger than life, superbly assured of themselves as they thunder against the barbarians or set in order the conflicting loves of men. These patriarchs who thought nothing of writing a hundred books in the intervals of violent action belong to a race that has apparently passed: there were giants in those days. The greatest of them lived at a time of utter despair, when the Roman Empire was crumbling and there seemed no hope at all that civilization would survive the nihilism of the barbarians who slaughtered as they pleased for no discernible reason except the lust for conquest. The conquests of the Church Fathers were, however, more permanent. They conquered men's minds with their comprehension of God and with their knowledge of men, their faith in God and their faith in man. In those days men ranked higher than the angels, and through all the works of the Fathers there breathes a singular respect for the divinity within man. As we see the Fathers in the Italian paintings of the Renaissance, we see their dignity, their immeasurable wisdom, their solemnity even, but their stature is absent. Against a Tuscan sunset Jerome with his lion or Francis amid his circling larks looks almost human, almost ordinary. El Greco painted them better, with the smoke and the mist and the air quivering from the lightning-stroke, in darkness and battering thunder. In such a landscape, they looked what they were, heroes who drew strength from danger.

This was the spirit of the men who laid the foundations

for modern Europe at a time of fear and trembling—Augustine waiting tranquilly for death to come to him while the Vandals were hammering at the gates; Ambrose making the Emperor do penance for murder; Gregory shoring up the ruins of the Empire with his immense spiritual prestige; Bernard announcing the laws of love and leading a Crusade; Thomas examining the implications of God's law in the mind's farthest reaches; they were men of authority and goodness, and our own age has none comparable with these.

They were also hard men who would have agreed with Nietzsche's motto: "Be hard! Be stern! Be unyielding!" There were reasons for their hardness. Like the early anchorites they were athletes of God, *athletae dei*, tough muscled, without an ounce of fat on them. They fought to win. They had no desire to contain the devil or the enemy on their frontiers: the devil must be fought back and hurled into the pit. They were racing against time, even though they believed themselves citizens of eternity. They knew the barbarians were sweeping down from the forests of the North or massing in the deserts of the East: so they trained themselves with the discipline of love to destroy their enemies. The paradox lay there. They were hard because they demanded the utmost glory and the utmost tenderness of the people, and were not content with either the lesser glory or the lesser tenderness: so they imposed upon themselves and on others a rigorous discipline. There were psychological reasons why this was necessary. As William James observed, there is a hardness of the mind as well as of the fist, and to this hardness we owe the advances we have made from the brutes—even the long, tortured advance toward kindness, charity, tolerance, tenderness, and common decency. Consequently they acquired a way of thinking, a way of facing impenetrable mysteries, a posture which was truly heroic, until heroism became as natural as the air they breathed. Not only Francis walked casually across the battlelines and bearded the Sultan in his den.

It is strange that they are so often neglected. Like Will Durant, who managed somehow to write a popular history of philosophy without mentioning the Church Fathers, we tend to relegate them to the small corner where we relegate the obscure saints. It seems a pity. They lived in the Dark Ages, which were not dark but were in places brilliantly and dazzlingly bright, and though the thunderclouds played over them, they can be discerned easily enough in the lightning. We can hear their authentic voices, and until recently the very periods of St. Jerome, the way he breathed and spoke, were known to everyone who could read, for his voice re-echoes in the King James version of the Bible. We recognize the full-throated voice of Augustine, but the sweeter voice of Bernard is too often forgotten.

Rooted in ancient traditions, fearless, with penetrating minds, the Church Fathers discussed matters that are still of momentous importance to our lives, and they lived at a time of upheaval comparable to our own. Chiefly they sought for the assurance of man's dignity on earth and the processes of salvation. They were oppressed by the thought of the world's end. They knew what was at stake; with the strength of their passionate nerves, they fought against fatalism and to this end introduced a ritual and a way of life that enabled people to live with dignity, calm, and a gallant spirit amidst horror. They delighted in the operations of their minds and in what Kierkegaard calls "the movements of faith"; but they also delighted in the operations of the human animal, the presumptuous creature who had set himself up as the contender against God, and if sometimes they quarreled with extraordinary bitterness concerning whether God was one hypostasis or three, or even argued on the subject of how many angels could stand on the tip of a needle, these were problems that possessed a deep significance to them, and the appearance and nature of the angels was as worthy of discussion as the appearance and nature of God. It was not absurd to ask how many angels could stand on the tip of a needle; it was merely a way of reducing the whole problem of the angelic hosts to human dimensions. Could the angels enter the interstices of the soul? Could the beating of their wings be felt? Of what color were they? some of the Fathers asked. In the end they discovered, as they might have suspected, that angels were as various as men, possessing different powers and accumulating different virtues and protecting men from different sins and accomplishing different destinies in heaven. Then they asked concerning the nature and appearance of heaven, and they believed that heaven lay behind a curving sheet of blue crystals in the sky, and behind this crystalline heaven lay wheeling suns, choirs of angels, trumpeters, jeweled pathways, God seated on his throne amidst dominions and powers. Until a little while ago it was conveniently said against them that belief in a solid blue rim of crystals was absurd and against the evidence. We grow more humble as we grow older. Recently we have discovered that at a height of 50,000 feet there are sheets of ice crystals where none had been expected.[1] This is a small matter, but it should teach that there are dangers in believing our wisdom is altogether greater than the wisdom of the Dark Ages.

In his *Treatise on the Gods*, Mencken says of the Christians: "It is their fate to live absurdly, flogged by categorical imperatives of their own shallow imaginings, and to die insanely, grasping for hands that are not there." To this charge the Church Fathers, following Tertullian, would have answered that they believed in God because it was absurd to believe in God, it was beyond any conceivable gift, even beyond any plausibility, and yet it was true. As for the categorical im-

[1]An Associated Press report published in the *Christian Science Monitor*, January 18, 1950, mentions the discovery by the department of meteorology of the University of Chicago of "an obstacle to flying, ten miles up, which looks like a polar icecap but is merely layers of air filled with little ice crystals. They reflect light enough to dazzle the eyes and are due to moisture, though there is no explanation how the moisture came to be there. These layers lie at the base of the stratosphere, sometimes just below and sometimes a few hundred feet inside. Airmen have attempted to land on them."

peratives there were only two, and to these they held fast: to worship God, and to love one's neighbor as oneself. As for the "shallow imaginings," they would have said nothing, leaving their work as witness of the immense depths they had explored, and the immense heights. As for "dying insanely," they would answer that it was demonstrably untrue. In love with Christ, they died magnificently and quietly, even when they were tortured.

In the deepest sense, the Church Fathers were concerned to introduce a world of order where there was only chaotic disorder before. They were the mathematicians and surveyors of the landscape of holiness, and their weapons consisted of the sayings of Jesus, the creeds, and the strange surrealist use which they made of symbols. They possessed one weapon that is denied to us, a language more flexible and sonorous than our own. English words can only approximate the majestic simplicity of the creed: *Credo in unum Deum, Patrem omnipotentem, factorem coeli et terrae, visibilium omnium et invisibilium* . . . "I believe in one God, the Father Almighty, maker of Heaven and earth and of all things visible and invisible. And in one Lord Jesus Christ, the only begotten Son of God, and born of the Father before all ages; God of God, Light of Light, true God of true God. Begotten, not made; being of one substance with the Father, by whom all things are made. Who for us men and for our salvation came down from Heaven. And was incarnate of the Holy Ghost and of the Virgin Mary and was made man, was crucified also for us under Pontius Pilate, suffered and was buried and the third day He rose again according to the Scriptures and ascended into Heaven, sitteth at the right hand of the Father and shall come again with glory to judge the living and the dead of whose kingdom there shall be no end. And I believe in the Holy Ghost, the Lord and Giver of Life, who proceedeth from the Father and the Son, who together with the Father and the Son is to be adored and glorified, who spake by the prophets. And in one holy, catholic and apostolic church.

I confess one baptism and the remission of sins. And I look for the resurrection of the dead and the life of the world to come. Amen."

The bells ring; the congregation chants the words in great triumphant rolling waves of sound; and it is as though the earth herself were praising the glory of God, so heavy, so deep-rooted, and so august are the voices. Roman *gravitas* and Greek *sophrosyne*, the quality of holding to the impassioned middle way, are curiously mingled together in this creed which is at once hymn, psalm, and threnody, and the same qualities are to be found among the Church Fathers who orchestrate the music of Jerusalem. It is important to observe that when we are among the Fathers we are no longer in the innocent landscape of Syria. To the simple sayings of Christ there is added a new dimension: the whole of Mediterranean civilization is pressed into the service of the Fathers, and the words of Christ are heard not as they were spoken in Galilee or Jerusalem, quietly, but against the massed choirs of the Church. By the third century Christianity was no longer a song: it had become a symphony. And the symphony was very largely written by the Church Fathers.

There were also weapons of interpretation. They commented at length upon the Bible, seeing the whole of the Old Testament as no more than a prologue to the Gospels, Solomon announcing the presence of Christ in the Song of Songs as assuredly as Isaiah announced Christ in his prophecies. Inevitably, the text was sometimes tortured to make the resemblance felt; inevitably too the sudden confrontation between the past and the present led to extraordinary contrasts, strange beauties of phrasing, such as happen always when ancient texts are embodied in a new language, and since the Fathers allowed themselves infinite possibilities of interpretation, there was no end to the inferences that could be drawn.

In this the Church Fathers were the precursors of surrealism. The great fish of Jonah could become anything they pleased. It could become a pearl, a jewel, the Church, hell, even the beating of the angels' wings; it could become a symbol of ordinary life or a symbol of life eternal. The Garden of Eden became the Garden of Gethsemane or the Garden of Golgotha, though more often it became the Garden of Revelations, where there flowed the waters of eternity. Christ was prefigured in Adam, in Abraham, in Benjamin, in Moses, in all the Kings of Israel and all the Prophets: with the result that he came to acquire an extraordinary depth of meaning, as though all history was contained in him, and at the same time he existed beyond history, beyond legend, and beyond story, since all history, all legends, and all stories came at last to him. The Shulamite became the Church, with Christ garbed like Solomon as her perpetual lover.

What is astonishing is how easily, with what surefootedness the medieval mind walked in this tangled landscape. A burning faith encompassed all difficulties of interpretation, and in the end, of course, they found simple reasons for the simple mystery. "All things have the shape of Christ," said St. Bernard, and so he urged that all that was necessary was to repeat the sacred name: then all things would show themselves.

We tend to believe that the life of medieval man was hard and brutish. It is doubtful whether it was as hard and brutish as the life of our own time. His faith was real: he knew he could move mountains: and the Church, which ruled his inmost faith, consecrated his family, prohibited him from usury, set aside by inviolable law weeks when no man could lift his voice or his knife against another, and saw that no man starved. In the dark plague-ridden cities light came blazing from the soul of man, and by this light men saw themselves among the elect, for every man by virtue of God's grace contained within himself a part of the living God. Today science is power. In medieval times power came from God and the simple offering of the bread and the wine.

If the test of a civilization lies in its arts, then medieval civilization remains among the greatest there have ever been, comparable with that of the T'ang Dynasty in China or with Periclean Athens. The carvings, the stained glass windows, the bookmaking, the architecture, the hymns, even the tapestries were informed with divinity. Belief in Christ made them artists. Almost they had no need to draw or paint or write. As Brancusi has pointed out, all that they ever needed to do was to draw an outline round the things they saw in their daily visions. So the Cathedral of Chartres arose quite simply as a church where the Virgin might be reverenced, and the illuminated manuscripts, encrusted with jewels, were such as one might read when walking the jeweled pathways of the City of God.

Above all they worshiped light, for was not light "the intelligible nature of God." So the tall windows among the columns were carried up to the roofs in the great cathedrals, and through the stained glass there streamed the radiance of God. Light in these cathedrals seems to breathe, and this indeed was what they intended: for men should be aware that in the heavens they were blessed by a living and breathing God, and if his breath was light, so was the touch of his hands, and so was his shining face. God is "Light of Light," said the creed. So in Santa Sophia the inside of the great dome was painted to resemble the galaxies of suns and stars. So, too, in the paintings of the illuminated manuscripts, the gold background represents the face of God, as it does also in the paintings of Giotto and the Sienese masters. For the men of the Middle Ages "radiance" meant precisely "the coming of the rays of the living God," while "splendor" meant the reflected light from the Godhead, and the sun itself was reflected light. A man could shine with splendor: he was not bathed in sunlight, but bathed in the light of God. In the high Renaissance men began to believe that they shone with their own independent light, but by that time the work of the Fathers was already done. They had no successors. The saints who came afterward, even the greatest of them, like St. John of the Cross, are already life-size. After the death of Thomas Aquinas the outlines of dogma had been completed; all that was necessary was the filling in of detail.

Compared with the mechanical perfection of the twentieth century, the perfection of the Middle Ages belongs to another order. They strove for perfection of man, not for perfection of machines, or rather, since man was an indescribably divine machine operating according to heavenly laws, he needed only a little more of the oil of grace to proceed smoothly along the heavenly way. His life was woven into the life of the Church. There were wars and famines, and for a hundred and fifty years after the death of the last Carolingian king, St. Peter's was occupied by a succession of murderous and unworthy Popes, but in the villages and towns the influence of the priests, themselves the sons of peasants from the neighborhood, only increased: for the most part they were quiet and humble men who regarded the celebration of their ritual as a perpetual feast. In those times men believed in miracles and visions. If a man said he had seen the Virgin plucking roses in his hedgerows he was not immediately conveyed to an asylum: it was simply assumed that the Virgin was about her own business—the roses were sacred to her—and she had a right to be there. In medieval times no one would have been altogether surprised if the Virgin and Christ came walking arm in arm into a tavern and demanded wine. Though we live among miracles still, we have lost the capacity of being astonished. The medieval mind found God everywhere.

One of the advantages of living in an age of disbelief is that the necessity for belief is more clearly demonstrated. The argument does not flatter our pride. It is as though a man had to be sent to the Sahara before he appreciated a human thirst. But though we do our best to deny it, man is still a creature of beliefs. "We are born believing," wrote Emerson. "A man bears beliefs as a tree bears apples." Every man has these singing trees within his flesh: he believes or perishes, and often he believes *and* perishes. We have seen in our own day what belief in a mortal individual may lead to: the meat-

hook in Milan and the gasoline poured into the gutter of the
Berlin Chancellery offered no consolation to the survivors,
and it is unthinkable that the dead rejoiced. *Aut Caesar aut
Deus?* We have learned by hard experience that all Caesars
(by which we mean all politicians) go to Hell. It would seem
more profitable to believe in a merciful God who loves human
justice, and then to go quietly about our tasks.

In all this the Church Fathers have an appointed place.
They were the constructors and engineers of belief. Not all
believed the same things. They even quarreled among themselves, as Jerome's bitter words to Augustine and Ambrose
attest. They saw variously, fought different enemies, and
were often hounded by their own doctrines: but it is as be-
lievers rather than as doctrinaires that they reveal themselves
at their best. Though they were tumultuous men leading
furious lives, a monastic atmosphere surrounded them. From
the monastic calm and from the knowledge of God's abiding
presence, they derived their peace.

Though there are nearly half a million pages in Migne's
Patrologia we still know all too little about the Church
Fathers. There are huge gaps in our knowledge of them.
Those like Augustine whom we seem to know best are those
who in some ways have revealed themselves least. One should
beware of Augustine: he tells too much, and too few of his
friends have related what manner of man he was. There is a
sense in which we know Thomas Aquinas better, and Bernard best of all. To know Bernard it is not even necessary to
know his writings: it is enough to listen to Guillaume de St.
Thierry describing the valley of briers where Bernard meditated and worked:

I tarried with him a few days, unworthy though I was, and
whichever way I turned my eyes I marveled and thought I saw
a new heaven and a new earth, and also the old pathways of the
Egyptian monks, our fathers, marked with the recent footsteps
the men of our time left to them. The golden ages seemed to have
returned and visited the world at Clairvaux ... At the first glance,

as you entered, after descending the hill, you could feel that God was in the place: and the silent valley bespoke, in the simplicity of its buildings, the genuine humility of the poor of Christ dwelling there. The silence of noon was as the silence of the midnight, but occasionally the silence was broken by the chanting of the monks and the sound of garden and field instruments. No one was idle. In the hours not devoted to sleep and prayer, the brethren kept busy with hoe, scythe and ax, taming the wild land and clearing the forest. And though there were such multitudes in the valley, yet each seemed to be a solitary.

With such quiet joy the Fathers faced the world: almost it is the same joy you find inscribed on the walls of the catacombs where the brightly colored birds and fishes, palms and lilies, speak of a world that possessed a Christian delight in life. There may be once again in the history of the West a descent into the catacombs. It is possible—for the evidence is all around us—that the Vandals will once again sack Rome, and another Jerome in another Bethlehem will shout against the invaders and the massacres, and see no hope at all except among the conspirators for Christ. At a time when faith is weak and survival of itself is hardly worth fighting for, it would be well if we remembered the Church Fathers who shored up the ruins, and "in a time of awakening fed honeycombs to our mouths."

A vast history of controversy has arisen over the Fathers of the Western Church. Disputes concerning their lives, their beliefs, their theories, and their powers are still raging; and it is no part of the purpose of this book to fan the flames. I have attempted to show the Church Fathers as dramatic characters in the long drama of Christianity, and to strip them of the pedantry which is too often associated with an examination of Christian origins. So there is little or nothing here on some controversies which were important at the time: there is, for example, little about the Montanists and less about St. Jerome's involvement in the Origenistic controversy, and I have not thought it necessary to enter into a lengthy discussion of the Manichees. Since this book concerns the Western Fathers, there is little enough about the Fathers of the Eastern Church, who will be studied in another volume. And I have thought it better that the Fathers should be shown as living persons of great relevance to our own time, rather than that they should be smothered in footnotes. The plain reader may take comfort from the thought that the scholars disagree profoundly among themselves. Meanwhile it is surely necessary that we should come to know the Fathers in the same way that we come to know Christ: by the simple study of their lives and the words they spoke with such vehemence in their search for the Kingdom of Heaven.

II. ❧ THE FORERUNNERS

WHEN THE DEAD AND BLEEDING CHRIST WAS taken down from the cross, His life had only just begun. The young Nazarene had seen with terrible clarity that He was an emperor over men and the empire He had founded would endure with His perpetual presence in the Eucharist. Like another Alexander, but without stepping an inch out of Palestine, He had conquered immense territories of the human spirit; with His death the conquest was affirmed, and He remained, though dead, the living ruler of the conquered land. In His brief life there was no time for Him to speak at length: so He spoke in paradoxes, in wry fables and legends of the cornfields, hinting at blessedness and giving utterance to the stern laws of the Kingdom of Heaven, performing miracles and sometimes towering into sudden wrath, so that the wrath on His face was itself a kind of utterance. The words, so casually recorded, became His Testament, to be interpreted by those who came after Him; and it was the task of the Church Fathers to put order and precision into the undocumented laws He had announced as He walked quietly in Galilee or along the dusty roads that radiate like spokes from Jerusalem.

We are so accustomed when reading the New Testament to believe we see Jesus plain that we forget the influence of the Church Fathers in every detail. They added new dimensions to the original texts. They commented at length upon the meaning of all the important words, and gave their own interpretations to words that had long since lost their original meanings. The precise inflexions of Aramaic are lost to us. Words like *love feast, the Kingdom of Heaven, the Son of Man,* and *the Messiah* subtly altered their meaning as Christianity evolved in the hands of the Fathers, as the words lost their Jewish connotations and assumed new and ever-changing interpretations in the hands of men who were strangers to the Jewish cult. Sometimes the words shed their feathers altogether and assumed a plumage that would never have been recognized in Jerusalem; and if the process was inevitable, it made for dangers and heresies. A half-remembered utterance of Jesus recorded by one of the apostles could and did become a battleground for furious sects; and there followed in the long, unhappy, and glorious history of Christianity enormous processions of scholars and preachers only too anxious to interpret Jesus's words according to their own proclivities. At times one wishes desperately that the living God, the possessor of prophecy and the gift of tongues, had taught the apostles shorthand. We shall never see Him plain. We shall never know what He said. We see Him through a glass darkly, and the words are muffled, though sometimes, with extraordinary purity, a single phrase rings through the dark. At such moments the measured terror of the voice of God is heard upon our own heartbeats, a sound which seems to come out of the welling spaces of the stars: but this is not the voice the apostles heard.

What was the voice? Neither Paul nor the Fathers knew. At best they can hint at it, guess at it, attempt to reconcile one word with another, or play the scholarly game of matching phrase against phrase. Most of them were poets: poetic guesswork played a part; so too did the process of poetic creation. To call them poets is simply to call them what they are: *poetes* rather than *vates,* artificers of the word, which happened to be the Word of God.

Throughout his life on earth Jesus never strayed far from Jerusalem. He was a Jew speaking to Jews, with an intricate knowledge of Jewish ritual: but His words were intended for the whole earth, and in His lifetime He simplified or broke down altogether the complexities of a ritual which had descended from the time of Moses. So He became a foreigner in His own land; and it was inevitable that the apostles would have to travel beyond the frontiers of Palestine before the seed would bear fruit. In the West it was to bear its most abundant fruit in France, Italy, and North Africa. To reach these places the gospel had to pass through the Cilician gate; and there, close to the narrow defiles that separate Europe from Asia, in the shadow of the dazzling Taurus mountains, in a small fortress town on a hill surrounded by meadows of black earth and orange trees, in sight of the sea, Paul was born. His birth in Tarsus seems to have been almost as significant as the birth of Jesus in the royal town of Bethlehem where David was born.

Through Tarsus, then, the gospel traveled westward by way of the Cilician gates, where Alexander had emerged at the head of his columns to conquer Asia and where Antony held court in the marketplace and saw Cleopatra in her golden barge, wafted on lovesick winds. Here Paul grew up and spent his youth. He was a Roman citizen who spoke Greek, and his family came, according to Jerome, from Gishala on the shores of Galilee. Birth, nationality, language, and descent all conspired to make him the last of the apostles and the first of the Fathers. He may have been—he seems to hint at it—distantly related to the family of Jesus, and he had the exile's love for the Galilee he had never seen.

Paul is the first of the Christians whose features we recognize. The appearance of the twelve disciples is lost in legend, but Paul springs clear out of the mists. That short, bald, bowlegged man, with the grizzled beard, the grayish eyes and knitted eyebrows, long nosed, with stooping shoulders, looking now like a man and now like an angel, according to the *Acts of Paul and Thecla*, may have resembled a satyr. Luther, who adored him, called him "a poor tough little mannikin." A portrait made during the first century, when the memory of the man was still living, shows him with diseased eyes; it is what we might expect. He saw things in blinding flashes of colored light. His mind was savage for certainties, and it moved, though on another plane, with the staggering speed of Shakespeare's. Nothing quite like that mind had ever appeared before or was ever to appear again. Uncouth and gentle and winged and harsh and intolerant, it combined a mess of incompatibles; and half the time the flint was striking sparks and half the time it struck nothing at all.

To Paul was given the grace of being the first to shape the Christian doctrine as we know it today. He poured himself into Christ; he poured Christ out into himself; and Christianity will always bear the traces of that continual process of distillation which occupied his lifetime. There is rest with Christ; there is none with Paul. The fuses are always being blown, the electricity crackles, the blue light of doom and love burns overhead: so that when Paul says: "I am crucified with Christ; nevertheless I live; yet not I but Christ liveth in me; and the life which I now live in the flesh, I live by the faith of the Son of God who loved me and gave himself for me," we believe him implicitly, and like Luther we read with great vehemence the words *me* and *for me*. Yet something is lacking. Paul speaks about Christ, rarely of Jesus. The man who broke the bread and blessed the wine is exchanged for the Son of God on the right hand of the Father.

Perhaps it was inevitable. Paul lived in visions, forever blinded by the vision at Damascus. Erasmus talked of Paul "thundering and lightening and talking sheer flame." He seems to have been so conscious of the flame that he never talks about real people. He does not talk about the Crucifixion as something suffered: it is a blaze of divine energy, springing from a secret shame and a heavenly triumph. The final Epiphany of the Kingdom of God is about to happen, this moment or the moment to come, and forever on his lips is the prayer of the Aramaic primitive church, uttered at the end of the celebration of the Last Supper: *Maranatha* (Our Lord,

Come!). Afraid of the physical death, he desired only to die into Christ, a final outpouring into the final wine, and all the time he looks forward to the day when sin will have no dominion. On the day when all things are reconciled and united comes the blaze of peace.

For Paul peace is always a blaze. It is not only that he could not think except in vivid images lit by lightning, but he sets one lightning-lit image against another, and solves all problems with a dialectic of flashing swords. The pace is stupendous; the swords are continually clanging; there is no rest in the duel between Paul and Christ; and all the time he is tempering the doctrine against his own steel, with the result that Christianity as he sees it is lit not by the softer skies of Palestine but by the blinding skies of Tarsus, dazzling with the reflected snows of Taurus, their peaks like silver horns. Even his speech has the breathless, heady air of the snows, and more often than we realize he breaks out into poetry:

> *Who shall separate us from the love of Christ?*
> *Shall tribulation, or distress, or persecution?*
> *Or famine, or nakedness?*
> *Or peril, or sword?*
> *As it is written:*
> *"For thy sake we are killed all the day long;*
> *"We are accounted as sheep for the slaughter."*
> *Nay, in all these things we are more than conquerors*
> *Through Him that loved us.*
>
> *For I am persuaded,*
> *That neither death, nor life,*
> *Nor angels, nor principalities, nor powers,*
> *Nor things present, nor things to come,*
> *Nor height, nor depth,*
> *Nor any other creature*
> *Shall be able to separate us from the love of God,*
> *Which is in Jesus Christ*
> *Our Lord.*

It is a new voice, as one might expect in a man who called himself "reborn in Christ." The *koinê*, the common language of the people, became in Paul's hands a vehicle for poetry, just as the common language of the Roman soldiers was to emerge into the extraordinarily fluid accents of medieval French; and though there is no reason to believe that Paul spoke Greek well—he came from a part of Asia Minor famous for its barbarous accents, and we derive the word "solecism" from the town of Soloi, only a few miles from Tarsus—he wrote Greek poetry like an angel. The very vigor of Paul's prose sends it spinning into verse, and we shall see in Tertullian, Augustine, and Gregory the same phenomenon of the evangelist determined to write persuasive letters or concoct scholarly exegeses, only to discover that he is singing hymns instead. So Paul sings his hymn of love:

> *Though I speak with the tongues of men and of angels,*
> *And have not love*
> *I am become as sounding brass*
> *Or a tinkling cymbal.*
>
> *And though I have the gift of prophecy,*
> *And understand all mysteries and all knowledge,*
> *And though I have all faith,*
> *So that I could remove mountains,*
> *And have not love,*
> *I am nothing.*
>
> *And though I bestow all my goods to feed the poor,*
> *And though I give my body to be burned,*
> *And have not love,*
> *It profiteth me nothing.*
>
> *Love suffereth long, and is kind;*
> *Love envieth not;*
> *Love vaunteth not itself,*
> *Is not puffed up,*
> *Doth not behave itself unseemly.*

Seeketh not her own,
Is not easily provoked,
Thinketh no evil,
Rejoiceth not in iniquity,
But rejoiceth in the truth,
Beareth all things,
Believeth all things,
Hopeth all things,
Endureth all things.

Love never faileth.
But whether there be prophecies, they shall fail;
Whether there be tongues, they shall cease;
Whether there be knowledge, it shall vanish away.
For we know in part,
And we prophesy in part:
But when that which is perfect is come,
Then that which is in part shall be done away.

When I was a child,
I spake as a child,
I understood as a child,
I thought as a child,
But when I became a man
I put away childish things.

For now we see through a glass, darkly,
But then face to face:
Now I know in part,
But then shall I know
Even as also I am known.

And now abideth faith, hope, love,
These three,
But the greatest of these is love.

In these verses Paul is doing a number of things in an extremely complex way. He is singing a hymn in praise of Christian love—the word he uses, *agapê*, often translated as "charity," means love feast, a love of a most intimate kind and especially holy for its association with the Last Supper. He is relating himself to the hymn, for when he speaks of himself as a child, he is simply referring to himself before he "assumed the body of Christ." Finally, he is writing, as the Fathers of the Church were to do continually, an extended commentary on one or two brief texts from Christ's reported sayings. Implicit in the whole poem is a ceremony of the new innocence which had fallen to the lot of the Christians. Faith, hope, and love (*pistis, elpis, agapé*) were to become the watchwords of the Christians—faith in Christ, hope in the Resurrection, and brotherly love among people.

We are so accustomed to the sound of these words that we no longer realize how surprisingly they must have sounded in Rome or Athens. It was the time of Plutarch, Epictetus, and Seneca: the old destructive Stoicism and the crumbling walls: of the Pharisees and the quarreling Sadducees: of a fading Empire and a Jerusalem soon to be crushed in a Roman triumph. Not once in the hymn to love does Paul mention Christ, but Christ is implicit throughout. This hymn, which seems to have been composed for the celebration of the Eucharist, introduces a new dimension into Christianity. A simple statement uttered on the shores of Galilee had become a song.

As he wandered from one obscure gathering of Christians to another, Paul was continually changing, molding, improvising the shape of doctrine. "It is not permissible to go beyond the things that are written," he wrote in one of his epistles, but he was continually going beyond them, inventing interpretations according to the impulses of his flame-lit mind. He explains that the words about the ox which was not to be muzzled while threshing refer to the apostles. He points out that we are not to understand by "speaking with tongues" any miraculous gift in the use of language: the uttered words were unintelligible: the Pentecost plays no part in his dogma. He is continually evaluating, or hinting at evaluations. This statement is important, that is not. He develops theories which seem to fly in the face of the reported statements of Jesus, as for example in Galatians, where he comes to the conclusion that the Law was not given directly by God but by the angels. He elaborates on legends, as when he says that the rock which gave water to the Fathers followed them in their journeying in the wilderness. He is continually employing legal phrases, which in itself would seem contrary to the simple utterances of Jesus. He delights in discovering parallels between the sayings of Jesus and the Old Testament, and most of all he delights in the discovery of the parallel between Sarah and Hagar and the Two Covenants; and all the time he is dependent upon rabbinic tradition. He was the first to introduce irony, that commonplace of lawyers and Church Fathers: and this dangerous weapon was to remain. All was grist to his mill. "I am debtor," he wrote, "both to the Greeks and to the barbarians, both to the wise and to the unwise." He was so immensely skilled that he drowned all opposition in his rhetoric and his poetry, so that sometimes the deafened reader longs for the silence of which Ignatius spoke: "He that hath the word of Jesus truly can hear his silence." Sometimes, too, we are made conscious of Paul's pride:

I am the least of the apostles ... but by the grace of God I am what I am. ... I labored more abundantly than they all; yet not I, but the grace of God which was with me.

This pride he shared with the Fathers of the Church.

He had reason to be proud. As he explains in Galatians, with many omissions and a curious impetuousness, he had laid down the rule. It was not the rule as Christ had stated it, but it grew out of Christ's statements and perhaps owed more to conversations with Peter and James than to anything else. The rule demanded that the Christians should remember the poor, remain chaste and uncircumcised, humble and temperate, and live in the spirit of Christ; "but the fruit of the spirit is love, joy, peace, longsuffering, gentleness, goodness, faith, meekness, temperance: against such there is no law." In a sense it was as simple as that. And the letter, written in Rome, concludes: "As many as walk according to this rule, peace be on them, and mercy, and upon the Israel of God."

In Galatians the glitter of the swords and the snow is absent. Writing for the particular purpose of warning the churches of Galatia from following Hebrew practices, he is on the defensive, no longer concerned with the immense problems of individual salvation and sin and suffering, no longer the dialectician determined to sweep an opponent off his feet by an exhibition of anger or brilliance. It is enough, almost, to love Christ and be chaste. He does not ask the Christians to observe the Sabbath, and he does not even mention the love feast.

To understand Paul we need to know his Epistles to the Romans, with their harsh and complex annotations to the nature of suffering and sin, but to understand the growth of the Church Galatians provides a sensitive clue. A "third race," neither pagan nor Jewish, was being born in freedom from all except the simplest rituals. As St. Justin Martyr describes the celebration of the Eucharist, we recognize the same quiet fervor which Paul had indicated in his rule:

After the prayers we greet one another with a brotherly kiss. Then bread and a cup with water and wine are handed to the president of the brethren. He receives them, and offers praise, glory and thanks to the Father of all, through the name of the Son and the Holy Spirit for these his gifts. When he has ended the prayers and thanksgiving, the whole congregation responds: "Amen." For "Amen" in the Hebrew tongue means: "Be it so." Upon this the deacons, as we call them, give to each of those present some of the blessed bread, and of the wine mingled with water, and carry it to the absent in their dwellings. This food is called with us the eucharist, of which none can partake, but the believing and baptized, who live according to the commands of Christ. For we use these not as common bread or common drink; but like as Jesus Christ our Redeemer was made flesh through the

Word of God, and took upon him flesh and blood for our redemption; so we are taught that the nourishment blessed by the
word of prayer, by which our flesh and blood are nourished by
transformation, is the flesh and blood of the incarnate Jesus.
(Justin Martyr, *Apologia* I, c. 65, 66.)

The celebration of the Eucharist usually occurred in the
morning; the love feast, introduced by prayers and ending
with hymns and the bringing in of the lights, occurred in the
evening; and this was all. The simplicity of Christianity in
its beginnings is something to marvel at. There was communion, the love feast, baptism, and the observance of Easter,
and nothing more.

All through the first century of Christianity, and far into
the second, Christianity maintained its simplicity, its air of
gentle lovingkindness; and it did this in spite of persecutions.
It was a religion of the poor. The observances took place in
private houses, and the Christians were marked by their aloof-
ness from the things that preoccupied everyone else. They
were not interested in wealth or display; they had no liking
for games; they were content to watch and pray. Inevitably
they were misunderstood. They were assumed to be homosexual because they kissed each other. It was said that at the
love feasts there were prodigious bouts of drunkenness, and
that they worshiped the head of an ass stuffed with straw.
The Roman Senate, which feared foreign religions as it feared
the plague, demanded that Christians should give the oath to
Caesar. They refused: they would give only the oath to Christ.
There followed martyrdoms, yet the martyrdoms were incurred willingly: almost in their frenzy of love for Christ the
early Christians rushed upon the swords. "Shall tribulation, or
distress, or persecution, or famine, or nakedness, or peril, or
sword separate us from the love of Christ?" asked Paul; and
so they died.

Gibbon wrote glibly concerning the martyrdom of the
early Christians, but there was nothing in the least glib in the
Christian desire for the sacrament of the blood and fire. The

savagery of the persecution of the Christians in the first three centuries of our era was not comparable in numbers to the savagery of the Nazis against the Jews, but it was of the same vehemence. Total destruction of the Christian religion was attempted; and the fury of the persecutors was equaled only by the desire of the Christians to offer themselves as sacrifices.

It was the time of the catacombs, when the faith was young, and the symbols of the faith were childlike still. Sketched on the catacomb walls were paintings of ships and fishes, peacocks, lambs, doves, lamps, and palms; against white rock the paintings glowed in simple colors. Christ was Orpheus playing on his lyre, or a shepherd bearing a strayed lamb over his shoulders. The miraculous saving power of Christ, the water flowing from the rock, the burning bush, the land of milk and honey, all these were in the grasp, or almost in the grasp, of those Christians who inscribed the words "In peace" over the bones of the dead and possessed in Rome a peculiarly Greek tenderness. Clement, Bishop of Rome, the first of the apostolic Fathers, continued the dialogue with love which Jesus had begun in Galilee and Paul had prodigiously expanded in Asia Minor, but there is nothing Pauline in Clement's curiously quiet epistles. He stated the complete simplicity of Christian love, almost without rhetoric and with no violence:

He who has love in Christ obeys the commands of Christ. Who can declare the bond of the love of God, and tell the greatness of its beauty? The height to which it leads is unspeakable. Love unites us with God; covers a multitude of sins; beareth all things; endureth all things. There is nothing mean in love, nothing haughty. It knows no division; it is not refractory; it does everything in harmony. In love have all the elect of God become perfect. Without love nothing is pleasing to God. (Clement of Rome, *Epistola ad Corinthios*, 49.)

Rhetoric and impatience were to come later: they were to burst upon the world with Tertullian, yet even then there were to be long passages of carefully modulated argument.

The martyrs, as Tertullian stated in the most majestic of his sayings, were the seed of the Church, but they were also practical people who went about their daily affairs in solemnity and joy; and most of Clement's writings have the effect of calmness.

In this he was unusual. Most of the early Fathers spoke with a fierce urgency. Behind the Roman face lie the Roman nightmares; and with the Fathers who came later there is always a hint of a latent hysteria, and sometimes a terrible self-abandonment. Ignatius, third Bishop of Antioch after St. Peter, speaks as though the Second Coming was at hand; he has little to say of love, and more concerning blood and fire. Like Paul and Christ he spoke in apothegms, in taut memorable phrases colored by a flaring religious imagination. "Be diligent. Be sober. Be God's athlete. Stand like a beaten anvil." "Grant me nothing more than that I be poured out a libation to God," he says in another place. He says simple things with firmness —the firmness of the anvil. "I would rather die for Christ than rule the whole world," he taunted the Emperors, adding, according to the legend: "It is glorious to go down in the world in order to go up to God." "Where is the pure bread of God?" he asked, and answered: "Leave me to the beasts, that I may by them be made partaker of God: I am a grain of the wheat of God, and I would be ground by the teeth of wild beasts, that I may be found pure bread of God. I would rather fawn upon the beasts that they may be to me a grave. I would leave nothing of my body, so that, when I sleep, I shall burden none."

The bread of the angels and the bread of God were continually on the lips of the martyrs; and some who were lucky saw that holy bread, for when Polycarp, another of the early apostolic Fathers, a friend of Ignatius, was martyred, it was observed that during the burning the flames did not seem to touch the body, which "shone a glorious color, like white baken bread."

Polycarp was martyred at Smyrna, but Ignatius, arrested in

Asia Minor, was brought to Rome for his martyrdom. The long journey, which ended in the Flavian amphitheater, was one of the great pilgrimages of the time. It is attested by his letters, which are almost all we know about Ignatius. We have no records of his birth, his rank, or his education. He has, as we see him across the centuries, no visible appearance: he is the personification of the thirst for martyrdom. Accompanied by ten soldiers, whom he calls "ten leopards," he was driven "by land and by sea, by day and by night" from Antioch to Rome; but at every station he paused, to be greeted by Christians who received his blessing and his strange, willful utterances. He thirsted for glory. "Come fire, come iron, come grapplings with wild beasts, scatterings of bones, hewing of limbs, crushings of the whole body; come, assail me, O cruel tortures of the devil! Only be it mine to attain unto Jesus Christ!" The eyes roll, the temper rages, the solemn procession moves on, passing through Smyrna, where in a few days Ignatius wrote four fiery letters which smolder even now with somber fire, and after a brief stay in Philippi we see him next in Rome, an old man, "lusting," as he said, "after death," and at the same time sorrowing, for the virgins and the annointed ones came to greet him at the stations, and he had no desire to leave them; and then in Rome he may have been brought before the Emperor Trajan, who may have said: "Who art thou, poor devil?" and Ignatius may have answered with admirable simplicity: "I am he who bears Christ within his breast." The legend or the history—it is impossible at this date to evaluate the truth of the *Antiochene Acts*—goes on to relate that Trajan ordered Ignatius to be fettered, taken to the amphitheater, and thrown to the wild beasts, and that Ignatius thanked God for the greater mercy.

It may be true. We have no reason to disbelieve that there were men like this. The fires of Patmos burned in Ignatius, and Christian love inevitably changed its meaning. A new urgency was appearing. Paul possessed none of this fervent desire for death; or rather, he possessed a desire to die for

Christ, but he also possessed a greater desire to be among the living, working in love for Christ, hardly knowing why he lived, yet delighting in his hesitancy. Paul said:

For to me to live is Christ, and to die is gain. But if I live in the flesh, this is the fruit of my labor; yet what I shall choose I wot not. For I am in a strait betwixt two, having a desire to depart, and to be with Christ; which is far better. . . . Having this confidence, I know that I shall abide and continue with you all for your furtherance and joy of faith; that your rejoicing may be more abundant in Jesus Christ for me by my coming to you again.

Compare the diffidence of Paul with the violence of Ignatius:

For what value is all the world? Better to die for Christ than to rule over the farthest kingdoms. The pangs of a new birth are upon me. Do not hinder me from living; do not desire my death. Suffer me to receive the pure light, to become a man, to be an imitator of the passion of my God. Do not abet Satan against me. I write to you in the midst of life, yet lusting after death. You will not be showing love, but envy and hatred against me, should you procure the saving of my life. (Ignatius, *Ad Romanos*, 5.)

The strange saint, wandering slowly toward Rome, left his mark on Christianity. All the wilder elements descend from him, from the terrible look in his eyes. The other apostolic Fathers, called so because they lived in the immediate tradition of the apostles, were of a different mettle. Polycarp was all tenderness. He enjoyed the authority which came from having been an intimate of St. John, and wrote letters to the churches: only one has come down to us, and this is dull, but the gentleness shines through. He had known Ignatius, too, meeting him during that fantastic journey from Asia Minor to Rome, regarding him with reverence. Polycarp was an old man when he heard that a summons for his arrest had been issued. He went into hiding in the upstairs room of a small country cottage, and was found when the hiding place was

revealed by a poor slave-boy under torture. He served re-
freshments to the police, asked for an hour of prayer, and was
led on an ass to Smyrna. He knew he would be martyred: he
had dreamed three days before that his pillow was on fire.
Brought before the ruler of Asia, he was asked to say simply:
"Caesar is Lord." He refused. Then the Asiarch begged him
to remember his white hairs, surely it was only a simple thing
to swear by Caesar and curse Christ, what harm would be
done? "I have been the slave of Christ for eighty-six years,"
Polycarp replied, "and He hath done me no wrong. How can
I blaspheme against the King who saved me?" The Asiarch
tried again, begging him to reconsider his decision, but all
Polycarp would say was "I am a Christian." "Then tell us
what it is to be a Christian," the Asiarch went on. "It would
take a whole day," Polycarp replied. "Very well, ask the
people whether they will listen for a whole day." "I have no
desire to convince the people," Polycarp answered, and it was
as though a last flare of pride had risen in him and he was
afraid the crown of martyrdom would be taken from him.
Shortly afterward the faggots were piled high in the circus of
Smyrna. Polycarp did not burn well, and to kill him the executioner plunged a dagger in his side.

Polycarp was a Greek of the Eastern Church, though he
paid a visit to Rome and was treated with the highest honors
by the Pope. Irenaeus, though born in Smyrna, belongs to the
Western Church. He had sat at the feet of Polycarp on the
hills high above Smyrna, while the old graybeard spoke of
St. John and remembered the stories of Jesus. Then, as a
young man, Irenaeus had traveled to Lyons. He became a
presbyter, and seems to have traveled between the churches
of Lyons and Vienne as a kind of missionary. He may have
been in those places in A.D. 177 when Marcus Aurelius
launched one of the bitterest of all attacks against the Christians: the streets were red with the blood of the martyrs. Irenaeus, whose name means "peace," had none of Ignatius's fire.
He wrote quietly and humbly. "Faith is the body of Christ," he

wrote, "and charity is Christ's blood." He attempted patiently
to keep the Church together. He was concerned with making
a reasonable religion. He would have no traffic with the
allegorists who saw all kinds of secret meanings in the Old
Testamen* prefiguring the coming of Christ. "To do so," he
said, "would be like tearing up a mosaic of a King, and then
using the little bits of mosaic to make the portrait of a dog."
He wrote a book against heresies, but he interceded with the
Bishop of Rome on behalf of the Gnostics. He became Bishop
of Lyons, and it was due to him more than anyone else that
Christianity was firmly established in southern France. Unlike
most of the early Fathers, he died in his bed.

Perhaps the greatest of the early Fathers was Justin Martyr.
He, too, was arrested. Rusticus, the prefect of Rome, ordered
him to stand a little apart from the rest. Then he said: "I
order you to obey the gods and submit to the Emperor."
Characteristically, Justin made no declamation. He said
simply: "I see no wrong in submitting to Christ." "What are
your doctrines?" asked Rusticus. "Our belief in one God,
and Jesus Christ His Son, foretold by the prophets, Christ
being the herald of salvation and teacher of the good disciples;
and since I am a man, I cannot speak further of God's boundless divinity."

"How do you assemble?" asked Rusticus.

"Where each man chooses, and where we can," Justin
answered. "The God of the Christians is not circumscribed
by space."

"Are you a Christian?"

"Of course."

There were a few more questions. To all of them Justin
answered gravely and humbly. Finally Rusticus said: "So you
believe you will go to Heaven and receive your reward when
you die?"

"I not only believe it, but I know it and am fully persuaded
of it."

"Then I shall give you the opportunity to find out."

"Do as you will. We are Christians, and will not sacrifice to idols."

When the order for decapitation was given, he said: "We desire nothing more than to suffer for Our Lord Jesus Christ; for this gives us salvation and joyfulness before His dreadful judgment seat, at which all the world must appear."

His death followed the order of his life. He had written: "You can *kill* us, *injure* us you cannot." He was once a Platonist, and it was only comparatively late in life that he became a Christian. He employed for new purposes the old Stoic phrase: *Spermatikos Logos*, the Seminal Word, the God Who lies embedded like a seed within everyone's breast, a phrase which took wings among the Fathers of the Eastern Church, and all his life he wore the threadbare cloak of a philosopher, saying that this was a sign by which he might be known: anyone who desired to argue with him would find him in a crowd.

He tells of one of these arguments in his *Dialogue with Trypho*, which opens with a chance meeting in a pleasant colonnade near the sea, perhaps at Ephesus. As he walked up and down the colonnade, his eyes fell upon a venerable old Jew, who for some reason was following him. "When I see a man in a threadbare gown," said the Jew Trypho, "then I approach him gladly. But please tell me, what are you pacing up and down for?"

Justin explained that he was meditating.

"Then you are a theorist?" asked Trypho.

"On the contrary I am a very practical person. I don't see any reason to separate theory from practice. I was meditating the subject of happiness."

"What is happiness?"

"It seems to me that happiness comes from a study of philosophy, for philosophy is the full knowledge of reality and the clear perception of truth, and happiness is the reward of this knowledge and this truth."

The *Dialogue with Trypho* is an extraordinary document. Philo of Alexandria had attempted to marry Platonism to the

Old Testament: Justin was attempting to marry Platonism to the New Testament. The colonnade, the appearance of the stranger, even the method of interlocution, all are Platonic: the scented air of Athens bathes the scene. But soon enough the scene changes: there is no longer the uncertainty of inquiry: there follows the certainty of Christ. Justin explains how he had been led to read the Bible, and how "a fire was kindled in my soul, and a passion seized me for the prophets and those men who are Christ's friends; and so, discussing their words with myself, I found this philosophy alone to be safe and helpful." Trypho smiles, approving Justin's ardor, and there follows the long debate. Trypho assails Justin from all directions. He attempts to show that it is impossible for the soul to know God, and that no one can be happy when meditating on the Creator, for there is no Creator, and if there was a Creator visible to the soul, then what of the goats and the sheep, who injure no one—surely they see God? It is all spoken on these courteous and kindly levels. Neither convinces the other, but occasionally they ridicule each other, as when Justin realizes that Trypho as a Jew possesses a particular affection for the ritual of circumcision. "But surely, Trypho, if circumcision was indeed demanded by God, it would be demanded of all people, and therefore it would be demanded of women."

As the argument proceeds, the Platonic atmosphere fails and, contrary to the instructions of Irenaeus, Justin finds himself embarking on the most amazing allegories derived from the Old Testament. The two goats of Leviticus are types of the two Comings. Jesus is prefigured in the cornerstone of the Temple, but He is also prefigured in Jacob and Israel. "Who was the fourth figure in the fiery furnace?" he asks dramatically, and proceeds to enlarge on the prophecies of Isaiah. Did not Isaiah prophesy that Jesus would be born of a virgin? "Nonsense," says Trypho. "The scripture says that a woman shall conceive and bear a son. There is nothing about a virgin. And a woman *did* conceive and bear a son, and he was Hezekiah. You ought to be ashamed of telling a story which is no better (and no worse) than the story of Danaë conceiving Perseus in a shower of gold. You know, if you talk about miracles, no one is going to believe you." This is no longer Platonic argument: the certainties in Justin's mind crowd fast upon one another. It is quite clear to him that Christ was born of a virgin, and all this was prophesied, and he cannot understand why the argument is not clear to Trypho. He discovers that Moses had predicted the name of Jesus. If you will only read the chronology of the Book of Daniel, you will see that the exact date of Christ's appearance is made clear. Trypho remains unconvinced. When Justin has finished, having explained meanwhile that he will soon embark on a sea journey, Trypho says: "The trouble is that we came to this argument unprepared, but it was pleasant to see you, we have both learned more than we expected to learn, and we must return to the matter in greater detail. But since you may be departing any day now, then remember me as a friend."

Probably the long discourse does not end here: the battle had still to be joined. But all the rest of the *Dialogue with Trypho* is lost, if it ever existed. For its time and place it was an extraordinarily mature work; and even though Justin based his hopes of salvation on the prophecies of the Old Testament, and though his arguments are scorned by the Jew, the nobility of the man shines through. He held fast to his belief in the prophecies and devoted half of his *Apology* to proving that they were fulfilled in Jesus, yet he remained partly a Platonist to the end. "I delighted in Plato's teachings, but I heard Christians abused: and I saw that they alone were fearless in the face of death." In another place he says: "No man ever believed Socrates so much as to die for his teaching. But Christ, who was known to Socrates in part (for He was and is the Word and is in everything)—this Christ, I say, not only philosophers and scholars believe in, but artisans and artless men, and so they despise glory and fear and death." He had written once: "I hoped I should have the vision of God"; and it may be permitted to believe that at the moment of his martyrdom Flavius Justinus saw the vision he desired.

About the time when Justin was writing, there appeared—no one knows from where—a letter which we know as the *Letter to Diognetus*. We know neither who wrote it nor the occasion of its writing, though it might well have been written by Justin shortly before his death. It is one of the strangest and most beautiful of all the letters written during the early flowering of the Church. It moves with something of the casual grace of the opening of Justin's *Dialogue*. It is sunlit, and has the sparkle of the sea. It says gently and with the utmost certainty what needed to be said.

Who among men had any knowledge of what God was until God came? He came when our wickedness had reached its height, and thereupon God's Son was sent as a ransom for us, his holiness coming for the unholy, his innocence coming for the evil, his incorruption coming for the corruptible, his immortality coming for the mortal. How else might we, the evil and unholy, be justified but by the Son of God? O sweet exchange of favors! O unsearchable processes of God! O rewards beyond all expectation!

So the letter goes on, describing in a quiet voice which will be heard again in Minucius Felix and sometimes, but rarely, in Tertullian, the rewards of Christ. No translation is worthy of the original, and few manuscripts have suffered its peculiar fate. Nothing seems to have been known of it until Henry Stephens, a publisher in Paris, discovered the codex and issued it in 1592. The codex dated from the thirteenth century and was kept in Strasbourg, only to be destroyed during the siege of 1870. It was never photographed. Every kind of debate has followed its publication; speculations concerning its authorship have ranged from a certain Apollos of the first century to Henry Stephens in the sixteenth. Yet it indubitably comes from the time of Justin Martyr, and it is inconceivable that it is a later invention. Justin or someone very close to him must have written:

Christians dwell in their native cities, but are sojourners; they share in everything as citizens and endure all things as aliens; every foreign country is to them a fatherland, and every fatherland a foreign soil. They marry, as do others; they have children; they do not cast away their offspring. They have their table in common, but not their wives. They are in the flesh, but they do not live according to the flesh. They pass their lives on earth, but exercise their citizenship in Heaven. They obey the tabled laws, but they excel the laws in their lives. They love all, and are persecuted by all. They are unknown, and yet they are condemned. They are put to death, but they are raised to life. They are poor, but they make many rich. They lack all things, and yet in all things abound. They are reproached: they glory in the reproaches. They are calumniated, and are justified. They are cursed, and they bless. They do good, and are punished as evildoers. When punished, they rejoice, as being made alive. By the Jews they are reviled as aliens, and by the Greeks persecuted; and the cause of the enmity their enemies cannot tell. In short, what the soul is in the body, the Christians are in the world. The soul is diffused through all the members of the body, and the Christians are spread through the cities of the world. The soul dwells in the body, but it is not of the body; so the Christians dwell in the world, but are not of the world. The soul, invisible, keeps watch in the visible body; so also the Christians are seen to live in the world, but their piety is invisible. The flesh hates and wars against the soul, suffering no wrong from it, but because it resists fleshly pleasures; and the world hates the Christians with no reason, but that they resist its pleasures. The soul loves the flesh and members, by which it is hated; so the Christians love their haters. The soul is inclosed in the body, but holds the body together; so the Christians are detained in the world as in a prison; but they contain the world. Immortal, the soul dwells in the mortal body; so the Christians dwell in the corruptible, but look for incorruption in Heaven. This is the portion God has assigned to the Christians in the world; and it cannot be taken from them. (*Epistola ad Diognetum*, c. 5, 6.)

It was still the springtime of Christianity; once more the muted voice was to be heard; afterward came the thunderers.

III. ❧ THE WHISPERER
AND THE THUNDERER

THERE WERE CLOUDS IN THE WEST, BUT HERE
and there the sun shone through, a clear and trembling sun such as lit the fields of Syria when Jesus
walked through the cornfields, wearing His tenderness like a cloak around him. The tenderness of Jesus was not
entirely lost among the martyrs, who clamored for a sterner
sacrament than the bread and the wine; and the heady sun of
North Africa was nearer to the sun of Galilee than the softer
sun of Rome. "There were clouds in the West"—the phrase
comes from Polybius, who was perpetually conscious of them,
for he had seen with his own eyes the destruction of Carthage.
In the West, in the region of Carthage, Christianity had its
quiet rebirth: that Carthage where a quarter of a millennium
earlier the fields had been thrice cursed, and smoke rose from a
teeming city, and the Romans battered against a province
which defied the Roman power. Carthage was ruined: it had
sprung to birth again, as all ruined cities do in time: and still it
challenged Rome. Now, as the martyrs died in the Flavian amphitheater, Carthage flaunted its weapons. They were spiritual weapons, and they were used cunningly.

The clear sunlit landscape of Diognetus returns at intervals
among the Fathers who came from the neighborhood of Carthage. Even St. Augustine will talk wonderfully of a sunlit
world at peace with itself; Tertullian, in the midst of his
lawyer's briefs, talks more wonderfully still of the peaceful
moonlights of the North African coast; but it is Minucius
Felix who recaptured the freshness of early Christianity so

38

well that even now, seventeen hundred years later, we hear the authentic tones of an unknown author's tenderness. The *Octavius* of Marcus Minucius Felix is rarely mentioned nowadays. It seems a pity. It is not a great work in the normal sense of greatness, but if we knew nothing of Jesus except the Sermon on the Mount, would we recognize its greatness? The *Octavius* is a sermon by the seashore spoken by three disputants; and all the light and all the voices of Syria can be heard in the soft flow of its argument.

We know nothing of Marcus Minucius Felix except that he was a lawyer practicing in Rome who came from North Africa, from Cirta, and lived perhaps at the same time as Tertullian. He employs Tertullian's arguments, but without forcing them. He whispers where Tertullian thunders, but some of the images are the same, and he is recognizably of the same landscape. But the *Octavius*, following the Ciceronian practice, begins with the conversations of friends near Rome. There are three friends: Minucius Felix himself, Octavius Januarius, and Caecilius Natalis. The last was probably a magistrate of Cirta, for such a name has been found in Cirta belonging to that time. Octavius Januarius was a Christian convert. They have been walking along the seashore for some time when Octavius sees a statue of the Egyptian god Serapis and blows a kiss to it. The others are a little shocked, but they pass on toward the seashore, toward a mysterious landscape of rotting boats and flotsam and small boys skimming pebbles across the waves, each one trying to outdo the other. Throughout the conversation you are made conscious of the presence of these boys: almost it is as though disputation was no more important and no more enduring than the spectacle of boys on the seashore.

The three disputants are sitting on the edge of the baths when Caecilius points to the infamy of the Christians. They commit a host of crimes. Do not they gather for bawdy love feasts? The lamps are doused when the love feasts are over. Everyone knows they practice unlawful embraces in the dark. They worship the head of an ass. On the altars there are phalluses. Worse still, they have a practice—abhorrent to all men of good will—of wrapping babies in dough. They are given knives which they plunge into the dough, and when the blood begins to spurt out they suddenly become maniacs, tearing the baby limb from limb. As if this was not enough, they believe in an all-seeing Creator, a pure absurdity, since God can hardly be expected to go running around in every man's thoughts. They believe in the Resurrection—another absurdity. They swear that the world will end in blood and fire: a statement more stupid than absurd, since the natural law demands that the world should continue pleasantly its existence. Saying this, Caecilius beams. "The whole thing is monstrous," he says, and shrugs his shoulders.

When Octavius comes to the defense of the Christians, he points to the sea. "See how beautiful it is," he exclaims. "All the beauty of the world proclaims the majesty of God. Look at the animals. They, too, are beautiful. The beauty of these forms proclaims the art of God, and we ourselves, our faces and our eyes so appropriately placed and all the other senses —surely they speak of divinity! Is not the world a house where everything is kept in the utmost neatness and order, and surely this house has a master, and the master himself is more beautiful than the stars or any part of the known world." The recourse to the argument of beauty was especially pleasing to St. Augustine, and Octavius might have been expected to expatiate further, but he passes on to other arguments. He shows how all the old wives' tales of Caecilius come to nothing in the end: there are no asses' heads, no phalluses, no drunken brawls after the evening feast. The Christian is dedicated to quietness. He has no temples and no images. Almost he has no rites. He walks humbly along the silent ways of God. As for God—

He cannot be seen: for he is too bright to look upon: nor comprehended: for he is too pure to be touched: nor measured: for he is wholly beyond the reach of the senses, infinite, immense, measurable by Himself alone. Our hearts are too small for any understanding of Him, and therefore we measure Him only when we say He is immeasurable. He who believes he has knowledge of God's greatness only diminishes it; he who would not diminish it, knows it not.

Seek no name for God: God is His name. When we attempt to distinguish people from the mass, then we need vocabularies and titles, marks of distinction; but God, who alone is, is wholly summed in the name of God. If we should call Him "Father," then we introduce ideas of the flesh; and if we call Him "King" we reduce Him to the level of this world; and should we call Him "Lord," then we might believe He was mortal. But put away the list of names, and then you will see Him in His brightness. (*Octavius*, XVIII, 8-10.)

The sun is still shimmering on the sea as he proceeds with the argument which is formed upon the nameless beauty of God, who can never be seen—but who has seen the wind? who can bear to look upon the sun? God is everywhere the spectator, His energy flowing through all that He looks upon, present even in the darkness of men's thoughts. We cannot avoid Him; therefore we must love Him. Not God alone, but all nature gives promise of the Resurrection:

The sun dips down and is born again; the stars fade and return; the flowers fall and come to life again; the shrubs bloom even after they have died; even the dead seeds grow into life; the body lying in the grave is as a winter tree, which conceals its greenness in aridity. Why demand that in raw winter the trees should flourish? We must await the springtime of the body. [*Expectandum nobis etiam corporis ver est.*] (*Octavius*, XXIV, 11-12.)

This is no longer argument: some other element has been introduced: and meditation takes the place of rhetoric. All the time Octavius is saying: "There is nothing to fear, God is everywhere, it is only necessary to know Him." The martyrs are the blessed of God, they are not forgotten in their agony, nor does death end all—again and again Octavius returns to the theme of the death where there is no dying. "There is no mourning at our funerals," he says. "Why should there be? We adorn our funerals with quietness, as we adorn our lives. No fading crown of flowers is placed upon dead brows. We hope for God's eternal garland which is ever green. So in quietness and modesty, safe in the liberality of our God, we quicken with the hope of a future happiness with faith in God's present majesty. So we arise in blessedness and live in the contemplation of what is yet to come."

With such quietness Minucius Felix concludes his account of the meeting of friends by the seashore, promising to continue the debate later, though Caecilius has already embraced the faith; but of the later debates we know nothing, nor perhaps is there any need to know anything further, since he has said nearly all he had to say. He had introduced a new note into the Christian religion and laid the groundwork for a host of successors, who orchestrated the simple words spoken by the seashore, while the spring winds came over the sands of Rome and the African lawyers talked into the afternoon.

Minucius Felix was not a Father of the Church, Tertullian was, though many Churchmen would wish it otherwise. This furious windmill with a spinning brain combined the vision of Minucius Felix with the vehemence of Ignatius. His theology revolves around the great Pauline antithesis of sin and grace. One imagines him in his lawyer's gown, heavy browed and thickset, stern, querulous, and slightly mad, thundering and appealing to the heavenly justice which seemed always to elude him, a man who used words like brickbats and rejoiced when the brickbats drew blood, the perpetual thunderer, in love with lightning. He hated with a pure, exalted violence, cursing Plato, loathing Socrates, at odds with himself, so that he gives the impression of being never at rest, always at the mercy of his own scorn, his own boiling religious temper.

He had reason to boil. The martyrs were dying. The Roman Empire was at bay, yet still the orders for the holocausts were being given; and it was all a waste and a decay, for victory was never to be doubted. So he wrote on and on, equally at ease in Greek and Latin, uttering his solemn anathemas against the enemies of Christ from whatever corner they came: the thrice-damned tribune receiving the same curses as the morons of the marketplace. Because he was almost insanely determined to oppose the established order, and because he was compelled to invent out of rude Punic Latin a language fit for heroic impudence, Tertullian found himself speaking in words that clanged and jolted like armor.

No quotations can give the temper of the man. He must be read right through for the sustained bitterness, anger, rodomontade, and brilliance of his thoughts: the smell of the blood in the arena sand is on everything he wrote. He believed Christ deformed; it is possible that he was also deformed. The son of a centurion, he could speak sometimes like a coarse-mouthed soldier, and then at other moments he would speak of a sleeping child with a casual tenderness.

He brought into the history of the Church nothing new except the manner of his violence, but it was justifiable violence; and there are times when he speaks like an inmate of a concentration camp, choking in the smoke of the incinerators; for like the Jews in Germany, the Christians in Rome and North Africa were sometimes burnt alive in the *vivicomburia*. "At the present moment," he wrote once, "it is the very middle of the heat, the very dog-days of persecution—as you would expect, from the dog-headed himself, of course. Some Christians have been tested by the fire, some by the sword, some by the beasts; some, lashed and torn with hooks, have just tasted martyrdom or lie hungering for it in the prisons." He was talking of real prisons, real anguish, real blood falling in real sand. There were no dubieties.

But if Tertullian more than any of the Christian Fathers suffers from quotation, there are hints of his dramatic power in all the books he wrote. "The blood of the Christians is seed," he wrote, "*Semen est sanguis Christianorum*." He could say brief flashing things like this with tremendous power and urgency: rarely has there been a writer so lapidary and so dramatic: he is like a thundering white-capped wave which comes racing to the shore, while in the hollow of the wave rocks and stones and pebbles are ready to be flung on the sand. The force of the final impact, the shudder of the stones, the turmoil of the waves, can be seen, or guessed at, in a translation of the concluding passage of *De Spectaculis*, a short work in which he denounced the Romans who lived only that they might enjoy the stadium, the stage, or the amphitheater. A greater stage, a greater amphitheater await them! He shouts with joy:

What a spectacle there is already at hand, the coming of the Lord in His pride and His triumph no longer in doubt! What exultation among the angels, what glory among the risen saints! What a reign of justice there will be! What delights to be found in the new city of Jerusalem! And there are still other spectacles to follow on the last and perpetual Day of Judgment, that day which the gentiles refused, for they laughed it to scorn, when all this old world and all its generations shall be consumed in a single blaze! How vast the spectacle of that day! We shall wonder and laugh, know joy and exultation! Then, on that day, we shall see the Kings who have been welcomed into Heaven, and at the same time we shall see Jove and all those who told of his ascent groaning in utter darkness. From Heaven, too, we shall see the magistrates who persecuted the name of Jesus liquefying in fiercer flames than those they kindled against the Christians! Who else? We shall see the sages and the philosophers blushing before their disciples as they burn in a single conflagration, those disciples who were taught by them that God was pure nothingness, or men were without souls, or their present souls shall never return to their former bodies! And then shall come the poets trembling before the tribunal, not of Rhadamanthus nor of Minos, but of the Christ they never thought to see! And then there will be the tragic actors loudly declaiming their own tragedy, and then there will be the players whose limbs grow more urgent than ever in the fires, and you will see the charioteer now painted red all over in a wheel of flame, and after them the athletes, not in their gymnasiums, but hurled pell-mell among the flames, unless it be that we should find ourselves with the desire to gaze upon them with an insatiable eye, to see those heroes who damned the Lord. I shall point to God. I shall say: "Here He is, the son of a carpenter or a harlot (as you said), the Sabbath-breaker, the Samaritan, possessed by devils. Here He is, who was bought by Judas. Here He is, who was struck with a reed and with a fist, made beastly with spittle, given gall and vinegar to drink. Here He is, whom the disciples secretly bore away, so that it might be said of Him that He had risen from the dead, unless it was the gardener who removed the body, afraid his lettuces would be trampled down by a horde of visitors!" Such spectacles, such exaltations are about to come—what praetor, consul, quaestor, or priest could ever give so great a bounty? And yet in some way all these things are ours, represented by faith within the imagination of the spirit. And what then of the things the eye has not seen nor the ear heard? What of the things that have never yet entered into the heart of man? So there shall come blessings more joyous than any to be found in circus, theater, or any stadium anywhere! (Tertullian, *De Spectaculis*, XXX.)

It is magical invective, but supremely dangerous, as the Russian schismatics learned much later to their cost. Tertullian believed firmly in vengeance, and the Last Day, the flames, the groans, the travails of the awakened dead. He yearns to see the sinners in their nests of flame: and when Gibbon, commenting on the passage just quoted, says that it contains "a long variety of affected and unfeeling witticisms," he has missed the point, for Tertullian was never so earnest as when he reflected upon the punishments of the damned, and never so gay. Tertullian had no gift for wit, though he possessed the supreme gift of irony.

We can chart out the mind of Tertullian by his hates, his ironies, and his loves, but he loves only martyrs and sleeping children (who have the innocence of martyrs), and the coming of spring and all the seasons. He employs irony as a rapier, but sometimes he will employ it with all the delicacy of a man who puts dynamite under an immense rock which is then sent tumbling down on the invaders in the pass beneath: more than any other Christian apologist Tertullian appears to have the desire to squash his enemies flat. Minucius Felix gently shrugs off the accusations of the pagans; Tertullian carries the hot coals to the enemy's camp. One of the charges directed against Minucius Felix by Caecilius Natalis was the sad habit of the Christians of putting babies in bread and then cutting them to pieces. Tertullian denies the charge: "Take one baby, known to be tender, which knows nothing of death and can laugh under the knife. *Item*, one loaf, to catch the juicy blood. Mix with lampstands and dogs, and some sops to set the dogs running and knocking the lamps over. Enjoy the feast with your mother and sister." He gives complete details of the preparation of the feast. "Plunge the knife into the baby, who is nobody's enemy, who is guiltless, who is everyone's child; or, if the office of murderer belongs to another, simply take your place beside the baby who is dying before it has lived; then watch the young soul as it escapes; then catch the infant blood; then steep your bread in it; then eat to your heart's content." Swift said much the same thing when discussing famine in Ireland: Tertullian says it with a greater malice, and with his eyes closer to the target. Not Swift but Tertullian is the world's master in "savage indignation."

The wide-ranging acid mind of Tertullian was concerned with one thing, and one thing only: that the religion of Christ, who is God, should be upheld. He must celebrate Christ, and at the same time he must denigrate all other gods. It is as though he was walking down a gallery of the gods: one by one they fall before him. He proves to his satisfaction that the Greek and Roman gods were men: therefore they were not gods: also, they probably had no existence: also, if they existed, they are now unrecognizable, encrusted with impossible legends: also, if any of the legends is true, it is irrelevant or has been put to other purposes than those intended. As for the statues of the gods, the spiders weave their webs over them and the birds foul them, while those made of bronze are melted down, as everybody knows, so that Saturn becomes a cooking pot and Minerva a washbasin. It is a fate which Tertullian hardly deplores.

There are other gods beloved by the Romans, to be found among dead Emperors suddenly made holy by the fact of death. He has none of our modern veneration for Marcus Aurelius, who murdered Christians at his pleasure. "The state lost Marcus Aurelius," he wrote in the *Apology*, "at Sirmium on March 17, but on the 24th his holiness the arch-eunuch, offering his own unclean blood and slashing his muscles, issued the usual orders to pray for the safety of Marcus, whose empire had been taken from him by death. Oh, but the messengers were late, and surely the diplomats were sleeping!" For Tertullian, the rebuke was comparatively gentle: he could thunder in a louder voice when he desired, but he was an adept at keeping his ammunition dry and his reserves untouched and unharmed. He allows his enemies the privilege of blowing balloons and contents himself with a pin.

In that overheated world where Tertullian explores his own anger, there are occasional moments of coolness, of an unexpected tenderness. At such moments the lawyer's tricks fall away, and he is no longer inclined to gnaw bones or pick a decaying corpse to pieces with his teeth. A sense of magic and wonder hangs over the strange landscapes of Tertullian, so that often he gives the impression of living through a childhood nightmare: when the nightmare is over he will awake and see the face of his mother, or the face of Jesus. He slept badly. Even as a child he found difficulty in sleeping, so that his nurse was compelled to tell him stories about the towers of witches—he uses the word *lamiae*, which Keats celebrated in his wonderful poem "Lamia"—and the combs of the sun, and there were apples that grew in the sea and fish that grew on trees. Years later, when he thundered against Roman power, we still recognize the witches' towers, and what are the combs of the sun but the radiance of Christ?

Born and bred a pagan, Tertullian possessed a convert's cunning: he knew the enemy from long acquaintance and found no good in him. His arguments are often unfair. Only Christ exists in the majesty of the heavens: the Romans are shadows. Recalling Minucius Felix, employing the same arguments but on another plane, he will suddenly forget his horror of the enemy and embark upon a prayer or speak softly of the flowers and birds. He remembers how the small birds fly, "spreading out the cross of their wings instead of hands, and saying something that seems to be a prayer." Marcion condemned the God who created this world. Tertullian answers, like Octavius by the seashore: "One flower of the hedgerow by itself, I think—I do not say a flower of the meadows; a single tiny seashell—I do not say of the Red Sea;[1] one feather of a moorfowl—I do not say a peacock—surely they do not speak of a mean artificer." All the delicate things of nature appeal to him. On festival days the people in the Roman Empire were ordered to wear crowns of flowers. Tertullian, on behalf of the Christians, refuses, for surely flowers are more delightful when they are free, and not bound in arrogant garlands? To make God intelligible to man, he returns to the same theory of beauty which Minucius Felix found so absorbing. He delights in humble things:

Imitate if you can the hexagons of the bees, the barns of the ants, the webs of the spiders, the threads of the silkworm. Endure if you can those mean creatures of your bed and of your roof, the venom of the mosquito, the beetles' poison, the spear and trumpet of the gnat. Of what kind will the greater creatures be, when you are helped or harmed by such small things, that you may not even in small things despise the Creator? Make a circuit around yourself, survey man within and without. Even this work of our God will please you, because the Lord, the greater God, loved it so well, and for the sake of the human body toiled to descend from the Heavens among these poverty-stricken elements, for the sake of which, even in this little cell of

[1] He is referring to pearls.

the Creator, He was crucified. But see—up to this moment He has not disdained the water with which He washes His own people, nor the oil wherewith He anoints them, nor the mingled milk and honey wherewith He feeds His children, nor the bread which is the representation of His own body. (*Tertullian, Adversus Marcion*, I, 14.)

It is for such things that we are grateful to Tertullian. He fires the blood with his invective, then cools it with an appeal to beauty and the symbolic imagination, hardly knowing where to turn, so overcome he is by the indwelling of God and by the perfection immanent in man. "Make a circuit around yourself, survey man within and without." It is the Stoic temper. But though something of the Stoic remained with him until the end, and in every chapter we come upon the characteristic Stoic sign-manuals, as in Augustine we see the characteristics of the uncovenanted Manichee concealed behind the august image of piety, Tertullian's insistence upon the inquiry into the nature of man is balanced by the knowledge of man's ultimate paradise.

Before Minucius Felix and Tertullian the Christians spoke of men as though they were bodiless, spirits already in a coarse friable envelope. With Tertullian the word *homo* is everywhere. He had no particular belief in the ascetic life. He married, and almost certainly had children. He will have nothing to do with those who decry the flesh, and he has a peculiar sympathy for women. For him the soul is set within the body in such a way that "it may be questioned whether the flesh carries the soul or the soul the flesh, whether the flesh serves the soul, or the soul serves the flesh. What use of nature, what enjoyment of the universe, what savor of the elements does the soul not enjoy by the agency of the flesh?" How wonderful is man, he says, echoing Sophocles, and he points to the works of art as emblems of God, and to the human body previsaged long before the coming of Christ as the pattern into which Christ would be poured, and surely our living and our dying assume the shape of drama and of art. He calls himself "a sinner of every brand, fit for nothing but repent-ance," but he was at least as lusty as Bunyan. "Are they not men?" he says of the martyrs, "and was not Christ man?" "We say—and we say it openly—while you are torturing us, mangled and bleeding—we shout: 'We worship God through Christ.' Count Him man, if you will. Through Him and in Him God would have Himself worshiped." And again: "So we spread ourselves before God, while the hooks pierce us and the crosses suspend us and the fires blaze on us, and the swords slit our throats, and the beasts leap on us. Even the posture of the Christian at prayer shows his readiness for every manner of torture. Here lies the crime: where God's truth is, there is devotion!"

When Tertullian talks directly of God, he talks inevitably in a different tone. At such moments he meditates cleanly, with no sense of strain, with the voice of someone praying at the end of the love feast, after the solemn partaking of the bread and the wine, the ceremonial bathing of the hands in water and the lighting of the lamps and the singing, till the echoes fade away, and then the lamps are doused as one by one, secretly, the Christians leave the meeting place. Almost exactly halfway through the *Apology*, as though this was the hub from which the spokes radiated, comes his portrait of God:

We worship the One God who fashioned the whole fabric with the instrument of elements, bodies, spirits, and who by His word commanded it, by the reason with which He ordered it, by the power wherewith He formed it, making it out of nothing as an ornament of His own majesty: whence it came about that the Greeks also gave the universe the name of *kosmos*. Invisible He is, though He is seen. Incomprehensible He is, though He is by grace revealed. Inconceivable He is, though our human senses may conceive Him. He is true, and He is great. But what in the ordinary sense may be seen, comprehended, conceived, is less than the eye that grasps it, the hands that soil it, the senses that discover it: for the infinite is known only to itself. So it is that we may conceive of God, though He is beyond our reckoning. The power of His greatness makes Him known to man, but He is yet unknown. And this is the sum total of their sin who will not recognize Him even when they cannot fail not to know Him. Would you have us prove Him to you from the vast variety of His works, those works which contain, sustain, delight and terrify us? Would you have us prove Him to you by the testimony of the human soul itself? The poor imprisoned soul, confined by its own depravity, exhausted by lusts and desires, enslaved to false gods, nevertheless after recovering its senses, having spewed out the evil within it, or as though awakening from sleep or from illness, when it comes to its proper health, why then, it utters the name of God, for no other reason except that it recognizes Him as the only true god. O noble testimony of the soul which is by nature Christian! [*Testimonium animae naturaliter Christianae!*] And saying this word, the soul gazes not towards the Capitol but towards heaven. For it knows the abode of the living God; from Him and from heaven it descended. (Tertullian, *Apologius*, XVII.)

We hardly recognize in the slow music of the theme the voice of the thunderer, but there are a hundred places where he spoke as quietly. He could be tortuous; he could be brilliant for the sake of brilliance; he could shout so loudly that sometimes we even know when he is hoarse, but always he returns to the contemplation of the miracle of man confronted with a miraculous God, living in a miraculous world, possessed of the miraculous promise of the resurrection of the flesh; and like Gregory later, he will insist that the resurrection is worthless unless it is of the flesh indeed. He wrote in his book *On the Resurrection of the Flesh*:

Gaze now on these exemplifications of divine power. Day dies into night, and is everywhere entombed in shadows. The glory of the world has is obsequies, all its substance is tarnished. All things grow dull, voiceless, dumb; everywhere there is a holiday and a rest. And so we mourn for the lost light. And yet once more with all its own beauty, its dower, its sun, the same, and unharmed, and complete, it revives for the universal world; slay-ing night, which is its own death, rending asunder its own sepulture of darkness, extant as its own heir, until night too revives herself with her own retinue. For both the rays of the stars are rekindled, which the rising of the dawn had extinguished, and the distant groups of constellations are brought back, which a temporary separation had removed, and the specular mirrors of the moon are readorned, which her monthly course had worn down.

Now winter and summer roll round in season, and the blessings of spring and autumn with their power and their fruits, while the earth receives from Heaven the knowledge of how to clothe the trees after they are stripped bare, the knowledge how to give color to flowers and spread the herbage over the earth again, and then those same seeds which were parched by the sun display themselves till at last they are consumed. O marvellous method of God, which preserves after denuding, which cuts only to restore, which destroys only to retain, which spoils only to renew, and diminishes only to enlarge. Indeed, by this miracle, greater and riper blessings are received than any which were taken away—so that destruction becomes increase, what is taken away is restored, and all loss is gain. Let me say again: the condition of all things is renewal. All things when they have departed return to their first condition, all things begin when they have ceased, they are ended only that they may be born. Nothing perishes save into salvation. Therefore the whole revolving wheel of existence bears witness to the resurrection of the dead.[2]

Here, in a language which would be understood by the Taoists and the Chinese poets, having once more thrown his lawyer's briefs aside, Tertullian surveys his own immortality and the immortality of all Christians, and finds it good, and easily explained. The cleverness has vanished in the contemplation of natural miracles. It was characteristic of him that he should inquire further: to attempt to discover what shape the embodied soul would possess on the Last Day. He was not a visionary. He could only report what he had

---

[2] Tertullian, *De Resurrectione Carnis* (Quoted from the translation by Bishop Pearson from Frederic W. Farrar, *Lives of the Fathers*, New York: Macmillan, 1889, I, 183).

learned from those who were. In his book *On the Soul* he reported the story of a woman who lost herself in ecstasies while the Scriptures were being read or psalms were being sung. She said that the soul she had perceived possessed a bodily form, seemed to be spirit, but was not empty; on the contrary it could be touched, it was soft, shining, and of the color of air, "and in every detail possessed a human form."

Of Tertullian's life we know almost nothing. We know he journeyed to Rome and wrote the *Apology* at a time when the Christians of Carthage were being slaughtered, and we know that he fell into the hands of the Montanists, a puritan sect which committed heresies in the eyes of Rome; he delighted in his heresies, and the Church has long ago forgiven him for them. We know that he was earthly, of the earth, if only because he saw God corporeally, unlike Clement of Alexandria, who could not find images enough to describe how incorporeal God was. We know that he was impatient and could become on occasions excessively angry, for he confesses as much. We know he never reached a higher rank than presbyter, that he loathed all Greek philosophers ("What has the Academy to do with the Church? What has Christ to do with Plato? What has Jerusalem to do with Athens?"), and his horror of the Greeks was surprising enough, since he evidently knew Greek well and had read widely among the philosophers. We know that as he grew older, becoming more and more a Montanist and less and less a Catholic, his temper, always sharp, was enflamed by puritanism, so that in time he came to regard the body with loathing, as a burden.

But to the end he retained his characteristic effrontery, his desire to shock, his amazing gift of satire and irony. We think of him as the author of *credo quia absurdum*, and it is true that the phrase represented one of his closest and dearest ideas. But he did not write: "I believe, because it is absurd." What he wrote was something far more complex. He said: "The Son of God was born, I am not ashamed of it because it is shameful. The Son of God died, I believe it because it is absurd. The Son of God was buried and rose again, I am sure of it because it is impossible." By asserting the shameful, the absurd, and the impossible against the evidence of good taste, probability, and reason, he was hurling a defiant challenge in the face of the classical world, and particularly in the face of the Stoics, whom he half admired. But it was a dangerous challenge. If Christianity was nothing but shame, absurdity, and impossibility, then all the cautious reasoning with which he attacks the gods of Rome in the *Apology* falls to the ground, for these were precisely the faults he found in Jupiter, Mars, Bellona, and half a hundred other gods. His greatest words do not lie in the most memorable of his statements: they lie in his defense of martyrdom.

"*Corpus sumus*," Tertullian once wrote. "We are part of the body of Christ, being members of the society of Christians." It was his proudest boast. At another time he talked of the two fires: the one that burns, and the other which is sent from heaven to prevent men from burning, so that they can never be reduced to ashes. And certainly he believed himself possessed of the second fire. The huge, robust, hot-tempered man was all his life aflame. He was not alone in this. It was characteristic of the North African writers, who shared the same brilliance, the same sense of impatience, and the same sense of some impending doom.

Like Tertullian, Cyprian was born near Carthage. We know almost nothing of his early life. He may have been a senator. He was certainly not a lawyer. He was a heathen until late in life, and like Augustine he seems to have spent some time as a teacher of rhetoric. He was proud, cautious, unforgiving, and not over generous; he rarely spoke about love, and continually honored good works; he was—though he passionately denied the charge—something of a coward. He was a good administrator, he could be inordinately dull as he imitated Tertullian without Tertullian's fire, and he would probably have gone unmarked if the Emperor Decius had not launched a plan to exterminate the Christians in 250 A.D., two years after Cyprian was elevated to the bishopric of Carthage with the title of *pappa,* or pope. When the martyrdoms began, Cyprian took to flight, saying that he had seen in a dream that he was needed elsewhere and could better look after his flock from a distance.

He never entirely lived down his flight from Carthage. Wealthy, possessing senatorial or near-senatorial rank, belonging to a famous family universally respected, Cyprian returned from exile with the evident desire to place himself in the path of the Roman tribunal. He would suffer as the other Christians suffered. He would lead more strictly than ever a life of voluntary poverty, abandoning his gardens and vineyards for the bare walls of a cell. The Christians had fought bravely; he would fight more bravely. From the moment of his return he was like a man resolved upon martyrdom.

The times were desperate. The Decian massacres were followed by the plague: the dead and the dying littered the streets. It was at this time that Cyprian wrote his tract *On Mortality,* with its fervor for a holy death. He wrote:

Only in the heavens above are to be found true peace, sure repose, constant, enduring and eternal safety. There is our dwelling, there is our home. Who is there who would not hasten towards it? There a great multitude of the beloved await us: innumerable hosts of fathers, brothers, daughters and sons. There, too, is the glorious choir of the apostles, and the exulting prophets, and the countless multitudes of martyrs, crowned now with victory after their wars and their sufferings, and there you will find the triumphant virgins, and the merciful enjoying their rewards. So let us hasten thither with ardent desire, coming face to face with Christ. After the earthly comes the heavenly; after the small comes the great; after the temporary comes the eternal. (Cyprian, *De Mortalitate.*)

It is not great music, but it is authentic music nevertheless. There are few subtleties in him. He had neither Tertullian's anger, nor Tertullian's sympathy with the human race. He quarreled often, but not violently. He quarreled with the Pope in Rome, demanding under what rule the Pope regarded himself as the successor of St. Peter, since all bishops were the apostle's successor, and surely the bishops of Carthage and Alexandria were of equal rank? There were schisms; he did his best patiently to heal them. Some Christians had been carried off by Numidian warriors; he helped to raise the ransom money. Decisions had to be made concerning the lapsed Christians, those who had saved their lives by receiving from the magistrates certificates showing that they had renounced their God. Cyprian's decision to allow them to return to the Church was made with good sense. But the quarrels continued; and in long, loose, flowing sentences full of redundancies he thundered from the pulpit at the characteristic evils of the time, never brilliantly and perhaps nearly always ineffectively. When he heard in 257 A.D. that a new edict against the Christians was on its way, he once more went into hiding. Yet his mind was made up. He determined to show himself. About this time he wrote the greatest, as it is the most beautiful, of his letters, a paean in honor of the martyrdom which now awaited him:

O feet most blessedly bound with irons, not to be loosed by the ironsmith, but by the Lord! O feet most blessedly bound, guiding me along the way of salvation to Paradise! O feet which are bound to the world for the present time only to be made free by the Lord! O feet, which linger awhile among the fetters and the prison-bars, only to run more quickly to Christ along a blessed road! Let envy, malice or cruelty hold you here in chains as long as they will, yet from the earth and from these sufferings you shall speedily enter the Kingdom of Heaven.

The body is not comforted in the mines with soft chairs and cushions, yet it is comforted with the peace and solace of Christ. The body weary with labor lies prostrate at last, but there is no evil in lying down with Christ. Your unbathed limbs are foul and discolored with filth, yet within are they spiritually cleansed. The bread is scarce, but men live not by bread: they live by the word of God. Shivering, you look for clothing: but he who puts on Christ is abundantly clothed and adorned. (Cyprian, *Epistola*, LXXVI.)

It is almost the voice of Clement of Rome, sad, truculent, full of a sad weariness of the flesh, but with no great desire for death and with no fear of death either. He knew exactly how the Christians were treated. Not all were martyred. Some were imprisoned, others were sent to work in the mines, others were loaded with fetters, still others were punished by being made to lie on the ground through all weathers. But for himself he knew there would be no alternative to death. On September 14, 257, he dreamed that a tall youth had taken him by the hand to the throne of the Proconsul. Then the youth stood behind the Proconsul, entering some words on a tablet. The Proconsul spoke, but Cyprian could not hear his words: he saw only the troubled look of the boy who shook his head and made a gesture that suggested the stroke of the headman. Cyprian begged for a day's delay, which was granted to him. On the anniversary of the dream Cyprian came out of hiding, two officers came to arrest him, and he was taken in a carriage to the Proconsul's court, a few miles outside Carthage. The Proconsul, Galerius Maximus, asked the inevitable formal questions:

"Do you say you are Thascius Cyprianus?"

"Yes."

"Who has made himself *pappa* of a sacrilegious sect?"

"Yes."

"Though the most sacred Emperors have ordered you to sacrifice to them?"

"I refused."

"Consider the matter well."

"I have considered it. Your task is plain."

There was a brief discussion between the Proconsul and his assessors; then he said: "I command that Thascius Cyprianus be beheaded by the sword."

"Thanks be to God," Cyprian answered quietly, while the Christians shouted: "Let us die with him!"

He had not expected to be beheaded; he had hoped indeed to be thrown to the lions; but the choice was no longer in his hands. He was taken to a plain near the city walls of Carthage. There he removed his red bishop's cloak and knelt in prayer, while the crowd gathered, and it was noticed that some of the onlookers climbed the trees to see better. After he had knelt he rose again, and this time he removed his dalmatic and asked his friends to give the executioner twenty-five pieces of gold as a sign of forgiveness. He knelt again, covered his eyes with his hands, whispered a word to the executioner, and was martyred. The Christians came running forward to dip their handkerchiefs in his blood—it was the first recorded instance of such a practice—and late that night his friends removed the body and buried it. Augustine, in one of his sermons, painted an elaborate parallel between the death of Cyprian and the death of Christ.

The death of Cyprian shocked North Africa: he was the first African bishop to be martyred; but the martyrs continued to die, and the Roman Empire continued its long progress of decay. In the same year that Cyprian died, Valerian took his armies across the Taurus Mountains into Persia, where the Sassanian King Sapor defeated him. The Roman Emperor was made prisoner, to be used as a footstool by the Persian King and later, stuffed with rags and straw, propped up in a corner of the palace to amuse the harem women. Not far from Persepolis, they made a carving of the Roman Emperor's surrender on the bare rock. Valerian is kneeling, but his hands do not shade his eyes: they are flung forward in an obscene gesture, demanding pity. It is as though the Persians had avenged the Christian martyrs.

The explosion of Christianity in North Africa continued until the death of Augustine. North Africa was the greenhouse where the plant flowered prodigiously; strange new heretical plants grew up overnight. But the main impetus of

Christianity was directed elsewhere. Along the coast of southern France and northern Italy the roots were gripping deep. There followed a long period of persecutions, and the Roman Empire, ill led, seemed about to perish, leaving nothing except anarchy in its place. Almost a hopelessness descended upon the Christians, a hopelessness already visible in Cyprian's words: "The world herself proclaims the evidence of universal decay. No longer is there sufficient rain in winter to nourish the crops, or heat in summer to bring them to maturity. Spring no longer makes provision for the sowing, nor autumn for her fruits. Less and less are blocks of marble wrested from the exhausted hills; less and less do gold and silver mines yield their wealth; and gradually the impoverished veins of earth must fail." In this letter to Donatus Cyprian was perhaps talking of his own powers at the same time as he spoke of the earth's exhaustion. But the period of exhaustion was short lived: in the next century arose three giants, born within a few years of one another, to defend the fort. One was named after a Roman Emperor, another was called Holy Name (*Hieronymus*), the third was named after the nectar of the gods. Between them, in various ways, Augustine, Jerome, and Ambrose laid the foundations for the renovated Church.

IV. ❦ AMBROSE: THE PATRICIAN

FOR A LONG PERIOD OF HIS LIFE AMBROSE WAS THE arbiter of the Empire. He humbled Emperors; he lived in visions, he thirsted for righteousness; and he left on the Church the stamp of his Roman austerity. The small slight man with the grizzled beard, drooping mustache, and pale yellow hair, whose portrait in the Church of Sant' Ambrogio in Milan shows a remarkable resemblance to the poet Rainer Maria Rilke, was all iron: now black, now glowing. He had the aristocrat's contempt for the middle way and the patrician's delight in ruling men. He was inflexible. Someone said of him: "If he says to the sun, 'Stand', it stands." Yet he had no physical presence. With his large, melancholy eyes, his tall forehead, his long nose and arching eyebrows, one perceptibly higher than the other, he looked what he was— the descendant of princes, the last of his line. His father, Aurelius Ambrosius, was Prefect of Gaul, who from his palace at Treves administered all Britain, France, Spain, and Portugal as well as part of Germany and the islands of Sardinia, Corsica, and Sicily. Born to the purple, Ambrose continued to live in the purple throughout his life, and long before his death he was regarded as a saint, so wearing the purple for eternity.

There are mysteries about Ambrose, as there are with all the great Fathers of the Church, but he was the least mysterious. He suffered no tortures; he seems never to have been wounded in the side; and he never needed to fight for his position or power. When he was a child, the Pope and high ecclesiastics paid visits to his mother's palace in Rome. Once, when the ladies of the household were kissing the hands of these dignitaries, Ambrose mimicked them and held out his hand, saying: "You should do the same for me, since I am going to be a bishop." The faithful Paulinus, who records the incident, finds nothing surprising in the story. Ambition ruled Ambrose. When he became bishop with vast ecclesiastical and political influence he was merely pursuing the ambitions of his father, but with a wider scope. Aurelius Ambrosius held power over men's bodies; the son held power over their minds as well.

When Ambrose returned to Rome to study, probably after the death of his father, the city which called itself "the capital of the world" still remembered its ancient destinies. The son of a Prefect, Ambrose could look forward to being a Prefect in his turn. But it was noted that he was strangely studious, in love with Vergil, and there existed a strange sympathy between him and his sister Marcellina and his brother Satyrus. The children had no need to talk together: each knew what the other was thinking: and the bond between them—that tight bond which exists so often in aristocratic families—increased with the years. When Marcellina took the vow of virginity, Ambrose also dedicated himself to virginity and religion, leaving Satyrus to continue the family fortunes. Satyrus became a lawyer and rose to be governor of a province; and though Ambrose, after completing his studies, accompanied his brother to Sirmium in Illyria, where they both became barristers in the Court of the Praetorian Prefect of Italy, it is clear from the beginning that Ambrose's heart was not in it. He missed Marcellina. He preferred the air of chastity which hung over his mother's palace in Rome, where religion was discussed in muted whispers and where he had come to love an old Christian teacher called Simplician, who took the place of his dead father. He had no love for wrangling in the courts or for any kind of rhetoric. "Away with the finery and paint of words, which weaken the force of what is said," he said later. The ringleted rhetoricians and the lawyers in their ceremonial togas were equally distasteful to him: only the presence of Satyrus comforted him a little. Probably he accompanied his brother because he had no idea what to do. His mind was clear, but he was ill read, given to moodiness, conscious of superb talents, proud, but possessing no spark or fire.

But gradually the fire was being ignited. Perhaps it was because he was nicknamed "the Bishop," and was therefore perpetually reminded of the role he would have to play, but it is more likely that the spark was ignited on the day when Sextus Petronius Probus summoned him into the marble office of the prefecture and solemnly discussed with the rising barrister the subject of Ambrose's advancement. Extremes met. Probus was a millionaire whose vast fortune according to rumor had been acquired by questionable methods; he was also unusually generous and sympathetic to the young. This strange Maecenas, "whose lavish hand," said Claudian, "surpassed the rivers of Spain in pouring out floods of golden gifts," found in Ambrose all the qualities he himself lacked. It was not only that Ambrose was an aristocrat, the son of a famous father. There was something stern and unyielding in him, a hint of the coming fire, an awkwardness and an apparent hesitancy. Satyrus was already governor of one of the thirty-six provinces. Probus appointed Ambrose governor of the province of Aemilia-Liguria. Ambrose appears to have begged off, but Probus cut him short: "Go, conduct yourself, not as a judge, but as a bishop." The governor's headquarters were in Milan; and there, by the waters of the Ticino, among the cornfields and the low hills, with only the briefest excursions outside the city, Ambrose spent the rest of his life. At the time of his appointment Ambrose was about twenty-nine.

In those days Milan was the principal seat of the Imperial Government of the West. The governor of the province was therefore in a position of quite extraordinary power. Inevitably he would come into contact with the Western Emperor. Still more inevitably, since Valentinian I was a brutal bigot, the new governor would find himself in conflict with the Emperor. Valentinian, with his steel-blue eyes, his flaxen hair, and his diabolical temper, was everything that Ambrose was not. He came from the people, he delighted in violence, and he was accustomed to say: "Authority must be enforced with severity." He was not simply stating a commonplace. His severity took the form of outrageous punishments. He ordered that a youth who let loose the royal hounds too soon at a hunting party be beaten to death. He kept two she-bears called Innocentia and Mica Aurea (Gold Flake). It was rumored that he threw condemned criminals to the bears and watched them being torn to pieces, and if his other actions are believed, the rumor was probably true. But Valentinian was handsome, he possessed considerable presence, and though he had few accomplishments, he at least looked like an Emperor, unlike his brother Valens, who was swarthy, pot-bellied, and bandy-legged. Valens had been elected to the purple at the same time as Valentinian. Valens ruled the East, Valentinian the West.

It was the time when the Roman Empire was shaking to its foundations. The barbarians were breaking through in the north, and Valentinian was spending his time with the army on the field, now in Gaul, now in Pannonia, where the tribes of the Quadi were rising. It was Ambrose's opportunity. As governor, he ruled firmly and wisely. He was popular with the people. He had reached the height of his ambitions, and he was gentle where his predecessor had been unscrupulously hard. He was still known as "the Bishop." When Auxentius, Bishop of Milan, died, there was confusion in the city, for there were two claimants to the see, and when a meeting for the election of the new bishop was being held in the cathedral, Ambrose attended in the role of governor and in the hope that his presence would enable the election to take place without bloodshed. He spoke some soothing words to the people. He was listened to in silence, and he might have stepped down and gone quietly away if a child had not suddenly cried out the well-known nickname: "Ambrosius bishop!" Then the cry was repeated by the people, and Ambrose found himself facing a mob crying: "Ambrosius bishop!" as though it had gone insane.

He had no desire to be a bishop. He was not an ecclesiastic; he had not even been baptized. He was only a catechumen, a candidate for baptism at some future time. He was thirty-four, with a brilliant government career before him. Why exchange a governorship for a bishopric? Something of the madness of the crowd seems to have been communicated to him. He pushed his way out of the cathedral, and prepared for the first time in his life to make himself hated. He already possessed a reputation for sanctity. Then let them know he was brutal, evil, even sinister. There followed a strange interlude during which he did everything in his power to convince the people that they judged unwisely when they acclaimed him bishop. He ordered torture to be applied to some prisoners, hoping to persuade the people that he was as cruel as Valentinian. The crowd, who followed him, cried: "Your sin be on us!" He ordered loose women to come to his palatial apartments. The crowd again cried: "Your sin be upon us!" Sickened by their fervor and by their display of emotion, he announced that he intended to retire from the world and give himself up to solitary meditation, but the crowd knew better. Deciding to take to flight, he left his palace by a side door at midnight, intending to go to Pavia, but it was a moonless night and he took a wrong road: in the morning he found that he was once again in Milan, entering by the Roman Gate. His secretary Paulinus, who relates these incidents, is not always trustworthy, but his description of Ambrose's attempts to escape the elevation to the bishop's see ring true; and nothing is more likely than Ambrose's arrest on his return. He was kept under guard in the palace. A message was sent to Valentinian, explaining what had happened and asking for the imperial seal on the verdict of the people. Valentinian appears to have been delighted by the turn of affairs, and by fast courier dispatched his assent. It is not improbable that he had his own reasons for wishing Ambrose removed from the governorship, nor is it improbable that the removal came about as the result of an imperial plot. But if the people thought they had won their victory outright they were mistaken. When news of Valentinian's delight in the elevation reached Milan, Ambrose had already disappeared. Now there was no governor and no bishop.

Ambrose had not gone far. He was merely staying in the country house of his friend Leontius. He had not, however, counted on the Pope, who ordered that anyone harboring Ambrose should immediately give him up under pain of severe punishment. Leontius, frightened, betrayed the secret. Once again Ambrose was arrested and led back to Milan.

During the following week the catechumen rose to be bishop, and in six days he passed through all the successive stages of the ministry, being first baptized, then appointed doorkeeper, then reader, then exorcist, then subdeacon, then deacon, then presbyter, then bishop. No one had ever before gained such high ecclesiastical rank with such speed.

On his bishop's throne, Ambrose felt lonely. Almost his first act was to write to the great Basil of Caesarea requesting that the body of the saintly Dionysius should be brought to Milan Cathedral. Basil, who had some knowledge of Ambrose's remarkable career, ordered that the relics of the saint be disinterred and taken to Milan. With the relics he sent a letter praising Ambrose, calling him "a man of noble birth, of high office, of lofty character, of astonishing eloquence." He added that in the relics of Dionysius there was to be found a part of the divine providence: "Here you have the unconquered athlete. These bones, which shared in the blessed soul with the conflict, are known to the Lord." The remark was perhaps a warning or a rebuke. Ambrose had attained to power too easily to show signs of asceticism, and he was too much the aristocrat to show signs of wrestling with the angel. There were no wounds. There were never to be any deep wounds. But the smaller wounds were perpetual.

Ambrose's troubles began as soon as he was mitered. The Empire was falling to ruin, the public buildings were decaying, the highways were falling into disrepair, trade was languishing, the population was declining, and Christianity was a hotbed of sects, with the Arians bitterly contesting the supremacy of the Catholics. Most of these problems he had been forced to meet as governor. He had increased taxes: as bishop he was compelled to use other expedients, and quite soon he decided to sell the church plate in order to give the money to the poor. When the Arians charged him with sacrilege, he answered: "Which do you consider more valuable, church vessels or living souls?" To save money, he lived simply and fasted frequently. He had always been retiring: now he became almost a recluse. It was observed that he was often distant with people and seemed not to hear what they said, and he would fall into unaccountable fits of silence. Augustine, who met him a little later, suspected pride in his silence; it was probably weariness.

Ambrose's brother fell ill, the result of being shipwrecked in the dead of winter and then helping to rescue the survivors in ice-cold water, but when Marcellina heard of the illness she was concerned less with Satyrus than with Ambrose, who had fallen into a kind of stupor the moment he heard what had happened to his brother. Marcellina rushed to Milan. Ambrose seemed to be dying. She comforted him as best she could, and reminded him that Satyrus was still alive. Her consolations were unavailing. When Satyrus died on his way to Milan, Ambrose's grief knew no bounds. Like Bernard, he was like a weeping child before the dead. The funeral oration delivered in the Cathedral of Milan on the day of his brother's burial was a wild cry of distress. He does not mention God's grace, for God has refused His grace. He is wild with horror. "What can I do now?" he exclaims. "What is there worth living for? O, those last kisses, so cruel and so dear! O terrible embraces, and in the midst of them I felt thy body stiffening in my arms, and the sound of thy last sighing." This is not the well-tempered *oraison funèbre* of Bossuet: it is the pagan horror of death rising to the surface:

Thou art present, I say, and art always before me, and with my whole mind and soul do I embrace thee, gaze on thee, speak to thee, kiss thee, grasp thee, whether in the quiet of the night or in the light of day, when thou dost vouchsafe to visit me and console my sorrow. And now the very nights, which in thy lifetime seemed irksome, because they denied us the power of looking on each other, and sleep itself, once hated as an interruption of our intercourse, have begun to be sweet, because they have restored me to thee. . . . Thus recently, when evening drew on, and I was complaining that thou didst not visit me in my rest, thou wert in truth all the time wholly and inseparably present with me; so that, as I lay with limbs bathed in sleep, but with mind awake for thee, thou didst live to me, and I said, "What is death, my brother?" For indeed thou wert not separated from me for a single moment; nay, thou art so present with me everywhere, that the enjoyment of each other, which we could not have always in this life, is now everywhere and always ours. . . . Therefore I hold thee, my brother, and neither death nor time shall tear thee from me. Tears themselves are sweet, and weeping itself is pleasant, for by these the ardent longing of the mind is assuaged and affection is soothed and quieted. For I cannot be without thee, or ever forget thee, or remember thee without tears. O bitter days which show that our union is broken! O nights of tears, which reveal the loss of the gentle partner of my rest, of my inseparable companion! What agonies would you cause me, were it not that the image of my ever-present brother comes to me, were it not that the visions of my mind bring vividly before me him whom in the body I may look upon no more. (Ambrose, *De Excessu fratris sui Satyri*, I, 19.)

There was a great deal more in this strain. He pretended to find comfort in death, but found none, gazing at the uncovered face of his brother as it lay in the coffin beneath the high altar. He begged his brother to bless Marcellina, and after saying a final *Vale* he gave a last kiss to the face he had loved. It was a week before he was able to talk of Satyrus in purely Christian terms, and then he found consolation in the thought of the resurrection of the flesh. "Why doubt that the body shall rise again?" he said. "The fruit falleth, the fruit cometh to life again. We see the grape-stones decay, but the vine springeth to life again." He quoted from St. Paul: "This corruptible must put on incorruption, and this mortal must put on immortality." But he seems not to have been completely convinced of his own words. He became even more somber, even more reserved. Satyrus had left no will. His immense fortune descended to Ambrose and Marcellina, and they gave it to the poor.

To distract a mind almost insane with grief Ambrose turned to work, to reading, to study, to long nights spent in prayer. He had read little when he was young. Now he made up for lost time. He summoned his old tutor Simplician to Milan, and under his guidance charted out a course of reading which made him, if not a learned man, at least a wiser one. He threw himself into his charities, and came to discern between those who deserved of his charity and those who did not: he could be scathing when he discussed false beggars. And he continued to sell church vessels in the marketplace for deserving causes. When the Goths ravaged Illyricum after the disaster of Adrianople in 378, he sold still more plate, and when once again he was charged with sacrilege, he answered: "Behold the gold that is approved! behold the gold that is profitable! behold the gold of Christ which saves men from death! behold the gold with which modesty is ransomed and chastity preserved! This great company of captives is more glorious than the splendor of cups!" A new note entered his prose when he spoke of the redeemed captives; and thereafter Ambrose always wrote well when he was exulting about some particular victory of the Church.

More and more Ambrose took to writing. It allayed his grief, and he increasingly liked to be alone with himself. He said once: "I never felt less alone than when alone, and never less at leisure than when at leisure," but he adored his own loneliness, and for this reason never or rarely employed a secretary: he wrote his books with his own hand. Also in writing he could forget the body and let the spirit soar. In his advice to the virgins he said: "Learn to be in the world, yet above the world; even if you carry about a body, let the bird within you soar." The bird within him soared. He wrote superbly on a host of subjects, and partly this arose from the fact that his mind was not encumbered with too much learning. He could write about drunkards as beautifully as he wrote about the bread of the angels. Of drunkards he wrote with considerable feeling, perhaps because Milan was famous for its drinking feasts:

Strong drink alters the senses and the forms of men. By it they are turned from men into neighing horses. A drunken man loses voice, he changes color, he flashes fire from his eyes, he pants, he snorts, he goes stark mad, he falls into a foaming pit. . . . Hence come also vain imaginings, uncertain vision, uncertain steps: often he hops over shadows, thinking them to be pits. The earth acquires a facial expression, and nods to him; of a sudden it seems to rise and bend and twist. Fearful, he falls on his face and grasps the ground with his hands or thinks that the mountains close in on him. There is a murmur in his ears as of the surging seas; he hears the surf booming on the beach. If he spies a dog he imagines it a lion and takes to his heels.[1]

The Ambrose who wrote of drunkenness cannot have been completely humorless, yet evidence of humor is rare in his work. He had neither Jerome's sharpness nor his patience, but he possessed something which Jerome only rarely possessed: a vein of pure poetry. He employed allegory freely. He even wrote a justification of allegory, pointing out that the Egyptians and the Greeks as well as the Hebrew prophets

[1] Ambrose, *De Elia et Jeiunio*, 15, 59-61 (translated by E. R. Rand, *Founders of the Middle Ages*, Cambridge: Harvard University Press, 1928, p. 84).

employed symbols. Was not Moses a symbolist? Hilary of Poitiers had extractly from the Bible "stories with archetypal and interior significances." He does the same, and like Jerome he will sometimes find himself confounded by his own suave brilliance in deducing anything he pleased from an ambiguous text. For him the words of the Bible were to be understood in five senses: literal, moral, allegorical, mystical, and anagogical, the last referring to the life to come. He could write wonderfully concerning the simpler symbols, as when in his *Catechisms* manna becomes the bread of the angels and the flesh of Christ:

See now which is the most excellent: the bread of angels or the flesh of Christ, which is the body of Life. The manna came from Heaven: this flesh is above Heaven. The manna was from Heaven, the latter is the flesh of the Lord of Heavens. One was subject to corruption if it was kept to the following day; the other escapes all corruption, and whosoever shall taste of it in pious disposition, shall not know corruption. For the former, water gushed out of a rock; for you, the blood of Christ is poured forth. That water changes them, but only for the moment: this blood satisfies you for eternity. You, when you shall have drunk, shall have no more thirst; for on the one side is the shadow, but here is the reality.[2]

Perhaps his quiet mastery of prose comes from his love for music. He did not invent the antiphonal chant, but he encouraged it; he loved the sounds of words and liked repeating them aloud to himself; and allegory gave him wings. But though he could write gently, he could also write with a fierce horror about poverty, about the rich who held back their corn in years of drought, about usurers everywhere. He wrote of a poor debtor compelled to sell his children:

I have seen with my own eyes a poor man being led, nay, dragged to prison, in order to force him to pay what he had not got; I saw him putting up his children at public auction in order to gain a delay in punishment. Chance permitted him to find

[2] Ambrose, *De Mysteriis*, 48 (P. de Labriolle, *The Life and Times of St. Ambrose*; St. Louis: B. Herder Book Co., 1928, p. 262).

someone who would lend him assistance in his extremity. He returned to his own roof with his family—and found everything had been pillaged; there was nothing left for him to procure a mouthful of bread. His children were dying of hunger under his eyes. He regretted not having sold them to some master, who could have fed them. He hesitated, and then came to the decision to sell them. But a battle took place in his heart between poverty and love. Hunger urged him to give them up, nature to continue the duties of a parent towards them. Quite ready to die with his children rather than to be separated from them, he went forward, then drew back. But in spite of his desire necessity triumphed, and love was overcome.[3]

He could be ferocious when he inquired into the causes of poverty. He had given his own wealth away; he could not understand why the rich did not give their own wealth away. He had nothing but contempt for the rich who, having acquired the earth, seemed desperate to acquire the sky, the air, and the sea. The rich flaunted their jewels before the poor: even their horses were equipped with golden teeth. They rejoiced when the harvests failed. They traded in human miseries. Such attacks on wealth are familiar in our own times, but they come from Ambrose with added freshness and with the authority of his sanctity. "The earth was created for all, for rich and poor in common," he wrote. (*In commune omnibus, divitibus atque pauperibus, terra fundata est.*) "Nature knows no rich," he thunders. "She creates us all alike, and alike she encloses us in the sepulchre. What more resembles one dead man than another dead man?" As for charity, what were largesses but duties performed, renderings paid to those who not only deserved the gifts but were the original owners? Had not God so designed the universe that the earth belonged to all, and there was food enough for all, only the rich had come first to take the food away. It was the ancient socialist thesis, shared by the Greek Fathers of the Church but rarely announced with such authority by the Fathers of the

[3] Ambrose, *De Nabuthae Iezraelita V*, 21 (P. de Labriolle, *The Life and Times of St. Ambrose*, p. 230).

West. All property is arbitrary, all riches are vanity, all usury is criminal, says Ambrose, and though Augustine and Ambrose echo these words, their echo comes from a greater distance. Perhaps of all these things Ambrose detested usury most. What is the use of making a man pay interest? He comes to you only when he is starving. He requires a remedy, and you offer him poison. He asks for bread, and you hold over him a sword. What kind of world is this where riches are power?

Partly, Ambrose's socialism arose from his own sensitivity, his delight in the poetry of living things, but it was something he shared with the early Christians, with Tertullian and Cyprian. Like Tertullian he half worshiped the beauty of the human body, seeing its divine proportions as only one more proof of the existence of the Godhead. All natural objects delighted and absorbed him. The moon proclaimed the mystery of Christ. He had a passion for wandering in flowering fields among "purple violets, white lilies, scarlet glowing roses, the grasses painted now gold, now orange, now all colors, and you do not know whether the beauty or the perfume delights you more." And then there was the sea: "the white foam lifting and scattering over the rocks like snow, while over the calm depths purple colors play." The music of the sea was like the music of the spheres. But it was man he delighted in most, and man's death he feared most, even though he pronounced a complex belief in the Resurrection and the Last Judgment. Perhaps it was because he loved men and wished them not to die that he placed so much stress on the protecting influence of the martyrs and the angels.

When he first became bishop, Ambrose begged the body of a saint. As he grew older, he seemed to feel the need for a kind of protecting wall of relics. The times were troubled. Valentinian had died, to be followed by the young and handsome Gratian who possessed, according to his tutor, the poet Ausonius, all the gifts which kingship demanded. He rode well. He was popular with his soldiers. He fought vigorous battles. He had his father's beauty. He was in love with the life of the camp. He had, however, two faults. He surrounded himself with a bodyguard of fair-haired Germans, and he had no particular interest in ruling the Empire. Ambrose loved him, wrote books for him, treasured his few letters, and pronounced him perfect, but the fair-haired Germans were regarded with distaste by some of Gratian's commanders, and his lack of interest in government made him careless. When the usurper Maximus raised the standard against Gratian and crossed over from Britain to take over Gaul, Gratian took to flight; he was captured in Lyons, promised his freedom, requested to attend a banquet in his honor, and there murdered. His last words were for Ambrose.

Then, with Maximus in power at Treves and Justina, the wife of Valentinian I, acting as regent for her son Valentinian II in Italy, the great unwieldy Empire began to split from the top. Justina hated Ambrose. She was an Arian, denying the true divinity of the Son and the Holy Ghost; and Ambrose felt himself called to thunder against her power with the same breath that he thundered against her heresy. Justina struck back. Ambrose took refuge in the Cathedral, where thousands gathered round to protect him. When Justina relented, Ambrose took it as a sign from Heaven. He had been in real danger. He had been accused of all crimes, including the crime of bewitching the people with his hymns, which he wrote astonishingly well. Auxentius, the adviser of Justina, an Arian like her, had determined long ago on his death and had threatened a general massacre. Now, in the momentary respite, while the rage of the Arian heretics was calmed, Ambrose proceeded to the dedication of the church that would later be called the Church of Sant' Ambrogio. The dedication provided an opportunity for a display of the powers of the Church. He ordered the martyrs to come to his aid. The people appealed to him to dedicate the church forthwith. He refused, unless the martyrs would immediately appear; and at the moment of his refusal, as he said in a letter to his sister, "my heart burned within me with a sort of presentiment."

It was a kind of white magic. Exhausted by the long argument with the Empress Justina, conscious that he had won over her only a temporary victory, he was suddenly aware of prophetic powers. The martyrs were there, not far away, urgently attempting to present themselves though they were under the earth. The clerics around him were trembling. He said: "Dig a hole before the railing of the Church of SS. Felix and Nabor." The hole was dug, but there was no sign of the dead martyrs. The blind, the halt, and the lame were taken to the place: they were immediately cured. Then they dug further, and found the bodies of two men. "They were," said Ambrose, "of surprising stature, like those of the old legends. The bones were intact and there was much blood." The heads had been severed from the trunks. The bodies were taken up, placed in biers, and brought to the Cathedral. The translation of the relics was attended by miracles. A blind man was cured; others were cured by touching the pall with their hands, while still others were cured by standing in the shadow of the holy relics. For Ambrose the appearance of the relics was a triumph; and with one eye on Justina, he declared: "The champions I desire are those who will defend, and not attack. So I have gained these champions for you, O holy people, and they will help all and injure none. Such are the defenders I desire. We have patrons, and we knew it not. In this we excel our ancestors, for the knowledge of the holy martyrs, which they lost, we have regained."

The story of the two martyrs, who were shortly afterward recognized as SS. Gervasius and Protasius, martyred in the reign of Nero, is a strange one. Ambrose's presentiment came at a useful time. That they were "of surprising stature, like those of the old legends" suggests that they may have been tall Cro-Magnons stained with red ochre which suitably counterfeited blood. It is impossible to believe that Ambrose played a trick, bringing martyrs out of the ground simply because it suited him to do so: but at the same time it is perfectly possible to believe he was mistaken in their origins.

Ambrose kept searching for relics. He found many. On a visit to Bologna he discovered the remains of SS. Agricola and Vitalis. In a garden outside Milan, toward the close of his life, he found the body of the martyr Nazarius, the blood still fresh, the hair and the beard still on it, so that it looked as though it had just been washed and laid in the tomb. Not content with one martyr, he returned to the spot a little later and began praying, according to the testimony of Paulinus, in a place where he had never prayed before. Thereupon he indicated that the body of another martyr lay near by; and this body was disinterred and taken to the great Basilica of the Apostles in Milan.

If the authority of Ambrose were not so great, the discovery of so many relics, always in pairs, might seem suspicious. There is no explanation for them; nor did Ambrose demand that they should be explained except by the visitation of God's providence and mercy. More than any of the Fathers, more even than Augustine, Ambrose suffered from his griefs over the dead; and there is at least a suggestion that he was in some strange way in touch with the dead.

By a curious coincidence, one of the observers of the translation of SS. Gervasius and Protasius was Augustine. Augustine was still a pagan. He had come with his mother Monnica on a visit to Milan in order to hear Ambrose, of whom so many were talking in Rome. He listened to Ambrose's sermons and found them convincing: it was the first time he had heard the doctrine of the Trinity sufficiently explained. He delighted in Ambrose's summons to preserve the spirit rather than the letter, and he took pleasure in Ambrose's hymns. He attended one of the famous morning audiences. Ambrose received his African visitor casually. Augustine was naturally shocked that so little attention was paid to him. He imagined that Ambrose must have heard of him, but Ambrose's mind was lost in his books, and he said nothing memorable at that time or even later. The famous reserve of the Roman patrician was evident. Augustine remarked that it must be a sorrowful thing for a man so wise to be continent; he almost pitied the bishop, who looked dried up and a little morose. Monnica had the habit of bringing cheesecakes, bread, and wine on her interminable visits to the martyrs' tombs. She would eat a little of them, then give the rest to the poor, but when Ambrose ordered that the practice should cease, probably because he was tired of hiring sweepers to sweep up the mess, Augustine found himself approving. God should not be worshiped with cheesecakes. Monnica, too, was overjoyed by the ordinance, which suggested a saintliness in Ambrose she had long suspected.

Towering in the pulpit, white-haired and stern, already a legend, living close to death and legend, himself the inventor of legends, Ambrose was the model Augustine followed. It was Ambrose who baptized Augustine. The young acolyte always regarded this as an act of peculiar providence. Long afterward Augustine wrote: "I venerate him as a father, for in Jesus Christ he begat me through the Gospel, and through his ministry I received the washing of regeneration—the blessed Ambrose, whose grace, constancy, labors, perils suffered for the Catholic faith, whether in words or deeds, I have myself experienced, and the whole Roman world unhesitatingly proclaims with me."

When Augustine spoke of the perils Ambrose suffered for the Church he was not exaggerating. Ambrose rarely knew any peace. The confused history of the period, the murders, the executions, the threat of the barbarians on the frontiers, made it essential that one man at least should stand firm for Christian principles. The Empire was split in two; it was in danger of splitting into a thousand fragments; and the times called for strong men. Theodosius, who had distinguished himself as a general in Spain, Britain, and Thrace and who had brought the Goths within his army to avoid fighting them, was elevated to the purple. This thickset middle-aged Spaniard shared the Empire with the young Valentinian II. Theodosius was deeply religious; so was Valentinian; and Ambrose hoped to exercise his power over them. It was not easy. Like Valens, Theodosius was handsome, unscrupulous, given to unmerciful rages. A small incident in Thessalonica resulted in a contest almost to the death between Ambrose and Theodosius.

It could hardly have begun in a smaller way. All that happened was that Botheric, the governor of Illyria, threw a handsome charioteer into prison. The charioteer was accused of homosexual practices by his own cupbearer. Botheric could hardly do otherwise; but he had not taken the power of the people into account. The charioteer was well liked. The chariot races were about to begin. The people asked for the charioteer's freedom. This was refused. So they rose in arms, murdered Botheric, freed their favorite, and went on to murder a few more of their overlords. Theodosius, then in Milan, was incensed. He ordered that the people be punished. When Ambrose came to interview him, he wavered. He would not punish, he would punish, he was not sure. Ambrose left him with the feeling that peace and order would be brought about in Thessalonica with no great harm done. He was mistaken. Theodosius gave secret orders that the Thessalonians be punished with a general massacre. He had hardly given the order when he relented again and sent a courier to countermand the original decree, but it was too late. There was to be another great chariot race in the circus at Thessalonica. The gates were closed. The soldiers of Theodosius were stationed at the entrances. At a signal they fell upon the people who had dared to drag the body of Botheric through the streets. In three hours seven thousand Thessalonians were put to the sword.

A cry of horror rose through the Empire, and Ambrose, who regarded himself as the imperial conscience, felt utterly ashamed. He had believed in Theodosius's word, trusted him, genuinely admired him. How had this come about? He wrote a letter to the Emperor, meant for the Emperor's eyes alone, a strange, cautious, hesitant, pleading letter, which said in effect and with many periphrases: "Thou art a murderer. Now, O Emperor, repent." As an example of Ambrose's diplomacy, it is one of the greatest letters he ever wrote:

I exhort, I beg, I entreat, I admonish you, because it is grief to me that the perishing of so many innocent is no grief to you. I suffer at seeing you (who up to now have been a model of exceptional virtue, whose clemency rose to such a high pitch that you found it hard to consent to the punishment of the guilty) incapable of regretting the murder of so many innocent people. The devil is envious of your chief excellencies—overcome him while you have the means. Do not add another sin by following a course which has been the ruin of so many.

As for me, debtor as I am to your benevolence in all things, grateful as I must ever be—for your goodness has been unsurpassed by all Emperors except one—I say, that I have no cause to be intractable towards you, but I have every reason to be apprehensive. I dare not offer the Sacrifice if you are present. Can it be permissible to offer the Sacrifice which is refused when the blood of a single man is shed, when the blood of many pours on the ground? I believe not.

I cannot deny that you have a zeal for the faith, and that you fear God, but you have a naturally passionate spirit which, when mitigated is easily moved to compassion, but becomes ungovernable when you are excited. I would gladly have left you to the workings of your own heart, but I dare not either keep silence or make light of your offense. So bloody a scene as that in Thessalonica is unheard-of in the world's history. I have warned and entreated you against it; you yourself recognized its atrocity; you endeavored to recall your decree. And now I call on you to repent. Remember how David repented for his crime. Will you be ashamed to do what David did? You can only atone for your sin by tears, by penitence, by humbling your soul before God. You are a man, and as you have sinned as a man so you must repent. No angel, no archangel can forgive you. God alone can forgive you, and He forgives only those who repent.

You have my love, my affection, my prayers, and if you believe me, then do as I tell you to do. If you do not believe me, pardon me for preferring God to you. (Ambrose, *Epistolae*, 51.)

Theodosius appears to have been deeply moved, and to have desired to perform an act of contrition. He came to Milan and presented himself at the porch of the Cathedral. Ambrose faced him and demanded: "How can you uplift in prayer the hands which are still dripping with blood? Depart, I say." Theodosius mentioned the letter he had received from Ambrose. "David sinned," he said, "yet David was forgiven." "Yes," Ambrose replied slowly, "you have imitated David in your sin; now imitate David in your repentance."

Ambrose was determined to bend Theodosius to his will. The Emperor would not be allowed to attend Mass and he would live under a curse until he prostrated himself before the high altar. It was no laughing matter, as Theodosius knew, to be deprived of God's mercy. When one of his courtiers tittered and asked him why he was so melancholy, he answered: "You do not feel my misery. The Church of God is open to slaves and beggars; to me it is closed, and with it the gates of Heaven." Some time later Theodosius came to the Cathedral again. Ambrose asked what penance he had performed. He answered that he was awaiting Ambrose's instructions. Thereupon Ambrose led him among the penitents, reminded him that according to law there must be a period of thirty days between the commission of a crime and its absolution, then ordered him to prostrate himself, having put aside all his emblems of royalty. Wearing a shroud, Theodosius begged for mercy. "My soul cleaveth to the dust," he cried. "O God, quicken Thou me according to Thy word." Until his death Theodosius remained faithful to Ambrose's command. Now, for the first time, the Church had triumphed over the Roman world.

But still, in this Roman world at odds with itself, the struggle for empire remained. Valentinian II was a weakling like Gratian. All imaginable gifts had been poured on him except

the gift of command. His mother Justina had died; he regarded Ambrose as his father. But this helped him little. The
capital of Gaul in those days was the city of Vienne, lying on
the banks of the Rhone: now a town of sleeping streets and
garish shadows, small parks and promenades, then glowing
with imperial marble. The palace of Valentinian looked out
over the mustard-colored hills, but he wielded no power.
Theodosius had placed a Frank called Arbogast in charge of
the young Emperor. Arbogast seems to have been as evil as
the sound of his name. Valentinian could not fight him; he
could only threaten suicide, make ineffectual gestures of command, dream of his sisters whose company he enjoyed above
all things. He had large soft eyes, high cheekbones, a petu-
lant mouth. He was a prince from a fairy tale, full of generosity and an impatient desire to please; Arbogast was the
perpetual hangman. Valentinian prized justice; Arbogast
prized murder. Valentinian was so weak that once, when a
man called Harmonius, accused of taking bribes, ran to him
for protection against Arbogast and concealed himself in the
folds of the Emperor's purple robe, Arbogast simply drew his
sword and plunged it through the robe. When Valentinian on
another occasion drew his own sword, Arbogast laughed and
asked whether he intended to take vengeance. "No," said
Valentinian, "I would be content if I could kill myself."

Yet he kept remembering Ambrose. He wrote a letter urging Ambrose to make the journey to Vienne. Ambrose temporized. He could not leave Milan, but he loved the boy-
emperor. There was another inroad of the barbarians on the
frontiers, and now it was urged on Ambrose that he should
go to Vienne and bring Valentinian back, not so much because he was Emperor but because with his youth and skill
he would form a symbol for the people, now that danger was
increasing. Again Ambrose temporized. There came another
appeal from Valentinian. This time Ambrose decided to obey
the imperial command and set out toward the Alps; but the
barbarians, who seem to have had spies in Milan, suddenly

withdrew, the danger decreased, Ambrose once more deferred the journey, and Argobast saw his opportunity. In one of the small hunting lodges on the banks of the Rhone Valentinian was smothered in his sleep and then hanged, Argobast apparently desiring to give the impression that the boy had hanged himself.

Ambrose never recovered from the shock. He realized that he was guilty of a supreme act of carelessness. Two young Emperors, both full of immense promise, had died during his reign in Milan. He ordered that the body of Valentinian be brought to Milan in a porphyry sarcophagus, and when he delivered the inevitable funeral oration, he could not forget Gratian.

O Gratian, O Valentinian, so fair, so dear, how short were your lives! How closely your deaths followed upon one another! How near are your sepulchres! I love to repeat your names, Gratian, Valentinian, to take solace in your memory. Gratian, Valentinian, so fair, so dear, so inseparable in life, death has no power to separate you. The same tomb will unite you who were united in affection. O Gratian, my son, to me most sweet, I grieve for you. Very many signs of affection have you shown to me. And I grieve for my son, Valentinian, to me truly beautiful!

With the death of Valentinian the war for the Empire was waged in earnest. Arbogast and the usurper Eugenius prepared to descend on Italy at the head of the Western army of Franks and Gauls, then encamped in Lombardy. The new Emperor, under the promptings of Arbogast, revived the pagan ceremonies in Rome; the old processions, which had not been seen for fifty years, were resumed; and instead of the purple-embroidered banner with the jeweled monogram of Christ, Eugenius decided to fight under the standard of Hercules Invictus. Theodosius was in Constantinople. He gathered his armies together, drove west, and found himself along the Alpine heights with the armies of Eugenius and Arbogast in the plain below. On September 5, 394, Theodosius gave the order to his troops to descend the Alps.

The first attack on that autumn day melted away. In despair, Theodosius's generals counseled retreat. Theodosius, stung to the quick, answered that he cared for nothing except victory and could not bear that the standard of Hercules should fly above the standard of Christ. They counseled a Fabian strategy of withdrawal, hoping or pretending to hope that Eugenius's armies would follow them up the mountains, but Theodosius refused them even this consolation. He prayed fervently, and afterwards, using exactly the kind of words that Ambrose had used when he was in mortal danger, he said: "We must follow the saints, our champions and leaders, considering their power and not the number of the enemy." It was also said that while he was praying or sleeping he had seen in a vision John the Evangelist and Philip the Apostle, who ordered him to lead his troops against the enemy at dawn.

On September 6 a long, costly battle was fought on the banks of the river Frigidus. It proved indecisive until the miracle which Theodosius had been expecting occurred. The miracle took the form of a blasting wind which suddenly came from the northeast, blinding the soldiers of Eugenius with clouds of dust, tearing their shields and lances from their hands, turning their weapons back upon themselves. The storm decided the battle. By nightfall Eugenius had been captured and his head had been struck off; Arbogast lasted a little longer. He escaped from the battlefield in disguise, wandered over the mountains for two days, and then fell on his sword.

When Ambrose heard the news he was overjoyed. The death of Valentinian had been avenged, and paganism had submitted to the cross of Christ. He proposed to offer a solemn *Te Deum* in thanksgiving. At the High Sacrifice he carried Theodosius's letter to the altar, and all the time that he was offering the Sacrament he held the letter in his hand.

It was the last battle fought by Theodosius, who was already ill when he returned to Milan. He had ordered that the partisans of Eugenius should be exterminated; Ambrose succeeded in obtaining an amnesty except for those who had held high office under the usurper. Strange weather fell on Milan. A fog hovered over the city, the rain fell monotonously, and earthquakes were felt. In this melancholy damp Theodosius weakened. He appointed his sons to rule the Empire—Honorius in the west, Arcadius in the east—and then one night in the depth of winter he called for Ambrose and shortly afterwards died in the bishop's arms. He was fifty and a few months.

Ambrose had never refused the opportunity to deliver a funeral oration, and now once more, standing in the cathedral beside the uncovered face of the Emperor, he declared that a prince had entered Paradise:

I loved him, who sent for me in his last moments, whose shattered body summoned me while he gave more anxious thought to the Church than to his own peril. I confess I loved him, and felt the sorrow of his death in the abyss of my heart, and thought to find some consolation in speaking of him—I have spoken too long. I loved him, and dare to hope that God will hear my prayers and receive this pious soul.

Theodosius lives now in the heavenly light: in joy he mingles with the assembly of the saints. There he embraces Gratian, whose soul, though taken in a shameful death, has also entered into the joys of paradise. So together these two noble men taste the heavenly rewards. To them we apply the words of Scriptures: "Day to day uttereth speech." Elsewhere, within the pit of hell, Maximus and Eugenius declare to one another: "Night to night showeth knowledge." So the pious have passed from the darkness of the world to light eternal; and already the wicked man is no more found, for the time of his iniquities has ceased. (Ambrose, *De Obitu Theodosii Oratio*, 6, 7.)

With the defeat of Eugenius, there came to Ambrose the wild hope that the Empire would become truly Christian at last. Augustine in Africa noted that all the idols of Rome had at last been overthrown, while Jerome declared: "The Capitol is dusty and neglected, the temples of Jupiter and their ceremonies have perished. The city has been stirred to the depths, and today the people pour past the half-ruined shrines to visit the tombs of the martyrs. Paganism is banished into solitude."

It was almost true. The joy that came over Christendom was something palpable, felt on the nerves and the spirits of men. They had not taken into account the armies which had left the borders of China two hundred years before and were now making their way toward Europe, pushing the tribes closer to Italy. Also, the Empire was still divided. Honorius was still a boy. The regent was the Vandal Stilicho, who had enlisted as a private and risen to the command of the Imperial armies. He had married the adopted daughter of Theodosius, and he was in a position to make his will prevail. But Ambrose was already weary of political entanglements. Once when Stilicho was celebrating in Milan, putting on a show in the circus which entailed throwing condemned prisoners to the lions, a prisoner called Cresconius escaped and fled for sanctuary to the cathedral. Stilicho sent soldiers after the prisoner, whom they found clinging to the pillars of the altar. Ambrose and his clergy gathered round to protect Cresconius, but the soldiers pushed them aside, arrested Cresconius, and returned to the circus. Ambrose flung himself down before the altar in helpless tears. Once again, as so often in the life of Ambrose, a miracle occurred. At the moment when Cresconius was about to be thrown into the arena, some leopards jumped the fences and proceeded to maul the spectators. Stilicho wisely took this as a sign from Heaven and returned the prisoner to the protection of Ambrose.

Two years after Theodosius, Ambrose died in winter. All that winter for him was a kind of death, though he did not breathe his last until Easter. Now, as he whispered out his letters or attempted to recite a commentary on the Scriptures, he was surrounded by well-wishers only too eager to write down on tablets the words he had always written with his own hand. Paulinus, his secretary, was writing one day when he suddenly saw a flame shaped like a small shield covering the bishop's head; then it was sucked down into his mouth, and the face became dead white for a few minutes. It was almost what they had expected. All Italy was praying for his recovery. Even Stilicho issued an Imperial order, which read: "Ambrose must recover." "When Ambrose dies," Stilicho said prophetically, "we shall see the ruin of Italy." When Ambrose heard of this he answered: "I have not so lived among you as to be ashamed to live on; but I am not afraid to die, for our Lord is good." A few days before he died, he said he saw Jesus coming by his bedside. He lay with his arms outstretched in the form of a cross, all the time whispering quietly to himself. He died on the dawn of Easter Eve, being fifty-eight years old and having been Bishop of Milan for twenty-three years and four months.

He left behind him no great body of doctrine. "The will of God is the measure of all things," he wrote once, and he was content with simple things, the more austere the better. All through his writings there are oddly Roman phrases. "The wise man does not shun exile," he wrote, echoing Vergil, "for he knows that the whole world is his fatherland." Even his sense of guilt and miracle seems to derive at least partly from Vergil: the dead father, the battles never seen but always imagined, the cadences of Vergil he had heard when he was a young student, the consciousness of a coming doom, flames towering on the walls and muted cries coming from the empty streets, all these were familiar, recollected not in tranquillity but in the utmost urgency. He had known these things in the *Aeneid* and he proceeded to act them out in his life. Even the two martyrs of enormous stature, stained with red blood, discovered a little way below the earth: these, too, seem to come out of the sixth book of the *Aeneid*. But in a sense they had not come out of the *Aeneid* at all. They were portraits of himself, or of his guardian angels.

In fear of death, in love with solitude, possessed of all the

Roman virtues, Ambrose towers over his century. He was the first of the four great Fathers, and only Gregory can rival him; it is significant that both of them found their consolations in music. Jerome hated him, but that was to be expected: it is hardly possible to conceive of two men possessed of more contrary talents. We remember him because he recalls the Ambrosian chants. He would have approved the irony.

When Ambrose in turn lay with his face uncovered below the altar, the bodies of SS. Gervasius and Protasius were placed in coffins and put on either side of him, while another bishop read a funeral oration, and miracles occurred. Then the bodies were separated. In the ninth century Archbishop Angilberto conceived the idea that Ambrose was restless in his solitude; the bones were disinterred; the three saints were laid together in a porphyry sarcophagus; and so they remain. It is hardly possible to imagine that Ambrose would wish it otherwise. He lies with his guards in an ornate silver shrine in the Church of Sant' Ambrogio which he loved above all others.

V. ❧ JEROME: THE HERMIT

"MY HAIR IS WHITE AND MY BROW FURROWED with wrinkles," Jerome wrote in old age, "and I have a dewlap like that of an ox hanging from my chin." Indeed, he had always been an old man, with an old man's addiction for solitude and an old man's tart tongue. He seems to have known no youth. He hated women, except those who were virgins, and he could choke with horror at the thought of what went on inside a woman's body. From women and the plagues of the devil he found refuge in scholarship. "He is always reading, always buried in books: he doesn't rest day or night: he is always either reading something or writing something." So said his friend Sulpicius Severus, and it was true enough of the man when he was a youth as it was true of the days spent in Bethlehem, when the mountains of books tumbled from his pen, so many that they were past counting, and he confessed he had re-read few of them and had forgotten half their titles. He was the greatest scholar of his age, and among the greatest scholars of all time.

It is the fashion nowadays to decry scholarship, to say that men who live entombed among books are remote from life, but it is possible—and certainly Jerome believed it to be true —that the waters of life flow through books, and the living force of civilization shows itself in style and written wit and learning. Jerome had all three. He trained himself like an athlete for scholarship. He wrote superbly, without Augustine's fire or Gregory's rages, but with a tremendous sense of the richness of the Latin tongue; and by translating the Bible he placed his seal upon it, so that even today the King James version reflects the rhythms he employed. He modeled his prose on the poetry of Vergil, and so he became the greatest of the mediators between the Roman past and the Roman present, for the language of the Church is still the language he hammered out, its rhythms still essentially his own. Even the words employed by the Church are often his—at least 350 words, used commonly today, were unknown until he coined them. And all the time the quiet scholar in his Bethlehem study concealed his own passions and his welling hysteria, his direct violence and devastating sensuality, behind the orderly rows of his own books. Sometimes the books fall down, and for a brief moment we see the tormented man jumping and quivering like a twisted nerve. "We war not against flesh and blood," wrote St. Paul, "but against principalities and powers." Jerome warred against both. He hated the flesh, but he wept with uncontrollable abandon when his closest friends died. He was atrociously inhuman, and yet human. The man who squandered so much of the richness of his mind on the impeccable translation we know as the Vulgate could fume and rant about women waving their hair, or putting rouge on their lips. He said that a man who called a girl "honey" (*mel meum*) was committing sin. He had no love for common humanity, but he had a great sorrow for poverty amid the splendor of Rome and wrote: "We have gold-gleaming walls and delicately painted pillars, but when we allow our poor to die, Christ, too, dies naked and hungry before our doors." When he took a dislike to people, he would always find absurd reasons for making them appear monstrous, as when he attacked the priest Onasus for his disfigured nose, his stammering speech, and the name he was born with. He was particularly vicious concerning the nose, which was evidently large. It got in the way of the man's eyes. It was a kind of thicket, which shut out the light, and what, asks Jerome, is the thicket doing there? What is it protecting? Why not cut it off? The name Onasus, a short form of Onesimus, means "helpful," and on that point Jerome becomes almost hysterical with savage laughter. Helpful, indeed! Well, it is the Roman custom to call Negroes "silver boys," and everything nowadays is called by its opposite, and since you are so ugly let me pretend you are beautiful, let me sing you a little song from the poet Persius, and thereupon Jerome sings, as if in a piping childish voice:

> The King and Queen have a daughter:
> You are the man she chose.
> And all the girls lay hands on you,
> Wherever you tread is a rose.

But as soon as he has finished singing Jerome says in hopeless disgust: "Oh, cover your nose and shut your mouth: that's the best thing for you."

There is a great deal of that kind of thing in the saint's letters. "Truth is bitter," he said once, but the bitterness overflows. It is not envy, but part of his scholar's temperament, the bile running free. "What a lot of fools people are!" he exclaims. "Everyone thinks he can interpret the Bible. . . . Gossipy old women, old men in their dotage, long-winded sophists, they all consider themselves as masters in the art, they tear the Scriptures apart and teach others what they have learned in the process. With knit brows and big words, they philosophize on the holy words to women. Others—oh, the shame of it!—learn from women what they teach to men. And as though that were not enough, they boldly declaim to others what they do not themselves understand. They do not even trouble to find out what the prophets and the apostles have meant, but they fit passages arbitrarily together to suit their own meaning, as if it were a splendid method of teaching, and not the worst, to corrupt the real meaning." He was not himself entirely guiltless of arbitrarily selecting passages and dovetailing them to suit what he considered to be the real meaning, and he was never more revealing than when he exclaimed against the preachers who learn from women. Preachers and women, indeed, were an ever-present occasion for mockery; and if his friends disagreed with him, he would turn the loaded battering-ram of his mockery against them, as when he drew a picture of Rufinus who addressed his students with long, weighty pauses between his words, hiding behind the books on the table, suddenly snapping his fingers in the hope of electrifying his audience, frowning and drawing his fingers down his nose with all the air of a wise man among fools; but the fool, says Jerome, was Rufinus himself, "whose front was a lion, whose backside was a dragon and whose middle was a goat." The quotation is taken from Lucretius. Jerome is always quoting. Like Rufinus, he loves to demonstrate the flowers of his learning; he inveighs against the use of flowery speech and quotations from the classics in an unusually long letter which is inordinately flowery and contains six quotations from Vergil, six from Cicero, one from Petronius, and another from a source unknown to us. He was tender and violent, gentle and rude, viciously proud and childishly humble, a man of deep hates and morbid passions whose brain was nevertheless permanently clear. He was a tissue of contradictions, and he seems to have been perfectly aware of it himself.

We know him by the name of Jerome, but he was born Eusebius Sophronius Hieronymus, the son of a small landowner somewhere in the region of the Julian Alps in what is now Yugoslavia. No one knows the date of his birth or where he was born: the town of Strido, which he mentions as his birthplace, has disappeared from the map, destroyed in the endless wars of the Illyrian frontiers. Though Jerome wrote voluminous letters, which are now collected in an edition comprising 1700 pages, he hardly ever refers to his parents in them. His father seems to have been a freedman. There was a maternal aunt whom Jerome detested, but we have no idea why. There was a sister who committed some terrible sin in her youth. There was an earthquake. There were slaves on the estate, for Jerome remembered running in and out of their cells, playing with them when he should have been working. Of his childhood this is all we know. Years later, when he was in Bethlehem and he needed to sell his inheritance to support the hospice he had founded there, he described how he had sold without the least regret "some half-ruined cottages which have escaped the hands of the barbarians," and perhaps—though no one can be certain—those half-ruined cottages were all that remained of the town of Strido, destroyed by the barbarians at some period in Jerome's youth.

Yet though we know so little, a great deal is already revealed. The earthquake, the nameless sister who committed a nameless sin, the habit of wandering among the slaves, even the hatred for the aunt, all these form part of the familiar pattern of his life. Loneliness, a sense of evil, and a brooding terror were his companions through most of his days, to be dissembled in a flash of wit or in ceaseless inquiry among books, but always there, like the devils of the noonday and of the night.

A spare, pale youth with large eyes, country bred, he came to Rome only to meet the horrors he thought he had left behind. Sex tormented him. His friend Rufinus was baptized "pure as the driven snow," but of himself he said he had sinned "with unclean lips and with the eyes and with the foot and with the hand and with all his members," and he added that he deserved a second baptism of fire because he had defiled his baptismal robe, meaning simply that he had defiled his body, for in those days the candidate for baptism stood naked before the priest. Caught up in the gay activities of the students, he seems to have sinned quite casually and then to have suffered terrible bouts of repentance: at such times, like many others who were conscious of their sins, he would visit on Sundays the sepulchers of the martyrs and the apostles in the catacombs, and he remembered the horror of it when he was an old man:

Often I would find myself entering those crypts, deep dug in the earth, with their walls on either side lined with the bodies of the dead, where everything was so dark that almost it seemed as though the Psalmist's words were fulfilled, *Let them go down quick into Hell.* Here and there the light, not entering in through windows, but filtering down from above through shafts, relieved the horror of the darkness. But again, as soon as you found yourself cautiously moving forward, the black night closed around, and there came to my mind the line of Vergil, *Horror ubique animos, simul ipsa silentia terrent.* (Jerome, *Commentarius in Ezechielem,* c. 40, v. 5.)

"The horror and the silences terrified their souls." There were many similar phrases he liked to repeat from Vergil. Indeed he rarely quotes Vergil in any other but a somber mood, and these somber rhythms were to return to him when he came to translate Isaiah, where occasionally he has shifted a phrase of Hebrew to allow the Roman poet's voice to be heard. He learned Vergil at the best school, for he attended the lectures in the Athenaeum where the great grammarian Aelius Donatus dictated to his students an intricate commentary on the poet. He studied logic and rhetoric and attended the law courts, where he heard the greatest orators of his time. He collected a library and copied out manuscripts with his own hand, a habit which remained until he could afford secretaries. Quite suddenly he disappeared from Rome and wandered with his friend Bonosus to Gaul. He stayed for a while in Treves, copied more manuscripts, including Hilary's *Commentary on the Psalms*—a work for which he had no very high regard, saying it derived almost wholly from Origen—and at some place along the banks of the Rhine he decided that it was his wish to serve God. Though his parents were Christians, he was too conscious of his sins to embrace Christianity openly. His friend Bonosus, who was wealthy and saintly, came from the neighborhood of Strido and decided to live a life of meditation on one of the bare islands in the Adriatic off the Dalmatian coast. Jerome was full of envy; it was the first time he had come face to face with a dedicated recluse. Jerome bewailed his own fate and his own worldliness. "Bonosus," he declared, "has become a true son of the Fish, and makes for the watery wastes. For myself, defiled by my ancient sins, I seek the dry places like the basilisks and the scorpions. Bonosus treads the serpent's head beneath his heel, while I am still food for the creeping monster who by God's decree devours the earth."

The capital of Venetia in those days was Aquileia, which is now a small ruined seaport. In Jerome's time it was a large city with vast colonnades and marketplaces, with perhaps half a million inhabitants; a center of learning and headquarters for an army. Here Jerome met Heliodorus, a former officer of the Roman army who became his lifelong friend, and the layman Innocentius, who first encouraged him to write, and Paul, a hermit who had known Cyprian and who declaimed at length on the advantages of the monastic life. Jerome had written in Gaul a *Commentary on Obadiah*. He was heartily ashamed of it, but now, with Innocentius prompting him, he decided to write in earnest. Paul may have told him the story of the strange dreams suffered by Cyprian before his martyrdom. Cyprian had seen a youth who imitated with his hand the stroke of a headman, a tall and impassive youth who had stood there silently behind the Proconsul, saying nothing except with his hand. Jerome decided to write another story of a martyrdom, and though he was to write many strange things he was never to write anything stranger or more revealing than the story he called *The Woman Struck Seven Times with an Ax*, for in this story all his sense of guilt, all his desperate desire for purity, all his eagerness to imitate the saintliness of Bonosus are revealed with quite extraordinary precision and with a wonderful dreamlike quality. In the introduction of the story, which takes the form of a long letter to Innocentius, Jerome explains that it happened "*in my lifetime*," and he complains that as he sets to work on it he feels as though he is embarking on a dangerous voyage far from land, "on every side of the sky, on every side of the sea," darkness roughening the waves, the sea boiling into white foam under the storm clouds, himself lost in a perilous boat. Then follows the strange surrealist story, which can be explained only by the identification of Jerome himself with the woman struck seven times with an ax. He wrote:

In ancient days there was a city in Liguria called Vercellae near the foothills of the Alps, once powerful, now lying half in ruins with only a handful of inhabitants. When, according to his custom, the Consul came to visit the place, a woman and her lover were brought before him, accused by the woman's husband of adultery. The Consul assigned them to the torture chamber of the public prison. A bloody claw was inserted in the boy's bruised flesh and drawn along his flanks, to make him reveal the truth under torture. Unable to bear the long agony, lying in his own blood, he decided to take the short road to death and accused the woman and so made himself deserving of death, for he gave her no chance to deny the sin. But the woman was stronger, and though stretched out on the rack, her hands tied behind her back and filthy with the prison dirt, yet because the torturer could not bind her eyes she gazed heavenward while the tears rolled down her cheeks, and said: "O Thou Lord Jesus, be my witness. From Thee nothing is hidden, Thou dost search the loins and the heart, and Thou knowest it is not from fear of dying that I deny the sin. As for you, O unhappy youth, if you are in haste to die, why should you take two innocent lives? I have long desired to die and to strip my body of its hateful flesh, but not as an adulteress. I offer my throat to the shining sword and welcome it with no shuddering, but I must take my innocence with me. He does not perish who dies in order to live!"

The Consul meanwhile gazed upon the bloody scene like a wild animal who has once tasted blood and is ever afterwards athirst. He ordered her tortures to be redoubled, gnashed his teeth and threatened the executioner with a similar fate, unless he made the woman confess a crime which the strong man had been unable to conceal.

The woman cried: "O Lord Jesus, help me! How many tortures are being inflicted upon this single creature who is wholly Thine!"

Her hair was fastened to the stake, her body bound more tightly to the rack, and then the fire was put to her feet. The executioner stabbed her thighs and did not spare her breasts; yet she remained firm, her spirit untouched by bodily pain, and in the enjoyment of a good conscience she forbade the torture to rage within her. The cruel judge started from his seat as though defeated, while she prayed to the Lord. Then her limbs were torn from their joints, but still she raised her eyes to heaven. Another had confessed their common guilt, but she denied his confession and though herself in danger she tried to save him in his hour of danger.

Her single voice continued: "Beat me, burn me, tear me. I am innocent. If you do not believe my words, the day will come when the crime will be carefully examined. My judge is known to me."

Now the torturer was sighing and groaning, for there was no more place on her flesh for fresh wounds. He was terrified by the sight of the mangled body and his ferocity abated. The Consul was aroused to fresh anger. He shouted: "Does it surprise you, O you onlookers, that this woman prefers torture to death? It seems to me that an adulterous act is committed by two people, and it is more credible that a guilty woman should deny a crime than that an innocent youth should confess one."

So the same sentence was passed upon both. The executioner dragged away these two people condemned to death. All the people came rushing out to see the spectacle, coming in dense flocks through the crowded gates, so that it was as though the entire city was migrating. At the first stroke of the sword the miserable youth's head was cut off: the rest of his body rolled over in its own blood. Then came the turn of the woman. With bent knees she sank to the ground, and over her quivering neck a gleaming ax was raised, and with all his strength the executioner brought down his powerful arm: but the moment it touched her body the deadly blade was stayed, so lightly grazing her skin that it did no more than draw blood. Seeing his hand defeated, the executioner gazed in amazement at his conquered arm; and once again the fearful ax was raised above his head. This time the ax fell feebly on her, quiet and harmless on her neck, as though the iron had feared to touch her. Thereupon, panting with rage, the executioner flung his cloak back over his shoulders, so that he could employ his whole strength, but this action of his only loosened the brooch fastening his garment. Unknown to him, the brooch fell to the ground and he poised his arm for still another blow. Then the woman said: "Your golden brooch has fallen. Take it, or else you will lose something for which you have worked hard."

I ask you, why was she so sure of herself? She had no fear of the death which hung over her, she rejoiced in her wounds, it was not she but the executioner who turned pale. Her eyes did not see the sword, they saw only the brooch; and she who felt no terror of death thought only of how she could help the furious man. Then the third blow fell, only to be made harmless by the sacred power of the Trinity. Now the executioner was absolutely terrified, and placed the cutting edge of the ax against her neck, believing that though it would not hack off her head, the pressure of his hand would slit her throat. But then—O miracle unheard through all the ages!—the ax bent back upon its haft, and seemed to be gazing helplessly at its master, confessing defeat.

The woman had been condemned by the Consul, but she was acquitted by the sword. And so it came about that the people took up arms to defend her. There were people of all ages and both sexes, all attempting to put the executioner to flight. They formed a ring round her and there was not one who could believe the evidence of his eyes. The news of the miracle threw a neighboring city into confusion: the lictors came together: from among them there came the officer charged with the execution of condemned criminals, "pouring," as Vergil says, "corroding ashes upon his fouled gray hairs," and this officer exclaimed: "O citizens, you are making me her substitute, it is my life which you are seeking. Even if you feel that mercy and clemency should be shewn to her, even if you want to help a condemned woman, surely I, an innocent man, should not have to pay for it!" The people were astonished and moved by this terrible appeal, a strange torpor settled upon them and their feelings were suddenly changed. Previously they felt it was an act of piety to defend her: now it seemed to them an act of piety to allow her to be executed.

So a new ax was brought and a new executioner appeared on the scene. The victim took her place, protected only by the favor of Christ. The first blow shook her. The second made her shudder. The third hurled her wounded to the ground. O sublime majesty of the divine power! Previously she had received four strokes without injury: now for a while she seemed to die, so that an innocent man might not be condemned.

The priests, whose duty it is to perform this office, wrapped her blood-stained body in a shroud, and then prepared to dig a grave and cover it with stones. That day the sun set in haste, and God's mercy was concealed in the darkness. Suddenly her breasts heaved, her eyes opened and sought the light. Life flowed into her. She sighed, she looked around, she rose, she spoke, and then at last her voice broke through the silence: "Lord, who art on my side, I shall not fear. What can man do to me?"

At this time an old woman, who had been kept alive by the bounty of the church, rendered back her soul to heaven, and her body was placed in that grave which had previously been occupied by the martyr. Before dawn there came to this place the devil in the guise of the executioner, and he looked for the body of the slain woman, and asked to be shown her sepulcher, thinking that she might be alive and wondering how she could have died. He asked the priests, and they pointed to the place where there was fresh turf and heaped-up earth. The priests said: "We will dig up the bones which have been laid to rest and make new war on the sepulcher—what kind of thing is this? If that doesn't satisfy you, shall we scatter her limbs for the vultures and the wild beasts to gnaw at? One who has received seven strokes of the ax deserves better than death!"

Shame sent the executioner away in confusion. The woman was secretly cared for in church, and so that the doctor's frequent visits should cause no comment, she let her hair be cut short and in the company of some virgins went to a place of retreat in the country. Then, until the scars formed on her wounds, she wore men's clothes. And yet today—for true it is that supreme legality is supreme injustice—even after so many miracles the laws are raging against her. (Jerome, *Epistolae*, I.)

Jerome does not explain why the laws raged against her, but he adds a note to say that the saintly Evagrius, who was staying with Eusebius, Bishop of Vercellae, traveled to Gaul and appealed for mercy to the Emperor Valentinian, and then "the Emperor restored to freedom the woman who had thus been restored to life."

Jerome was writing in an age when credulity was widespread, but the story as he relates it baffles the wildest credulity. There are too many signs that Jerome is saying something out of the intimacy of his heart, speaking indirectly of himself, the boy who had gone down to the catacombs and been wounded so often by his own sins—were the seven strokes of the ax the seven deadly sins? We do not know, but for the first time we are in touch with a living man with a furious sensual imagination and a taste for blood and all the details of execution. The incident of the falling brooch reads like something seen and seen again within a nightmare, and the harsh shuddering style suggests a man at the end of his spiritual resources, terrified and ill. There was no doubt of the terror. Quite suddenly, some months after writing the story, he left Aquileia with a few friends. He never revealed the reasons for his departure. All he says is that a sudden whirlwind—*subitus turbo*—descended upon him and he could no longer breathe the poisoned air. He hints at the presence of an "Iberian viper" who had threatened him with death, but it is all mystery. He left his native province, and he was never to return.

The small band of friends wandered over Asia Minor, intending to make their way to Jerusalem. They were sick when they reached Antioch. There Innocentius died of a fever, and there one by one Jerome's friends left him. In a foreign land he was alone.

He had perhaps hoped to be alone. The instinct of the hermit had been deeply ingrained within him ever since Bonosus had departed to his craggy island in the Adriatic. The rage of his heart must be stilled somehow, and how better could it be stilled than by a long apprenticeship to silence? "To me," he said once, "a town is a prison, and the desert loneliness is paradise." He joined a community of hermits who lived on the edge of the desert of Calchis in Syria. There he slept in a bare cell, clothed himself in sackcloth, and for five years submitted to rigorous penances, praying and studying the Scriptures.

Lying at night on the bare ground, drinking only water and eating only uncooked food, his shriveled skin turning as black as an Ethiopian's, with scorpions and wild beasts for his companions, keeping his body awake by banging his bones against the ground, he lived a life of perpetual austerity, and though he desired peace above all things peace was not easily come by. "I have damned myself to such a prison against the fear of Hell," he wrote, but there were moments when the desert prison was singularly attractive, when the cares of the body were exchanged for visions of perfect blessedness. At such moments he would write to his friends, Heliodorus and others, urging them to join him, and there came from him a peculiar fiery prose which shows that a poet was concealed in him. Begging Heliodorus to leave his family and come at once to Calchis, he suddenly takes wing and sings, as he says, "like a sailor singing a happy song":

O desert enameled with the flowers of Christ!
O solitude issuing forth the stones of the city of a mighty king!
O desert rejoicing in God's familiar presence!
O brother whose soul is greater than the universe, what doest
    thou in the world?
How long shalt thou remain beneath the shelter of the roof-tree?
How long shalt thou repose within the smoky prison of the city?
Have faith in me, I see a wider light!
How sweet to cast away the burdens of the flesh and soar in
    purest air!
Art afraid of poverty? Christ calls poor men blessed.
Art afraid of labor? No athlete but is crowned with sweat.
Dost think of food? Faith feels no hunger.
Dost dread the touch of worn bruised fasting limbs upon the
    ground?

I say Christ lies by thy side.
Dost dread a wild beard and disheveled hair?
I say thy head is Christ.
Dost fear the eternal vastness of the desert?
I say thy spirit takes a gentle walk through Paradise.
Dost dread rough skin and unclean scurvy limbs?
I say those bathed in Christ need never bathe again!

(Jerome, *Epistolae*, XIV, 10.)

In another letter, written long afterward, he explained that these moments of illumination came after nights of weeping when he would set out from his cell and explore the desert alone. "Then whenever I came upon a hollow valley, a craggy mountain or a steep precipice, there was my oratory, there the slave-prison of my most wretched flesh; and as the Lord Himself is my witness, after many tears and a long gaze upon the sky, I felt myself in the presence of the angelic hosts, and in joy and gladness I sang: 'Because of the savor of thy good ointments we will run after thee.'"

But these moments seem to have been rare. There were devils to be fought. Pale with fasting, he was assailed with desire for the beautiful dancing girls who came creeping into his imagination, and it puzzled him that they came when his limbs were cold. He never explains entirely whether he was able to banish them, but he tells the story of a young Greek who had entered the desert and suffered from the same incandescent imagination. To take his mind off his dreams, the youth's spiritual instructor ordered one of the older monks to curse and revile the youth, so making his life intolerable, and then he would be charged with having committed innumerable sins he had never committed. There were continual trials, and the witnesses came forward with their accusations. The spiritual instructor would cleverly put in a plea on behalf of the youth, saying "our brother must not be swallowed up by too much sorrow," but the trials went on for over a year. At the end of that time the youth was asked whether he still suffered from his hot dreams. "Good heavens," the youth replied. "How can I want to fornicate, when I am not even allowed to live?"

Jerome fasted assiduously, went on his lonely wanderings, fought off the disease of the spirit known as *acedia*, the utter listlessness which attacks even the best of monks at times, and found solace in reading. He began to learn Hebrew: it helped him to preserve his serenity. He had observed that people when they are weak in body sometimes suffer from fits of giggling in the desert, and he was determined upon a high seriousness. "You must have a solitude of the mind, a Sabbath of the heart, a calm of conscience and inward aspirations if you go down into the depths of the forests or the summits of the hills," said Ivo of Chartres. "Without these all solitude is attended by listless despair, vainglory and perilous storms of temptation." Jerome saw the dangers, avoided them where he could, and even succeeded in being able to forget the vast temptation of reciting Vergil and Cicero to himself. To this time belongs the dream he recounted years later. About the middle of Lent he was attacked with a fever, which brought him near to death. His funeral was prepared. As he lay on the verge of death, he dreamed that he was standing before the Judgment Seat. The judge asked: "Who art thou?" Jerome replied: "I am a Christian." "No," said the judge, "you are lying. You are a Ciceronian, not a Christian, for where thy treasure is, there is thy heart." The angels were ordered to beat him. Then, the fear of Hell which had been so vivid when he went down in the catacombs returned, and like hammer-beats he heard the words "In Hell who shall confess to thee?" He begged for pardon, none was given to him, the angels re-doubled their fury until he cried out: "O Lord, if I ever possess secular manuscripts, if I ever read them, I have denied Thee." When he woke up he was bathed in tears and there were welts on his shoulders where the angels had beaten him.

It is one of the constant themes of the early Fathers that the Church and the Academy, prayer and pagan poetry, can have nothing in common. Jerome followed an accepted tradition and, like the other Fathers, cursed the pagan poets all the more fervently because he was never able to escape from them. "What has Horace to do with the Psalms?" he cried. "Vergil with the Gospels? Cicero with the Apostles? All things are pure to the pure, but we ought not to drink the cup of Christ and the cup of devils!" Though he promised to abjure the works of Cicero in his dream, he never succeeded in putting Cicero aside; and Rufinus relates, not without malice, that in his later years he would pay his copyists more highly for a transcription of a Ciceronian dialogue than for a book of homilies.

The desert weighed heavily on Jerome. There was madness all round him. He kept appealing to his friends to join him, but none came, or at least we have no news of their coming. He wrote earnestly to Heliodorus:

Away with prayers and blandishments! There are times when love itself must divulge its anger! You despised me when I begged you to come: now perhaps you will listen to my reproaches. O delicate-fingered soldier, what business have you in your father's house? Where are the ramparts, the trenches and the winter under canvas? Lo, the trumpet sounds from heaven. Lo, the armed Emperor comes forth from among the clouds to subdue the world, and from the King's mouth there issues a twice-sharpened sword to hew down all obstacles. Tell me, are you coming from your chamber to the battlefield, from the shade to the sun? Listen to the King's proclamation: "He who is not with me is against me, and he that gathereth not with me scattereth." Lo, the adversary in thy heart endeavors to slay Christ. Lo, the camp of the enemy sighs over the bounty you received before your service began. Though your little nephew is hanging round your neck, and though your mother with hair disheveled and rent garments shows you the breast that gave you suck, though your father flings himself down on the doorstep, trample him under-foot, go your way and fly with dry eyes to the standard of the Cross. (Jerome, *Epistolae*, XIV, 2.)

There came a time when Jerome grew ashamed of the letter, which he remembered vividly; and then he confessed that he had been "trying to curb the first tides of youthful wantonness in the hardship of the desert." He admitted that the letter was altogether too flowery, but he evidently hoarded it as he hoarded copies of so many of his letters, pleased with its fervor if not with its pride. As for his pride, it was to remain with him always, though he had learned in the desert that "pride pounces swiftly on a man who has fasted for a little while and seen no other human being."

He had learned other things. He had learned that even in the desert there were schisms and disputations on the meanings of words so violent that people came to blows when they discussed whether God was one *ousia* and three *hypostases*. Jerome was asked what he believed. He said: "I believe God is three subsistent persons." It was not enough. He was asked to define further, and he was sufficiently canny to realize they were trying to trap him. It was all unpardonable error and evil, and he complained against the sectarianism of the priests of Antioch, but without effect. "Every day," he wrote, "they question me about my faith, as though I had been born again without faith. I confess whatever they wish. Even then they don't believe me. For myself, all I care for is to leave them. So they have told me to go, and I have implored them to let me stay until the spring comes at least." As always, he was granting himself the permission to change his mind in the middle of a sentence.

At some time in the year 379 Jerome made his way to Antioch, and was ordained a priest. He had no particular duties to perform. Restless, he decided to go to Constantinople, where Gregory of Nazianzus was preaching. He admired Gregory, set to work on translating Origen's *Homilies on Jeremiah*, and wrote a tractate on the Seraphim for the Pope, Damasus, who had come to power only after a mob armed with hatchets and firebrands had surrounded the fortress where Ursinus, the rival Pope, had hidden himself. After the fighting, there were 137 dead lying on the ground, and

Damasus's belief in the felicity of his guardian angels soared. Jerome's tractate impressed upon the Pope the necessity of believing in the spiritual powers of the angels. The Pope was only too ready to obey Jerome's wishes and even summoned him to Rome. For his tractate and perhaps for other services he was made the Pope's ecclesiastical secretary. That was almost the highest honor Damasus could grant him, and Jerome, if he made no great errors, could expect to follow in Damasus's footsteps and wear the three-tiered crown.

Meanwhile, he threw himself into the life of Rome. He had a passion for mingling with the rich and saintly virgins of the city. In the intervals of collating manuscripts in the papal library and discoursing to the Pope on the meaning of the word "Hosanna," Jerome paid frequent visits to these saintly women who lived in marble palaces converted into aristocratic convents. There was Albina, a rich and noble widow, living in her palace on the Aventine with her widowed daughter Marcella, who wore the plain brown robe of the dedicated virgin. In the same palace lived Marcellina, the sister of Ambrose, another dedicated virgin, and there were perhaps twenty others, though we know by name only Paula, Sophronia, Felicita, Asella, and another Marcella. Over this community Albina ruled with a stern hand, but she allowed saintly visitors, and Athanasius had once stayed in the palace, speaking at length of the virtues of the desert and leaving as a parting gift for her daughter a copy of the same *Life of St. Antony* which was to have such a disturbing effect on Augustine. Of all these the most talented, the most brilliant, the most genuinely ascetic was Paula, whose four daughters were to become the joy of Jerome's middle age.

Jerome was lionized when he came to Rome, not only because he was the Pope's secretary, but because his fervent letters written in the desert were known to the devout. Many knew them by heart. They breathed a passion for incorruptibility. They were new. They spoke of asceticism in a way which made it exciting, and they were dangerously effective with young women. Jerome knew this. He deliberately kept away from young women for a while, but when Albina issued an invitation begging him to visit her palace on the Aventine, he accepted, and the rest of his life was to be spent among the women whom he first met in this palace in Rome.

Rome was a noisy, inflammable, decadent city, with a turbulent mob and a turbulent and dangerous aristocracy. There were senators who traced their descent back to the gods and who possessed incomes of half a million dollars a year, with a thousand slaves to do their bidding and twenty or thirty country houses from which to choose where they would spend their holidays. The rich were over-rich, the poor lived on the wheat from Egypt. The chief amusement lay in the chariot races fought among the Blues, Greens, Reds, and Whites. At the chariot races nearly the whole population assembled, shouting themselves hoarse, so that the traveler heard their voices even before Rome came in sight. The Church, growing in political influence, had acquired immense power. Marble basilicas were being erected every month. The most sumptuous festivals were held. Inevitably corruption penetrated even into the Church.

Jerome, tall and striking, with his pale face and large dark eyes, wandered through the Roman streets, his mind sharpened by the religious disputes in Constantinople, with all the freshness of a man who only a few months before had been living on locusts in the desert. He detested most of the Romans and did not apologize for detesting them. His savage indignation overflowed. He loathed bearded priests especially. He loathed the pious widows who were determined that their piety should be observed. He loathed the artifices by which the wealthy women pampered their flesh. He hated squeaking shoes, transparent silks, perfumes. But though he rains down curses on loose women and characteristically pays comparatively little attention to loose men, it is the rich clergy, the processions of monsignors and mountebank priests, who make his gall rise.

In anger Jerome writes like an angel. He has a ferocity and a controlled violence that have rarely been equaled. The sharply etched portraits—his letters are full of them—introduce us to a world as vividly decadent as anything in Proust, dominated by a Pope who achieved the nickname of "the tweaker of the ladies' ears" (*auriscalpius matronarum*). It is even possible that Jerome may have been describing the Pope when he drew the portrait of a high ecclesiastic going on his rounds:

The only thought of such men is their clothes—are they pleasantly perfumed, do their shoes fit smoothly? Their hair is crimped with the curling-irons; their fingers glisten with rings; and if there is the least trace of damp on the road, they walk on tiptoe so as not to splash their shoes. When you see such men, think of them as potential bridegrooms rather than as ordained priests. Indeed, there are some among them who devote all their devotion and all their energy to discovering the names and households and characters of married women.

I will describe briefly for you a master of the art so that you may more easily recognize from the appearance of the master the nature of his pupils. He rises and goes forth with the sun. He has the order of his visits duly arranged. He takes short cuts. Troublesome old man that he is, he makes his way almost into the bedrooms of ladies still asleep. If he sees a cushion, or a pretty tablecloth, or any little bit of household furniture, he praises it, he admires it, he fingers it, and then he laments that he possesses nothing like it, and begs—or rather, extorts—it from the owner, for all the women are afraid of offending the city gossip. He has two enemies whom he abhors—one is continence, the other is fasting. He likes to be served with a savory luncheon, and his pet weakness is a plump young crane vulgarly called "pipizo." He has a rough and saucy tongue well sprinkled with words of abuse. Go where you will, he is the first man you set eyes on. Whatever news is whispered abroad, he has either originated it or exaggerated it. He changes horses every hour, and is so sleek and so spirited you would think he was the brother of the King of Thrace himself. (Jerome, *Epistolae*, XXII, 28.)

Jerome is equally ferocious when he discusses the high-born
widows who receive these church dignitaries, women who
flaunt themselves in silk dresses, paint their faces with rouge
and white lead, and wear in their ears the most expensive pearls
from the Red Sea:

> Give a wide berth to those who remain widows of necessity,
> not of inclination. Though they change their raiment, their am-
> bitions remain unchanged. Their Basternian litters are preceded
> by cohorts of eunuchs. See their red lips and plump sleek skins:
> you would not think they had lost a husband, you would fancy
> they were hunting for one. Their houses are full of flatterers and
> guests. The clergy, too, are there—men whose teaching and
> authority should inspire respect—but no, they kiss the ladies on
> the forehead and stretch out their hands to bestow a benedic-
> tion, but also, mark you, to receive in their palms the reward for
> their holy salutation. These good women, seeing how the priests
> depend upon their munificence, are puffed up with pride. They
> know by experience what a husband's rule is like and prefer the
> freedom of widowhood. They call themselves chaste nuns, and
> after a seven-course dinner they dream of apostles. (Jerome,
> *Epistolae*, XXII, 16.)

Jerome has a habit of tearing the wings off the gaudy flies:
long practice made him expert. Already he has a woman's
sensitivity and a woman's malice. He knows exactly how
earnestly, with what degree of helpless passion the widows
greet the representatives of Christ. He likes to talk of the
wretched little women (*miserae mulierculae*) who minister
to the bearded ascetics. He observes that the ascetics come
bare-legged into the drawing rooms, their feet blue with a
holy chill. As for their beards, he regards them as signs of
their own interior dirtiness: "If there is any holiness in a beard,
nobody is more holy than a goat." But his best barbs are reserved for the decorated women who go to church with a
full consciousness of their own magnificence:

> There are many like her who pack their wardrobes with gar-
> ments, putting on a new dress each day, and even so never

getting the better of the moth. The more especially devout ones wear a dress until it is threadbare, but though they go about in rags, their coffers are full of dresses. Her prayerbooks are made of purple parchment, with melted gold for lettering and the cover is clothed with jewels, though Christ lies naked and dying at her door. When she extends her hand towards the needy, she sounds a full blast on the trumpet. When she goes to Mass, she hires the town-crier. I lately saw a very noble Roman lady—no names, or else you will think this a satire—on her way to the basilica of St. Peter, with a crowd of eunuchs guarding her. She was giving money to the beggars with her own hand to create, I suppose, a more extreme reputation for sanctity. She gave them a penny apiece. One old beggarwoman, weighed down with years and rags, ran in front of the line to get a second coin; but when her turn came, she got not a penny, but the lady's fist in her face, and was covered with blood for her criminal offence. Verily, avarice is the root of all evils. . . . Peter the Apostle said: "Silver and gold have I none, but such as I have, give I unto thee." But nowadays many say, in deed if not in words, "Faith and mercy have I none, but such as I have, silver and gold, that I do not give unto thee either." (Jerome, *Epistolae*, XXII, 32.)

There is a wicked gleam in Jerome's eyes as he tells these stories. Though he is wholly serious, wholly mordant, he is clearly enjoying himself. False piety he finds the most detestable of sins, and almost he pardons the young women of Rome who have so far forgotten themselves that they cut their hair short and lift up their chins as though they were proud of themselves. He mentions these in passing. They are, of course, despicable, but the women who wear hair shirts are more than despicable: they are damned. Of these pious women he wrote:

Some of these women disfigure their faces so that men will know they have been fasting. As soon as they catch sight of anyone, they drop their eyes and begin sobbing, covering up their faces and groaning, but all the time they have one eye open to see what effect they are making. They wear black dresses and girdles of sackcloth, their feet and hands are always dirty: only their stomachs—which can't be seen—are seething with food. Of these the Psalm is sung every day: "The Lord will scatter the bones of them that take pleasure in themselves." Other women change their raiment, and put on the dresses of men: they cut their hair short and lift up their chins in the most shameless fashion; they blush to be what they were born to be—eunuchs they are now, instead of women. Others dress in goats' hair, and becoming children again, put on babies' hoods and make themselves look like owls. (Jerome, *Epistolae*, XXII, 27.)

It is as though Swift were having a holiday in fifth-century Rome; and indeed there are many parallels between Jerome and Swift. Both accomplish their ends without any appearance of striving, and both are intoxicated with the evil in the world. Neither showed sympathy for the married state; and they regarded the stomach as a seat of evil only slightly less horrifying than the sexual organs. As for those organs, Jerome cannot contain himself when he speaks of them. To a widow called Furia who contemplated marrying again, he writes:

Surely you have learned the trials of marriage by now! Surely you have been surfeited to nausea as though with the flesh of quails! Your mouth has tasted the most bitter gall, you have evacuated that sour and unwholesome food and relieved a heaving stomach. Why stuff into it again something which has already proved noxious? "The dog is turned to his own vomit again and the sow that was washed to her wallowing in the mire." Even the brute animals and the wandering birds do not fall twice into the same nets and snares. Are you afraid that the Furian line will cease, and your father will have no child of yours to crawl and creep upon his chest and leave a nasty stain on his neck? (Jerome, *Epistolae*, LIV, 4.)

Jerome is for some reason nearly always horrifying when he talks about necks and stomachs; they are the enemies. He never explains why he has such a terror of the neck. He wages merciless war on the stomach, envying the monks who could live on five figs a year. For himself, he said he was content to feed on beans: only those who despised themselves fed on quail or truffles; and though he hated beards he admired St. Hilary whose one concession to custom was that he allowed his beard to be cut once a year at Easter.

What is the explanation of Jerome's peculiar horror of sex and the intestines, his adoration of virgins? It would be easy enough to envisage reasons based upon psychoanalysis, but it is possible that the clue lies elsewhere. He had lived for five years in the desert. In one of his letters he exclaimed: "The desert loves the naked"—*nudos amat humerus*. In the desert, against the dry bushes and the sheets of yellow sand, the bare broken rocks and the burning sun, few illusions remain to the human animal. He is stripped bare, becoming hardly more than a bleeding and twitching nerve, knowing himself dependent upon the streams of treacly black water from the rocks. To whom can he appeal except to a God as naked as himself? Those who have been in the desert never recover from the experience, and there remains with them, to the end of their lives, the vision of a perfect purity, a God who is close to them, a fever to be alone with the alone.

Jerome never forgot the desert: he is always referring to it: and when he came to live in Bethlehem he was, in a sense, returning to the desert. His study was a cave. Caves in Palestine have three purposes: they are tombs, or robbers' dens, or holy places. For Jerome his cave was all three, and from the robber's den he would lay siege to Heaven and rob it of its wealth.

In Jerome's famous letter to Julia, he points out that no soldier takes a wife with him to battle. A married woman takes care to please her husband; she has no time for God. All the saints were virgin. Neither Elijah nor Elisha nor Jeremiah took to himself a wife. He admits that in past days the law was: "Blessed is he who hath seed in Zion and a family in Jerusalem," but with the coming of Christ the old law has been changed. Today the word is: "Think not that you are a dry tree: for instead of sons and daughters you have a place forever in heaven." Though Paul had spoken as though the

Second Coming was at hand, as though the world had no need of being peopled any more, Jerome's arguments are based upon a continuing existence of the earth. He will even praise wedlock because it produces virgins, almost as one might praise whales for producing ambergris. He wrote:

I praise wedlock, I praise the married state, because they produce virgins for me. I take the rose from the thorn, the gold from the earth, the pearl from the oyster. Shall the plowman plow all day? Shall he not enjoy the fruit of his labor? Wedlock is all the more honored when that which is born from it is the more loved. Why, O mother, envy your daughter? She has been nourished on your milk, and drawn out of your viscera, she has grown strong in your arms: and your sedulous piety has kept her safe. So you are indignant because she refuses to wed a soldier, but will wed the King instead? She has rendered a great grace to you: you become the mother by marriage of God. (Jerome, *Epistolae*, XXII, 20.)

Reminded that Paul had said: "Concerning virgins I have no commandment of the Lord," Jerome rages against those who say that Paul was married, or meant what he said. Did he not say: "I wish that all men were even as I myself?" And did not that mean he was a virgin? Jerome rarely if ever refers to the text which Luther admired so abundantly that he produced a crop of children: "It is better to marry than to burn." Yet it is unfair to suggest that Jerome was morbid. For him virginity represented an almost unattainable purity, a part of heaven, even a pattern of heaven. The virgins are the desert in flower. So, at the very thought of virginity, he becomes extraordinarily poetical. Like some learned rabbis before him and like Bernard later, he will employ the Song of Solomon, and as though rewriting it in another mode, prove that God is the promised Bridegroom:

Then shall the secret places of your inner chamber keep guard over you forever, and forever shall the Bridegroom play with you within. When you pray, you are praying to your Bridegroom. When you read, He is speaking to you. When sleep falls upon you, He will come behind the wall and put His hand through the hole in the door and touch your belly, and you will tremble and awake and cry out: "I am sick with love." And you will hear Him answer: "A garden inclosed is my sister, my spouse; a spring shut up, a fountain sealed." Therefore do not go away from home or visit the daughters of a strange land, though you have Patriarchs for brothers and rejoice in Israel as your father. I would not have you seek the Bridegroom in the public places, or go about the corners of the city. You may say: "I will arise and go about the city: in the streets and in the broad ways I will seek Him whom my soul loveth," and though you ask them: "Saw ye Him whom my soul loveth?" no one will deign to answer you. The Bridegroom cannot be found in the public places of the city. "Straight and narrow is the way that leadeth into life." And it says also: "I sought Him but I could not find Him: I found Him but He gave me no answer." Let foolish virgins roam abroad: but do you stay within, alone with the Bridegroom, and if you shut your door and pray to your Father in secret, He will come and knock and He will say: "Behold, I stand at the door and knock: if any man open I will come to him and will sup with him, and he with me." And then immediately you will eagerly reply: "It is the voice of my beloved that knocketh, saying, 'Open to me, my sister, my nearest, my dove, my undefiled.'" (Jerome, *Epistolae*, XXII, 25.)

Jerome's ruthlessness conceals his delicacy; and to read his dissertations on virgins is to be horrified until we remember that he is at one and the same time composing a litany in praise of young women, demanding physical purity, composing a mystical treatise, and amusing himself with the game of rearranging ancient texts to suit his own purpose. It is a good game, and perfectly legal, as T. S. Eliot has demonstrated in our time. There are inevitable dangers. We do not know on what occasion the Song of Solomon was written. That it was sung to music and danced by hot-blooded boys and girls at the spring festivals in Palestine is at least as probable as that it was written in prophetical expectation of the union of the Church with Christ.

When Jerome speaks of virginity, he is on dangerous ground. He demands that the virgins should possess a holy pride. He wrote to Julia:

I would not have you consort overmuch with married women, or frequent the houses of the great. Nor would I have you look too often on those things you spurned when you were a virgin and desired to remain one. You must know that women of the world plume themselves if their husbands are judges or hold high positions. If an eager crowd of visitors flocks to greet an Emperor's wife, why should you insult your husband? Learn a holy pride: know you are better than they. (*Disce superbiam sanctam, scito te illis esse meliorem.*) (Jerome, *Epistolae*, XXII, 16.)

The trap is sprung in the last sentence. The mind rebels at all the possibilities the casual phrase implies. No one had spoken of holy pride before; but now, with the publication of Jerome's letter—for nearly all his letters were written to be published abroad—a seal was laid upon *hybris*, the unholy pride which the Greeks feared above other sins. In his *Commentariorum in Sophoniam* Jerome returns to the same theme and explains what he was about:

He who glories in dignities shall perish; he who is puffed up with pride shall perish; he who glories in the strength of the body shall perish. But he who shall arise and be proud with a sacred pride, he shall be with the apostles, and he who shall be worthy to suffer disgrace for Jesus Christ's sake, shall be glorified with the apostles who exult in tribulations, knowing that tribulations give birth to patience, patience gives birth to hope and hope confounds the enemies of God. (Jerome, *Commentarium in Sophoniam.*)

The distinction is clear, but it is permissible to suspect that the saint who invented the *fama de sanctitate* knew more about pride than he cared to admit. There are moments when Jerome conceals his pride only with the utmost difficulty. Indeed, he could hardly help being proud. He was surrounded by adoring women, who were mostly rich and patrician. They hung on his words and received his benedictions with a special fervor. It could hardly last forever. Rumors came to him that he was more concerned to surround himself with beautiful virgins than with the spreading of the gospel. He denied the rumors proudly, but when Blesilla, the most beautiful of Paula's daughters, died at the age of nineteen, apparently as a result of her mortifications, all Rome rose against him. In the middle of the funeral rites Paula fainted away. The people who saw her grief exclaimed: "She grieves because her daughter has been killed with fastings, because she has not married again, because no grandsons will be born into the family. How long are we to tolerate the presence of these detestable monks!" Such a shout was once heard from the lips of a King, and Jerome was in as mortal danger as Thomas à Becket. Then in 384 his protector, the Pope Damasus, died. His successor had no love for Jerome. He remained in Rome for seven more months and then fled to the East, perhaps with the intention of returning to the desert. He was evidently in a raging temper. He called on heaven to witness his innocence against the charges of immorality which were thrown at him, and he seems to have been content when his chief accuser, brought to court and put under torture, confessed Jerome's innocence.

He wandered to the East by slow stages, meeting Paula, Julia, and their virgins at Antioch, then going on with them to Jerusalem. Jerome was still unsure where he should settle. He went to Egypt with the intention of founding a monastery in the Thebaid. He had thought at one point of settling in Jerusalem, but the city was loathsome, full of "creeping heresies," almost worse than the "purple-clad harlot" of Rome. Eventually he decided to remain at Bethlehem, and there he spent the remaining thirty-four years of his life.

For Jerome Bethlehem in the autumn of 386 was everything he thought desirable. There were no wars. The Roman Empire seemed to be at peace; and as he set about building a monastery not far from the Cave of the Nativity, with Paula and the virgins by his side, he could look forward to long years of quiet study, with no temptations to trouble him except the temptations of scholarship. It was not to happen quite like this: but the piety of those early years, when they were still building the hospice and the nunnery, breathes through his letters, in which for the first time there is no sign of strain, no vast excitement, no intoxication of heresies.

Here [he wrote] we find humble and wholesome food: bread and milk, the herbs we grow with our own hands, and all the delicacies of the countryside. Living thus, sleep does not overtake us in prayer, satiety does not interfere with our studies. In summer the trees afford us shade, in autumn the air is cool and the fallen leaves give us a quiet resting-place. In spring the field is clothed with flowers, and we sing our songs the sweeter among the songs of birds. When cold winter comes and snow, we have no lack of fuel: I am warm enough when I sleep or keep my vigil. Let the Romans cling to turbulent crowds, let the arena be filled with cruelty, let the circus riot, and—since it is unpardonable to forget our friends—let the senate of the ladies attend their salons. Our happiness is to cleave unto the Lord and to put our trust in the Lord God. (Jerome, *Epistolae*, LVII, 2.)

Almost it was like a foretaste of Paradise under the overshadowing hills. Every path was sacred, every house was anointed, and it was enough to wander down tracks over the hills, listening to the hammering of the workmen building the wooden walls. He was especially pleased with the hospice, "for," he observed, "if Mary and Joseph should pass this way again, they would not go unprotected." It would not have surprised him in the least if Mary, Joseph, or Christ had entered the monastery. Everything was prepared for them. The quiet virgins read their psalters, attended six services every day, and slept peacefully at night, wearing in bed the same shaggy brown clothes they had worn during the day. They were severe, precise, methodical, with a pleasant dutiful gaiety of their own; and the life cannot have been unlike the life of the early Shakers in America. Jerome was completely charmed by the way in which the highborn patrician ladies obeyed the rules of the order. To keep them out of mischief, there was always work for them. They lit fires, trimmed lamps, shelled peas, boiled the vegetables, and laid the tables, and passed the cups. They were always running hither and thither in their mean dresses. None of them "breathed of Capuan odors or shone with flakes of Spanish gold in their hair." Silence and the psalms of David—it was the perfect background for a scholar, and with an oblique reference to Vergil's *Georgics*, Jerome wrote when the community was well established:

In this little villa of Christ everything is rustic, and apart from the singing of Psalms there is silence. As the plowman drives his share, he sings his *alleluia*. The sweating reaper diverts himself with Psalms, and the vine-dresser as he clips the shoots with his reaping-knife hums the songs of David. These are the only songs sung here. These are our popular love-songs. They are the songs sung by the shepherds, who come to hearten the tillers of the soil. (Jerome, *Epistolae*, LXXVII, 7.)

Jerome arranged his day with the tidy precision which was now to become characteristic of him. He began teaching the village boys Latin and Greek. There was nothing in the least strange in this. The Hebrew boys belonged to the Hellenistic *oikoumene*: there were Greek porticoes in Bethlehem: Roman rule had left its traces on the habits and language of the people: and the poet Meleager had been born near by. Jerome found them apt pupils. Also, he was provided with an excuse which permitted him to continue his studies in classical Latin, forgetting the angelic whipping he had received in a dream. Had not Paul quoted the Greek writers? With a smile he pointed out that he was doing no more than obeying the commandment in Leviticus, which said that if you marry a female captive you must first shave her head and trim her nails. He was, he insisted, following the spiritual meaning of the law. He had shaved the head and trimmed the nails of pagan Roman culture. Was he not pressing Rome into the service of Christianity?

Now there began in earnest the immense volume of correspondence with which Jerome bombarded his friends and enemies. Living in a glass house, he took pleasure in throwing stones. They flew in all directions. A controversy on the meaning of a text took place in Gaul. Jerome, the moment he heard of the controversy, would write his brief, his summing-up, and his judgment; and from his cave in the rocks there came a host of documents which thundered like encyclicals. He wrote commentaries on *Philemon*, Galatians, Ephesians, and Titus at the request of Paula and Julia. Sometimes, though he was in ill health and his eyes were already growing dim, he dictated a thousand lines a day.

His great work was the translation of the Bible, which he had begun in Rome and now continued in the intervals of a thousand other occupations. He wrote a book on *The Site and Names of Hebrew Places*, which he finished, and contemplated a huge history of Christianity from its origins, which he never started. He wrote a short life of St. Malchus which reads like a fairy story. Malchus was a venerable anchorite attacked by the Saracens and compelled to marry a Saracen maid, who was secretly a Christian. They escaped across rivers and deserts, pursued by their Saracen master, until the moment came when a heavenly lion barred the master's path and conveniently swallowed the Saracen. Thereafter Malchus and his bride established a monastery. Though Malchus was a historical character, Jerome had described his own life in the story, and indeed he was rarely capable of doing otherwise. All through his writing there are those strange hints toward an autobiography, so that we come to know him, with his humility and his pride, as we know no other of the Church Fathers.

He wrote histories, commentaries, guidebooks, dissertations on language, on names, on places, and inevitably he came to write epitaphs. *Epitaphium* was the name he chose for a long list of Christians with brief comments which he compiled in 392. Afterwards, for some reason, he changed the title to *De Viris illustribus* (*Concerning Famous Men*). It is an astonishing document. The first deals with Simon Peter, the last deals with Jerome himself, "who is placed at the end of the volume as one born out of due time and the least of the Christians." He includes Philo, Josephus, and Seneca among the Christian writers. He speaks honorably of Origen, and treats the heretics Tatian and Priscillian with commendable praise. His detestation of Ambrose comes clear through the guarded statement: "Because the Bishop of Milan is still writing, I shall deny myself the opportunity of casting judgment so that I may not be exposed to the charge of speaking with too great a flattery or too great an accuracy." The last four words were poisoned. It was not the only time Jerome had attacked Ambrose. In his preface to a translation of the thirty-nine homilies of Origen on St. Luke, he described "an upstart crow who is all bedraggled, yet laughs uproariously at the splendid shining feathers of the other birds," and it was known that this rebuke was intended for Ambrose.

Living calmly in his cave, Jerome was at the mercy of his genius for invective. It would come suddenly, when he was least aware of it, this passion for denunciation and abuse. He was an expert at it. There were no rules, though there were several models: and his beloved Cicero grinding out curses against Catiline supplied the supreme exemplar. As always, Jerome's curses were loudest against those who spoke against virginity, "that blessed vase which the Lord has filled." A Roman monk called Jovinian, whom Jerome described as a "sleek white-clothed incubus who stalks the world like a bridegroom, followed by pretty little fat boys with primped hair, all rosy," had announced that the elect would all receive the same rewards, while virginity, widowhood, and marriage were equally pleasing in the sight of God. He became the target of Jerome's abuse. That anyone should suggest that marriage was pleasing in the eyes of God was of course intolerable. Even more intolerable perhaps was the suggestion that there were no hierarchies among the elect. Jerome adored hierarchies. He thundered. He quoted text against text. With stupendous glee he revealed the weakness of the other side. When Jovinian quoted the verse of St. John: "He that is born of God doeth no sin," Jerome answered with the verse of James: "In many things we all offend." He was superbly sure of himself and nothing would make him change his opinion. Even Augustine had written a book called *On the Blessings of Marriage*. Jerome could see no blessings. He was not prepared to believe that marriage was wholly indecent and against God's will, though elements of indecency and devilry remained in it; on the other hand it was best to be avoided except by those who "by reason of the terrors of the night cannot sleep by themselves." He seems to have believed that marriage consisted of the perpetual repetition of the sexual act. So he argued that the married state was incompatible with prayer, and therefore with Holy Communion—how could such lewd animals deserve to receive the bread and the wine? He advanced the theory that marriage was regarded even by Noah with sacred horror, for did not the unclean animals go two by two into the Ark? He hated the number two. All should be singular and virgin.

As he twists texts to suit his meaning and searches through all literature for celebrations of virginity, his bile rises, the fulminations become unendurably prolix, and the high screaming note takes the place of the orderly procession of ideas. When Jovinian died, Jerome did not sigh with relief, but cursed all the louder, saying that he must have died from stuffing himself with too much food. "He belched out rather than breathed out his life," says Jerome, and adds significantly: "All this happened while eating pork and pheasants."

Meanwhile the work of translation and education went on, undisturbed by the frequent explosions of the half-blind monk in his cell. With Origen's *Hexapla* before him—a translation of the Bible in four columns together with two original Hebrew texts—he hammered out his own style. At immense cost he invited Hebrew scholars to come to his cell and dispute the finer points of interpretation. He had no particular fondness for the sound of Hebrew, saying that "it clattered along woefully," which suggests that he heard the music of his own translation with his inner ear and was curiously lacking in his knowledge of music, for chanted Hebrew possesses a grave music which has much in common with chanted Latin. Augustine and Ambrose knew their music well, and Augustine's treatise on music was one of the most accomplished of his writings. Perhaps, if Jerome had known more about music, he would not have surrendered to the coarse invectives he uttered with such profound abandon and such evident enjoyment.

He who raged against his enemies raged also against death. When Paula died he was grief-stricken. She had been ill for years, apparently from tuberculosis. She was all bone with a thin transparent layer of skin, and Jerome attended her with the gentleness of a mother. When she died, he could no longer continue with his studies. He beat his chest, he cried out for mercy, and it was observed that though he had almost continually crossed himself in the past, now he crossed himself even more often and with greater fervor. It was the year 404 and the eagles were gathering. Jerome seems to have realized that with Paula's passing, a whole age was passing. He gave orders for a splendid funeral. All the bishops of Palestine, with John of Jerusalem at their head, were summoned to carry her bier the short distance between the nunnery and a cave in the rocks close to the Cave of the Nativity. For three days psalms were sung antiphonally in Greek, Latin, and Syriac by virgins who stood around the undecorated coffin where her uncovered face, as white as alabaster, gleamed in candlelight. On the walls of the cave Jerome carved in Latin hexameters an account of her virtues, her graces, and her patrician origin.

He had loved and adored Paula as he did no other woman, and when he was very old he kept repeating her name. Julia, Paula's daughter, to whom he had addressed the most famous of his many letters concerning virginity, assumed her place.

Jerome never recovered from Paula's death. From this time onward his letters nearly always contain some phrase about "the weight of my grief." Yet the violence remained. There were still quarrels. A certain Vigilantius came to visit him from Gascony. This man, who had once been a tavernkeeper, came in time to possess an extraordinary affection for the old scholar. They prayed together and were rarely separated. Then inevitably they quarreled. As Jerome tells the story the quarrel occurred as the result of an earthquake. Vigilantius awoke in the dark, leaped out of bed naked as he was born, and went running to the Cave of the Nativity, where he prayed all night. There was nothing particularly dishonorable about such behavior, though, Jerome observed with some acerbity, he could have had the decency to clothe himself. What was dishonorable was that Vigilantius had taken a nip of some intoxicating liquor to steady his nerves. The man, upbraided for drunkenness and nakedness, was sent away. He was hardly on the ship when he began to denounce Jerome as an impostor and a heretic. When Jerome heard of this, he was almost speechless with horror.

You fool [he shouted in a letter], O cursed one, don't you know what you are saying? Once, as you knelt beside me, you remembered my sermon on the resurrection of the body, and suddenly you jumped up, clapped your hands and embraced me, saying that I was orthodox and worthy to be praised. Then you went away. No sooner on the ship, than the stench of the bilge flooded your brain, and you remembered me as a heretic. . . . Well, go to school again. They ought to call you Dormitantius (the Sleeper), not Vigilantius, for truly you are not vigilant, you slumber with your whole mind, and you snore, not because you sleep soundly, but because you are wholly given over to lethargy.

When Vigilantius wrote a book denouncing Jerome, the old man could only froth at the mouth, summoning the sternness of Elijah, the zeal of Simeon the Canaanite, the sword of Peter who slew Ananias and Sapphira, and the severity of Paul who struck Elymas with blindness to witness that evil had been committed and evil must be rewarded. "Let Vigilantius sleep," he said with disgust, "and while sleeping, may he be destroyed together with the Egyptians by the avenging angels who hovered over Egypt."

But if Vigilantius was damned, others deserved damnation even more. People came from all parts of the Empire to sit at Jerome's feet, bearing letters of introduction from high prelates and from monks only casually known to Jerome. It was impossible to sift these people. They would stay at the hospice; then they would announce that they had traveled on foot throughout Europe to be blessed by Jerome. He could hardly refuse them permission to stay.

Among those who stayed was a handsome ruffian called Sabinianus. He was notably religious, gentle, and inspired, or so Jerome thought. Later he began to have his suspicions. The suspicions were confirmed when he learned that Sabinianus had seduced one of the nuns while she was keeping vigil before the shrine of the Nativity, and thereafter he had communicated with her many times by means of letters tied to a rope that dangled from her window. They had met again at the Chapel of the Angel to the Shepherds a short way out of Bethlehem, and there too she had broken her vows. Sabinianus had stood under her window during many nights, silently exchanging love glances with her, writing letters, receiving answers, and all the time making plans for their escape from Syria. In the morning, worn out with sleeplessness, he would return to the monastery to read the gospel in the chapel. Unfortunately for Sabinianus his love letters were found. Jerome ordered an inquiry, and Sabinianus was summoned to the old man's cell. There was an affecting scene. The handsome ruffian threw himself down at Jerome's feet, begged for forgiveness, promised to retire to the desert, and swore that he would sin no more. Such contrition was seemly. Jerome prayed with him, fervently quoted the Bible to him, implored God's mercy on him, and then let him go. Afterwards Jerome regretted his clemency. He should, he declared, have beaten the man to death—such terrible things had he committed. It came to his ears that Sabinianus had made a profession of seducing virgins. He had even seduced a general's wife. This general, returning from the wars, discovered his wife's sin, ordered her to stand public trial, and even aided the executioner when she was beheaded. As for Sabinianus, Jerome's trust was entirely misplaced. The wretch made no effort to find a holy refuge. The last Jerome heard of him he was flaunting himself throughout Syria, "clothed in fine linen, his fingers laden with rings, his teeth carefully brushed, his thin hair elaborately arranged over his round forehead and his bull neck enclosed in rolls of fat."

Jerome's sorrows were always great, but the greatest was to come. During the Han Dynasty the Huns suffered severe defeats at the hands of the Chinese and began to turn westward. For nearly four hundred years they made their way across Asia, destroying as they went, reducing the tribes or pushing them deeper toward Europe. In 375 they overwhelmed the Ostrogothic Kingdom, and the Goths, who threw themselves on the mercy of Rome, were allowed to cross the Danube and settle in Moesia. Three years later they rebelled against the Roman tax-gatherers, brought up their army, defeated the Emperor Valens at Adrianople, and dictated their own terms. Occupying the land between the Adriatic and the Black Sea, they had both the Eastern and the Western Empires at their mercy. They chose to attack the Western Empire; and while the Vandals and Suevi burst into Gaul, the Visigoths plunged through Italy under their chieftain Alaric. By 408 Alaric was at the gates of Rome. His armies were thrown back. He besieged Rome again the following year, and was again thrown back. Finally, on August 24, 410, when the Tiber was low and the Romans were gasping in the heat, he broke through the Salarian Gate and put the city to the sword. For three days and three nights there was a massacre.

In far-off Bethlehem Jerome heard of the wars, and shuddered. Grief had become a habit, but this new grief exceeded all others. He wrote in 409:

A remnant of us survives not by our own merits, but by the mercy of God. Innumerable savage people have overrun the whole of Gaul. The whole country between the Alps and the Pyrenees, between the Rhine and the Ocean has been laid waste by Quadi, Vandals, Sarmatians, Alans, Gepidi, Herules, Saxons, Burgundians, and, alas for the common weal, even the hordes of the Pannonians. The once noble city of Mainz has been captured and destroyed, and in its church many thousands were massacred. The people of Worms have been cut down to the last man after a long siege. The powerful city of Rheims, the districts of Amiens and Arras, the Belgians who live on the outskirts of the world, Tournay, Speyer and Strassburg have fallen to the Germans. The provinces of Aquitaine, of the Nine Nations, of Lyons and Narbonne have been laid waste with the exception of a few cities; and those who are spared by the sword are the prey of famine. I cannot speak of Toulouse without tears. I am silent about other places, so that I may not seem to despair of God's mercy. . . . Now time has dried our tears, and save for a few graybeards, the rest who are born in captivity and siege no longer regret the liberty of which the very memory is lost. Who could believe that Rome on her own soil no longer fights for glory, but for her very existence; and no longer even fights, but purchases her life with gold and precious things? (Jerome, *Epistolae*, CXXX, 5.)

Worse was to come, for he wrote when Alaric was still outside the gates. When Alaric broke in, Jerome cast about for some supernatural explanation of defeat, and when he heard that a young woman called Demetrias had vowed herself to virginity in Rome against the wishes of her whole family, he came to the conclusion that her faith was equal to the loss of the city; certainly her profession of virginity mitigated his sorrow. Nevertheless, the sorrow was real. In furious, cascading prose he sings a litany over the Empire, which had died as empires die today, more from sloth and luxury than from the power of the invaders. "O shame," he cried to his friend Gaudentius, "the world is rushing to ruin. The glorious city, the capital of the Roman Empire, has been swallowed up in one conflagration. There is no part of the earth where exiles from Rome are not to be found." What is the explanation? He goes back to Moses, and the dying Christ who makes His presence known through the poor, the needy, and the hungry. His passion mounts, and he writes worthily of a tragedy which is not unlike the tragedies of our own times:

The once sacred Churches have fallen into dust and ashes, yet even now we set our hearts eagerly upon money. We live as though we were doomed to die on the morrow, but we build houses as though we were going to live forever in the world. Our walls glitter with gold, gold gleams upon the ceilings and upon the capitals of our pillars; yet Christ is dying at our doors in the persons of His poor, naked and hungry. We read that Aaron the high priest faced the furious flames and with his burning censer stayed God's wrath; this greatest of priests stood between life and death, and the fire did not dare to pass his feet. God said to Moses: "Let Me alone and I will consume this people," showing by the words "Let Me alone" that He can be stayed from carrying out His threat. The prayers of the servant hindered the power of God. But who is there now under the Heavens who can stay the wrath of God and face the flames and say with the apostle: "I wish myself accursed for the sake of my brethren." Flocks and shepherds now perish together: the priest is in the same position as the people. Moses in his compassionate love said: "Yet now if Thou wilt, forgive their sin; and if not, blot me, I pray Thee, out of Thy book." He wished to perish with the perishing, and was not content to save himself. (Jerome, *Epistolae*, CXXVIII, 5.)

Again and again, as though obsessed with the aching wound, Jerome reverts to the same theme. Now at last he posssesed a subject worthy of his raging pen. "Who could have believed it," he asks in the preface to his *Commentary on Ezekiel*, "that Rome, founded on triumphs over the whole world, could fall to ruin?—that she, the mother of nations, should also be their grave?—that all the regions of the East, of Egypt and of Africa, should be filled with the swarms of youths and maidens from the former Lady of the World?" Bethlehem was now crowded with refugees, once rich, now beggars at the gates. The hospice was overflowing with guests. Jerome attended them, inquired after their fortunes, learned that the statue of Virtus (meaning "manly courage") had been melted down to help pay the required tribute demanded by the invader, and shook his head sorrowfully. "The city is taken which held captive the world, perishing of famine before it perished of the sword, and scarcely were there any to be made captive." It was not quite true. For three days and three nights there was havoc; then Alaric abruptly demanded order in the city of Rome. But the harm was done; and once-proud Rome was beaten to her knees.

In time Jerome forgot Rome. He could not lament forever. The destruction of Rome was followed by a wild inroad of Bedouin Arabs from the south, but he says little of the attack: they appear to have been beaten off. As he grew older, he grew more garrulous, more certain of himself; and when Albina, the Christian wife of Albinus, arrived in Bethlehem, he was overjoyed.

As he worked quietly in Bethlehem, there came to him extraordinary prestige. He was like the Chinese sage who acquires stature by simply sitting still. He grew so old that there came a time when people could never remember when there had been no Jerome. His pride and intolerance remained, but a calm sadness began to overlay his work, and though Rome was never conquered completely, he never recovered from the days of horror when it seemed that the whole of western civilization was to be laid to the sword. His virgins died, but other virgins came to take their places. He began to complain that the monastery was overcrowded, there were too many people to attend to, he had no leisure for work, the scribes cheated him. Yet he worked on calmly, adding to his immense pile of books, having completely lost count of his own writings or the number of scribes who had worked for him. He had become an institution.

One of the advantages of being an institution is that the great men of the earth come to you for advice. Jerome was, as always, delighted to advise, but he also liked milking his visitors. He was always eager to know what was happening in the world. Orosius, the historian, came to visit him. He asked interminable questions of Orosius, who answered them to the best of his ability and complained that on matters concerning which he desired knowledge, Jerome was singularly inattentive. Orosius had his reward one day when there came a citizen from Narbonne. Jerome had prayed that the barbarians would turn Christian and make peace with the Roman Empire, and so it had happened; but no one quite knew how it had happened. In the hearing of Orosius, the unknown citizen from southern France told the story of Athaulf, the brilliant brother-in-law and successor of Alaric. This young Visigoth, who had carried the princess Placidia, the sister of the Emperor Honorius, into honorable captivity, dying in a brawl in Barcelona, with his last breath commanded his brother to restore Placidia and make peace with Rome. He said:

It was at first my wish to destroy the Roman name and erect in its place a Gothic Empire, taking to myself the place and the powers of Caesar Augustus. But when I found by experience that my Goths were too savage and untamable to obey the ministrations of the law, and that they desired to abolish the institutions on which the state rested, forgetting that they would thereby destroy the state, I chose the glory of seeking to restore and maintaining by Gothic strength the name of Rome, desiring to go down to posterity as the restorer of that Roman power which it was beyond my power to replace. Wherefore I avoid war and strive for peace. (Orosius, VII, 43.)

The death of Athaulf occurred in the summer of 415. For Jerome there remained five years of arduous work. There was one final blaze of his wayward genius for bitter controversy. Pelagius, a corpulent one-eyed Welshman whose original name was Morgan—Pelagius is simply a Greek translation of the Welsh word meaning "a man of the sea"—had announced the unreality of original sin. It was enough, Pelagius said, if we should keep God's commandments. By the will alone, and without grace, man could become pure. Had not Jesus said: "If thou wilt enter into life, keep my commandments." What else was needed? A man did not need to be baptized, or rather, if he was baptized, though there was no remission of sins, he was sanctified: yet by being born into the world he was already sanctified. Augustine had said that infants dying unbaptized were not saved, they were damned forever, for they had not entered the Church and the Church was in the world as the Ark floating on the flood. To all this Pelagius answered: "You blaspheme against the Holy Ghost, for you love evil and you consecrate it with your learning." He added: "A monk's life is vicious." Augustine raged, because Pelagius had stricken him in a place where he thought himself secure; and perhaps there was no one who knew more about damnation than Augustine. Jerome raged, because Pelagius attacked virginity. In the year after the death of Athaulf, while Orosius was staying with him, Jerome attended the Synod of Diospolis, where fourteen bishops came to judge the heresies of Pelagius. Tempers were at fever pitch. Jerome cursed mightily. He had had enough, he said, of the little maggots who denied original sin, for was not original sin the very foundation from which there arose the purity of the Church? Unfortunately, Pelagius had written in Latin. The Bishops knew only Greek. Pelagius was absolved of heresy, and Jerome wandered back to Bethlehem, cursing not only the synod but all the Greek bishops, and making curious references to his desire to meet the Pelagians face to face.

It was an unfortunate challenge, for the Pelagians took him at his word and advanced on Bethlehem. What actually happened no one knows. According to Jerome, who was evidently biased, the Pelagians took the law into their own hands, killed a deacon, set fire to the monastery, and behaved in such a way that Jerome, Julia, her niece Paula, and all the virgins were compelled to take flight into a nearby tower, which had been erected as a watchtower against the threatening invasions of the Bedouins. The people of Bethlehem came to their rescue and put the unruly Pelagians to flight. Jerome seems to have been in real danger of death. He communicated the story to Augustine, but otherwise held aloof; and though Paula complained to the Pope, the letter of rebuke addressed to the Bishop of Jerusalem arrived conveniently after the Bishop's death. Pelagius, however, was no longer allowed to preach in Palestine, and Jerome wrote contentedly, remembering the furious diatribes of Cicero: "Our Catiline has been driven out of the city and altogether out of Palestine." The last of all the letters of Jerome which has been preserved relates to the heresies of Pelagius, and it was written to Augustine and Alypius. It was as we might have expected: both of the great Fathers of the Church drew strength from their knowledge of original sin.

But Jerome was not always proud, nor was he always conscious of his own sinfulness. It is possible to read his letters to his virgins as though he was perpetually thundering at them, perpetually warning them, but his exaggerations were often playful. He could be tender, and when he was stricken by grief, he was as helpless as any sorrowing peasant. When Paula died he could only say that "my words go on the rocks" —he liked nautical expressions, constantly used them, and must have seemed to himself very often as a ship with all its sails blowing. But love, too, moved him to silence. In the desert, suffering from loneliness and the misery of having no one he loved around him, he wrote to three boyhood friends: "I have had more joy from your letter than the Romans felt when Marcellus conquered Hannibal at Cannae. . . . I talk to your letter, I embrace it, it speaks to me, it is the only thing here that understands Latin, and as I write this I see you here before me." At the close he says: "My words are all mixed up, but love knows nothing of order."

Surprisingly, since he detested the married state and all its fruits, he was most tender with children; and though his letters concerning the upbringing of children were filled with warnings of the terrible fate which awaits them if they misbehave, they were also filled with gentle and pleasant things. He wrote in old age to his friend Gaudentius a letter to be read to Gaudentius's daughter Pacatula. Jerome begins by saying it is a difficult matter to write to a little girl who will not understand what is being said and who might come to think the letter supplies a kind of warrant for her desires. Pacatula suffered from a disease common among children: an overwhelming desire for honey-cakes, which is against the law. She will not listen to the words of the Prophets, who have declaimed often enough against unwarrantable desires? Then what should be done? Jerome concludes, with wisdom, that the best thing is simply to give her the cakes if she repeats her lessons well, and if she repeats them especially well, she should be given a little jewel, a little doll, or even some flowers. Nor can he find any sufficient reason why Pacatula should not throw her arms round her mother's neck and be kissed by everyone.

It is not, of course, quite as easy as that, and Jerome immediately launches into a disquisition concerning all the things she *shouldn't* do. On no account must she wear bright dresses. No, she should wear black, for otherwise all the temptations of the flesh will come to her: bright-colored silken dresses are especially to be avoided. On her seventh birthday, when she has learned to blush, she must learn the Psalter, and she must never drink wine, and she must always, always be chaste. He recognized that the virtue which resides within honey-cakes, dolls, jewels, and flowers is part of the virtue of God.

He was nearly always wise with little children. For another child he wrote a delightful set of instructions. She was learn-

ing her alphabet, and he suggests the best manner in which it
should be done:

Have letters made for her, of box-wood or ivory, and let them
be called by their names. Let her play with them, and let the
play be part of her instruction. It is not only needful that she
should place the letters in their right order, and put them to
memory by singing their names, but sometimes she should mix
the letters up, putting the last in the middle and the middle first:
in this way you will know whether she has learned them by sight
as well as by hearing. And when she begins with her trembling
hands to engrave letters on wax with her pen, then let some older
person guide her fingers, or let the letters be graven on the slate,
so that she may trace the letters already formed, nor stray outside
their outlines. Give her some little present, something acceptable
to her tender age, as soon as she has learned to join letters and
syllables together. She should not be alone when she is at her
work, but she should have companions, whose accomplishments
she may envy and whose praises may spur her to shame. Do not
scold her if she is slow. Arouse her ambition by praise. Let her
desire victory; let her be pained by defeat. Above all, never let
her hate her studies, otherwise the bitterness learned in childhood
may last until she is of mature years. Then, too, you must carefully select the words she is to put together: let her form the
names of the Prophets and the Apostles and all the Patriarchs
from the time of Adam, and Matthew and Luke also. So it will
happen that while she is learning to write, she is also setting up a
store of goodly things in her memory. Choose a master of sufficient age and good conduct and sound learning. No really
learned man would blush to serve a child, especially a child of a
noble family. Did not Aristotle serve the son of Philip in the same
way, teaching Alexander the very alphabet, in spite of the fact
that teachers of such things abounded. We should not despise
the little ones, for without them great things cannot come to pass.
(Jerome, *Epistolae*, CVII, 4.)

The letter was written to Laeta, the wife of Toxotius, who
was the son of Paula. The girl who learned her letters from
ivory tablets later became the head of the nunnery in Bethle-

hem; it was as Jerome would have desired. He had cajoled
and threatened. To Laeta he told the story of the saintly
Eustochia, whose hair had been waved by the order of her
aunt Praetextata. That night Eustochia dreamed of an avenging angel who declared that those who had laid their hands
upon the hair of God's virgin would suffer the torments of
the damned. "Those hands this very hour shall wither," the
angel said, "and in torment you shall recognize your guilt,
and at the end of the fifth month you shall be carried off to
Hell." At the end of the fifth month Eustochia died, and
Jerome did not conceal his delight in the fulfillment of the
prophecy.

Though Jerome was human when he contemplated a child
learning her alphabet, he was mean and inhuman when he contemplated her growing to maturity. "Let her never look upon
her own nakedness," he thundered. "She should not read the
Song of Songs until she has read Chronicles and Kings, for
otherwise she might not observe that the book refers only to
spiritual love." But the crowning punishment occurs when
he gives advice about her serving-maid. "I would not let her
have a favorite serving-maid into whose ear she might frequently whisper: what she says to one, all ought to know. Her
companion should be no sleek and handsome girl with a talent
for singing sweet songs in a liquid voice, but someone who is
grave and pale and carelessly dressed and inclined to melancholy." It seems a pity.

More and more as he grew older, Jerome was called upon
for this kind of advice. He gave it willingly. One day there
came to him a monk from Gaul with a strange story, which
Jerome only half believed. The monk explained that he had
come to the Holy Land to see the sacred shrines, but there
was another reason for his coming, perhaps a more important
one. The reason was this. He had a virgin sister and a widowed
mother, and both of them had taken priests into their households. Tongues were wagging. If only Jerome would order the
priests out of the houses, and reconcile the mother to the

daughter. Jerome seems to have suspected that the Gaul was interested in his own property rights, which were being infringed by the mother and her daughter, and he fought shy of the commission. "Well, it's a fine commission," he said, "but what can I do? I am not a bishop. I live in a small cell away from the turmoil of the world, and here I lament my past sins and attempt to avoid temptations. Surely it would be inconsistent if I remained in hiding, and allowed my tongue to roam over the world."

"You are too timid," the Gaul answered. "Do you not remember the time when you spilt heaps of salt on the cities?"

The allusion to Jerome's famous sarcasm did not pass unnoticed.

"That's true enough," Jerome answered, "but it is precisely that which now leads me to seal my lips. Because I attacked crime, they think me a criminal. It's like the old saying:

> *All the world declares and swears*
> *Here is an old man without ears.*

That's why I won't have anything to do with them. Once I raise my voice, everyone rains curses upon me and says, 'He sings with the voice of a drunkard.' So you see I have learned to be silent at a hard school, I lock the doors of the mouth, as they say, and incline my heart to no malicious words for fear that, in censuring others, I might myself commit a sin."

The monk reminded Jerome that he had traveled across the sea for the express purpose of having the letter, and Jerome at last consented, reflecting that a letter addressed to a certain pair of sinners would hardly arouse the indignation of other sinners.

"All right," he said. "I'll do as you wish, but you must keep the letter private. Put it in your luggage, and if it is listened to, then we shall both rejoice, and if no one pays any attention to it—I rather think this will happen—well, I shall have wasted my words and you will have wasted your journey."

That night he wrote the letter by a single rush light, dictating it at enormous speed, so that he exhausted his secretaries—he kept three or four at all times, and bitterly complained of their slow speed at shorthand—and the letter was ready when his visitor knocked on his door in the morning.

It is a delightful letter, for as Jerome was clearly in some doubt about whom he was addressing, he felt obliged to summon up an imaginary mother and daughter, and inevitably, his mind running on, he painted them in the darkest colors though he says he is prepared to give them the benefit of all doubts—a sly hint, perhaps, that he did not altogether trust the Gallic priest. Characteristically, he called the letter a "scholastic essay," which it was not. All he knew of the sister was that she wore dark clothes and pretended to saintliness and occasionally went to parties. Jerome was concerned about the parties; he wrote:

Should it happen to you, wearing your dark clothes, that you should join a group of young people, married women and those who are soon to be brides, and pleasure-loving girls, and young men with long hair and close-fitting clothes, then I warn you to beware, for it may happen that some boy with a suspicion of a beard will give you his hand, and if you are tired he might even let you lean on him, and you may find yourself squeezing each other with your fingers, and then he may tempt you or you may tempt him. Or you will be sitting down at table with married men and women; you will of course wait till they have finished kissing and until they have finished tasting the dishes, and without making the least protest you may find yourself admiring the silk dresses and the gold brocade they are wearing. And when the dinner is served, you will of course pretend you are unwilling to share their meal, but they will compel you to follow their wishes. So that you will drink their wine, they will praise it as the gift of the Creator. And so that you will visit the baths, they will say that they, too, abhor the evil that lies there. And when, most reluctantly, you agree to do something they have asked you to do, why, then they will cry in chorus: "What a dear innocent girl—such a talented person!"

Meanwhile some singer will enter the dining room, and in the softest voice he will perform for them, and though he will not look at other men's wives, he will gaze upon you, who have no protector. He will make gestures. There will be little subtle inflections in his voice suggesting things he is afraid to put in words. . . . There you are, a healthy young girl, dainty, plump, rosy, all afire amid the fleshpots, amid the wines and the baths, surrounded by married women and young men, and even should you refuse their requests, you may come to believe that the mere asking of such things is evidence of your beauty. There are libertines who are ardent only when pursuing virtue, for they are excited by illegality. And may it not be that your coarse and somber robe expresses your secret desires? If it is completely smooth, if you allow it to trail upon the ground so that you shall seem taller, if the upper part is slit in order that something should be revealed within, concealing all that is unsightly, revealing all that is most fair, should you not beware? As you walk, your shiny black shoes go creaking in a way which deliberately excites young men. You bind your breasts in strips of linen, but the tight girdle gives amplitude to your chest. You allow your hair to fall over your forehead and over your ears, and sometimes it happens that your shawl drops, leaving your white shoulders bare, and then, very quickly, pretending that the dropping of the shawl was not deliberate, you make a motion to lift the shawl again. And should you ask me how I know all this, I say that your brother's tears have told me all. (Jerome, *Epistolae*, CXVII, 6-7.)

Jerome is not entirely convincing, nor is he ever quite convincing when he talks of vice. He hardly knows what advice to give her. He has conjured up the portrait of her, and indeed so much of the letter is concerned with the portrait that there is hardly space for advice. He warns her not to become any man's mistress, for men are deceivers, and she will be abandoned for another mistress soon enough. Best to remain a virgin. "Women soon grow old, especially when they have a man at their side." It is an odd statement, and probably the most inaccurate that Jerome ever made. He is on safer ground when he warns against the presence of a priest in the house.

Then once again he uses nautical phrases, saying that once he is thrown out, there will be calm waters and the ship may be steered away from all shoals. "Thus we may rejoice, and thus we may escape." *Ibi gaudemus, hic evadimus.*

Most of his life Jerome had hoped to "rejoice and escape." He would have been happier in a world of monks and nuns, forgetting that, as St. Hugo of Avalon wisely said, the world was meant by God to be inhabited by men and women. He loved God, learning, and virgins in that order, and outside the order encompassed by these three things he was like a child, and this was as it had to be. He towers as a scholar. No one else had such a feeling for the colors and the sounds of words, the landscapes and atmospheres in which they move. They come to life in his hands. He loved to trace their origins, and made the wildest and most improbable guesses concerning them, tracing in his book *Concerning Hebrew Names* the meaning of every Hebrew name, and sometimes finding six meanings, all different, for the names of the Patriarchs; and this delighted him, for he could go on to examine these meanings, and see how they explained the nature of the Patriarchy. He played the surrealist game of giving the most magical meanings to the most ordinary things, and he liked to match texts from the Bible, even when there was no similarity between them. Luther said of him: "He deserves Hell more than Heaven, and writes only of fasting, virginity and such things," but Luther was wide of the mark, and Jerome's heart-rending voice can be heard beneath the thunder of Luther's translation of the Bible. Jerome called himself proudly *trilinguis, Hebraeus, Graecus, Latinus,* and in truth he was all these, as well as the other things he claimed to be: *philosophus, rhetor, grammaticus, dialecticus.* In the last months of his life he went blind, and this too was inevitable: for a long while his eyes had been weak, and deeply sunken, and watery, and he regarded their weakness as a punishment for his sins. In his commentary to the seventh book of Ezekiel he spoke of the hardships of those latter times. The Hebrew texts seemed to fade when he tried to read them by lamplight, but he was determined to go on, if only because the sufferings and injustices of the time offered no other compensation for the scholar but the quiet of his study. He was aware that these commentaries written in old age were sometimes obscure, but he begged the reader to believe that the obscurity was not always in his own mind. It was due to the enormity of the task, the teacher's lack of skill, the indifference of his listeners (*rei magnitudine, doctoris imperitia, audientis durita*).

These three things had dogged him through his life. The task was so great that he had almost quailed before it. No one else had assumed the task of translating the whole Bible; no one else, not even Augustine, had written so many commentaries. "If," he said plaintively, "I am to be criticized for writing so much to women, then it should be remembered that no one asked me about the Scriptures, and I would have preferred a thousand times to discuss the Scriptures than talk to women." The indifference of his listeners was very real. In the end there was only misery. The last words he ever wrote, when he was suffering from indigestion, sleeplessness, and the creeping attacks of old age, were: "I am exhausted by grief and old age and torn by perpetual illness, and I can scarcely express myself at all."

When the battle was over he could remind himself that he belonged to the heroic tradition and had become a Patriarch while still living. His epitaph should be the proud boast he wrote soon after coming to Bethlehem: "It is not by the brilliance of great men, but by my own strength, that I should be judged."

VI. ✿ AUGUSTINE:
THE SENSUALIST

IF AUGUSTINE ENTERED THE ROOM, WE WOULD RECOG-
nize him instantly. The most wanton of the saints, the
man with the clearest mind, the most exalted opinion of
himself, the subtlest knowledge of himself, he belongs to
our own time. He speaks a language we know only too well,
and if we set him beside Marcel Proust or Dostoevski they
would talk together as equals. He belongs to the times of
crisis, when men's minds go wheeling after the final purposes;
there was no leisure in him: he burns himself up with the
fury to know all things, to determine all things. Like the
great modern psychological novelists, he is armed with a scal-
pel and is prepared to knife the soul until it reveals its secrets.
"Where is it?" he proclaims. "Where is the heart of the
mystery?" He runs after it, embraces it, squeezes the juice
out of it, utters threats and blandishments to it, and finally,
as it must, the poor mystery reveals itself. Is it God? Is it the
evil in men's hearts? Is it love? Why do the stars go round?
How did the angels fall? Where wast thou in the morning of
the world? He has known all these things, tested them against
himself, and found—he was never absolutely certain what he
found: himself and God, a world almost too beautiful to contemplate, an uneasy alliance between the soul and blessedness.
Though he traveled only from North Africa to Milan and
back again, he was the perpetual wanderer and gives the impression of having circumnavigated half a hundred globes. His
names Augustine and Aurelius commemorate two emperors,
both of whom were ruthless, and he was himself a ruthless

emperor, conscious of an imperial destiny. Unlike most emperors, he was guided by a furious intelligence, and like Tertullian, another African, he seems never to have used his intelligence until it was at fever heat.

Augustine was a Numidian, a brother to the Berber and the Tuareg, one of those strange people who have inhabited the Northern coastal plains of Africa from time immemorial, neither Negro nor European, but descended like the Basques from some earlier race of settlers. There may have been Negro blood in him. He was tall and long limbed, thin chested, with sloping shoulders. He had a long nose, a high forehead, thick lips, and tremendous eyes, and he did not walk so much as take large loping strides. His skin was a kind of dark bronze; his eyes were black. Throughout his youth and at intervals into middle age there was the flush on the cheeks and the flame in the eyes of the tubercular: there is the clarity and violence of the tubercular in everything he wrote.

He was born on Sunday, November 13, 354 in the town of Thagaste in what is now Algeria. It was a pleasant town with high white walls, set among wooded fields. Ilex and pines grew beside the streams; lions roamed in the forests; boar, hare, redwing, and quail were to be hunted a stone's throw from the city walls. The town, built by the Romans, had a theater, a forum, baths, long colonnades of marble columns, and was a marketplace of some importance. Among the wealthy patricians who ruled over the destiny of the town was a certain Patricius, a landowner who possessed a farm and a number of slaves. He seems to have been a stern taskmaster, who was never quite reconciled to having Augustine for a son.

There were good reasons for this. The child had an ungovernable temper; he lied often; he liked playing more than he liked study; he was also a thief, on his own confession. Worse still for Patricius, the son possessed a desperate affection for his mother, Monnica, and none for his father. Patricius, the stern old member of "the very splendid council of Thagaste" (*splendissimus ordo Thagastensis*), possessing all the privileges of the minor nobility, desired above everything that Augustine should become a man of culture: beyond that, he had little interest in the child, allowed the boy to do as he pleased, and cared nothing at all about his morals; and when much later Augustine drew up the balance sheet of his father's behavior, the greatest crime of Patricius was precisely that he allowed the boy to be immoral as he pleased. It is hardly fair. The scales were loaded from the beginning. Augustine, with his sharp North African mind, would have been just as immoral even if his father had attempted to whip immorality out of him. Augustine was pleased when Patricius was converted to Christianity by Monnica, but the conversion seems to have taken place for political reasons; and there is an air of grudging approval in Augustine's account of it, as though he was saying: "Well, the old fool knows what's best for him, but there won't be any treasures of heaven laid up for him."

Monnica was twenty-two when Augustine was born. There was already an elder son, Navigius, and a daughter, her name unknown, who became a nun. It is possible that Augustine deliberately omitted to record her name, for the same reason that he never mentioned the name of his mistress or of a young man he once bitterly grieved over: in some deep way she may have hurt him. He was easily hurt. He quarreled incessantly, and he lived in a house where quarrels were frequent. Monnica kept order with a smooth tongue, with a mother-in-law in the house and a brood of lying slaves. The tempest began in the cradle; for when Augustine tells the story of a baby he had seen—"I know, because I have seen, jealousy in a baby. It could not speak, yet it eyed its foster-brother with pale cheeks and looks of hate"—it is reasonably certain that he was talking about himself. There were more tempests later, when Augustine spent his time playing a curious game called "nuts." In this game three seashells and a pea are shuffled dexterously together, and the winner is the one who discovers under which seashell the pea is hidden. Augustine played the game well, but he bitterly denounces others with quicker fingers who cheated better than himself. He stole from the kitchen, from the cellar, and from the table. He was a convincing liar to his tutor and to his schoolmasters. He was an excellent shot with a stone and won "splendid victories" against schoolboys whose gashed and bleeding faces were evidence of his prowess: Dostoevski seems to have played the same game with the same success, for the description of the stone-throwing in *The Brothers Karamazov* is close to the bone and told with a horror too great to have been something observed from a distance.

As for his lessons, Augustine had an abiding horror of them, and most of all he detested arithmetic and Greek: Greek because it was difficult, and arithmetic because it was senseless. "What on earth," he asked, "is the use of repeating one plus two equals three?" He was thrashed repeatedly in school, for impudence and for playing dice and bones in class. Years later, when he was an old man and wore the miter of a bishop, the memory of those thrashings remained vivid in his mind; he would conjure up in an agony of remorse the stripes on the bleeding flesh. There was Monnica perpetually at her devotions; a stern father whipping slaves; wild games among schoolboys; laziness at lessons. In the beginning there was hardly anything else.

Probably Augustine's viciousness in his youth was an inevitable result of the disorderly affections within his household. There was little peace, little happiness. At twelve he was sent to school at Madaura, an old Numidian city, proud of its antiquity and pagan to the core. Here for the first time he fell in love with letters. He read Vergil, weeping over Dido's death, studied well, received an unusually large allowance from his father, and appears to have joined a pagan sect. Years later an old Madauran grammarian called Maximus rebuked him for deviating from paganism—*a secta nostra deviasti*. But he liked Madaura, and years later remembered the heroic proportions of the naked statue of Mars in the marketplace. He remembered, too, with a kind of affection, a statue of a man stretching out three fingers to offset the evil eye. Perhaps the statues sank deep in his consciousness: heroic nakedness and the warding off of the evil eye were among his main preoccupations later. Also, he read love poetry. His senses had always been keen; and in this hot city, known to Apuleius, his first experiments in sensuality occurred. It was not love, but raging lust. He speaks about these things openly, with little compassion for his own wayward youth. "I dared to roam the woods and pursue my vagrant loves beneath the shades," he says, perhaps referring to the woods surrounding Madaura or perhaps referring to no woods at all: only the shelters where lovers lie. "Lord, how loathsome I was in Thy sight," he says in the *Confessions*. "It stormed confusedly within me, whirling my thoughtless youth over the precipices of desire, and so I wandered still further from Thee, and Thou didst leave me to myself: the torrent of my fornications tossed and swelled and boiled and ran over."

It is possible that Augustine was making too much of his own sins; to have been chaste in Madaura must have been nearly an impossibility. But unchastity was not his only sin. Once, during his holidays, he robbed a pear tree. He tells of the event with a quite extraordinary psychological profundity. He desired to rob the tree, and he did rob it, but he was impelled neither by hunger nor poverty, and in fact he did not want the pears at all, there were better ones in his own orchard, and even after the theft he took no joy in what he had stolen. "But I took joy," he says, "in the theft and in the sin." His knowledge of sin was to increase prodigiously in later years.

Augustine's father died when he was sixteen. He would have been forced to become a workman if Romanian, a distinguished citizen of Thagaste, had not come to his help. Romanian was wealthy and given to fits of generosity, and he was so highly respected that even during his lifetime his statue was erected in the marketplace. Augustine worshiped him,

and was given an allowance. He had shown talent in literature already, and now Romanian sent him to Carthage to
study. "*Veni Carthaginem*," he wrote. It was the place he had
dreamed of, the greatest seaport of the western Mediterranean,
a place of legends, dedicated to Astarte and Venus, *Carthago
Veneris*, a softly shining city between the lakes and the sea,
with her Capitol and her Palatine and her teeming colleges.
"Carthage," wrote Apuleius, "is the heavenly muse of Africa,
the inspirer of the Roman people," and so it was. All the races
congregated there. Though defeated, she dictated to Rome.
The city was pagan. The goddess Tanit was worshiped, disguised now under the name of *Virgo Coelestis*, the Virgin of
Heaven. Augustine attended the ceremonies performed for the
goddess. "Our eager eyes," he said, "rested in turn on the
goddess and on the girls, her adorers." There were ceremonies
for the Phrygian Great Mother and for Isis. Talking in Punic,
mingling with the crowds, his blood rising to fever heat, his
father dead and his mother far away, Augustine threw himself into the delights of the city. Before he left Thagaste to
come to Carthage, his mother had solemnly warned him:

> My mother commanded me not to commit fornication, and
> especially that I should not defile any man's wife. This seemed to
> me no better than women's counsels, which it would be a shame
> for me to follow. . . . I ran headlong with such blindness that I
> was ashamed among my equals to be guilty of less impudence
> than they were, whom I heard brag mightily of their naughtiness;
> yea, and so much the more boasting by how much more they
> had been beastly; and I took pleasure to do it, not for the pleasure
> of the act only, but for the praise of it also. (Augustine, *Con-
> fessiones*, II, 3).

A change was coming over him. Though the fevers of the
flesh remained, there were now fevers of the mind. His
awakening mind found pleasure in exercise; he threw himself
into his studies as solemnly and as passionately as he seduced
women. He was becoming an excellent Latin scholar: he
went on to study rhetoric, mathematics, music and philosophy.

"My unquiet mind was altogether intent to seek for learning," he wrote. He even disapproved of the "Wreckers," those gangs of students who burst noisily into classrooms and jeered at the young students, though a little while before he would have joined them. He took a furious pleasure in the debating society, where he achieved some eminence for his wit and his brilliance. He made friends easily. Alypius, Nebridius, and Honoratus were friends he met at this time, and held to himself with bonds of iron. He read the book of Cicero called the *Hortensius*, which survives only in fragments, and began to ponder how he should spend his life: it occurred to him that one could hardly spend it better than in acquiring wisdom.

But what was wisdom? Some students spoke of Christ, others of Manes, the Persian who had suffered crucifixion and introduced the sacrament of the bread and the fruit. Manes had affirmed the eternal coexistence of two Kingdoms, one of darkness, the other of light. Eternal war was waged between light and darkness, between good and evil. Manes proclaimed that he was an apostle of Christ, and proclaimed the need to love and reverence Christ, who was not born, never became a man, and never died. Manichaeanism had much in common with gnostic Christianity. Its dualistic belief, its hatred of established Christianity and its oddly unconvincing demonology made Christians hold it in abhorrence.

Augustine confessed later that it was because the Manichees spoke of the truth that he was seduced into believing them; if they had used some other word he might not have fallen so easily. He had decided that he prized truth most, and he would rise in the Manichaean hierarchy, for he was already disposed to be ambitious. Having joined the sect he returned to Thagaste, only to discover that Monnica, who had grown even more fervent in her Christian faith during his absence, regarded him now as a sinner fallen beyond redemption. She threw him out of the house. Augustine simply walked to the house of Romanian, explained the situation, and was allowed to lodge in the rich man's villa as tutor to his son Licentius. There followed a long period of preparation. Dimly Augustine seems to have discerned that the Church was waiting for him and would enclose him in the end. Meanwhile, he would send his questing mind down all the pathways of learning. He continued to earn acclaim from his speeches; he played with astrology; he enjoyed the pleasant life of a rich man's adopted son; he acquired a taste for expensive things; and he knew perfectly well that in all Thagaste there was no one so brilliant, so promising as Augustine.

Then the bubble burst. It burst in the way which is common to exalted and clever youths. His closest friend, "the one who was sweet to me above all sweetness of this life," died. What was worse: shortly before he died, he received the Sacrament. Augustine was appalled. The boy had been a Manichee. They spent their leisure time together, discussed everything together: then why had he suddenly changed his religion? Why? Augustine never discovered the answer to the question. "I resolved to wait until he should regain his strength, then I would speak frankly with him." But though strength returned for a while, a few days later the boy died.

Confronted with death, Augustine threw himself into a wild panic of grief. This boy had been half of his soul, *dimidium animae*, and he was gone, and would never return, and there was no comfort anywhere. "This darkness fell upon my heart, and wherever I looked there was only death. My country became a torture, my father's house pure melancholy. All the pleasures I had shared with him turned into hideous agony now that he was gone. My eyes sought for him everywhere, and found him not. I hated all familiar sights because he was not there, and these places no more cried to me: 'Lo, he will come,' as they did when he was absent but still living." "Tears," he said, "were my only comfort," and he seems to have given way to an unrestrained, self-torturing grief entirely unlike anything he had experienced before, and far greater than the grief which followed on the death of his father.

This grief cleared the way for his conversion. He remained a little while longer a Manichee, but he could not prevent himself from thinking of the boy's sacramental death; and there followed the long struggle between the Manicheee and the Christian in Augustine's soul. From this moment he seems to have been continually exclaiming, like Melville in *Clarel*:

> *Nay, nay: Ah! God, keep from me*
> *Cursed Manes and the Manichee!*

Shortly after the death of his friend, Augustine found himself debating with Faustus, the most learned Manichee in North Africa, and doubts began to arise over the relevance of the Persian religion. Was evil a substance? Did the Manichees promise the resurrection of the flesh? He was restless: there were no satisfactory answers to these questions. Then where was truth? Monnica, who had forgiven him and now allowed him to live under her roof, insisted that the truth lay with Christ. Augustine thought the truth probably lay in a legal career in Rome: he would become another Cicero. He decided to leave for Rome as soon as possible, chiefly perhaps to escape from his dead friend. Monnica clung to him, refused to let him go. He was an adept at subterfuge, and when everything was prepared for the journey, he allowed Monnica to accompany him to the seashore. He pretended he had a friend on one of the boats in the harbor and promised to return in the morning. That night Monnica spent in a small oratory sacred to the memory of Cyprian, the protector of Carthage. When she woke up, he was gone.

In Rome Augustine still held to the remnants of his belief in Manichaeanism, a belief he shared with his old schoolfriend Alypius, who sought him out and stayed close to him during the ensuing years. Augustine fell ill, apparently of a malarial infection, and thereafter the debate with himself grew more eager, more relentless, more demanding. Where was the truth? In beauty? In God? In the war between the forces of light and darkness? There were moments when he gave way to a savage nihilism, and other moments when he flirted with Neoplatonism. All the time he continued his studies in rhetoric, until he became the most brilliant of the young disputants in Rome. The Roman Prefect was Symmachus, a Manichee, or at least closely connected with the religion. When the university of Milan asked through the Prefect for a new teacher of rhetoric, the choice fell on Augustine. One of the ironies of history is that the Manichaeans contributed to sending Augustine to Milan; and there, from the lips of Ambrose, he would learn the arguments which were to destroy Manichaeanism as a religious force in Europe.

By the time Augustine reached Milan he had come to the stage when he was prepared to abandon the Manichees. Their arguments were arbitrary, too arbitrary. Since everything in the world was either light or dark, evil or good, a huge catalogue of light and dark had been prepared. Some things were good, others evil. Some foods were good, others were fit only for the devil. "They say the golden melon comes from God's treasure-house, but the golden fat of the ham and the yolk of an egg are evil. Why so? And why does the whiteness of lettuce proclaim to them the Divinity, while the whiteness of cream proclaims only evil? And why this horror of meat? For, look you, roast suckling pig offers us a brilliant color, an agreeable smell, an appetizing taste—sure signs, according to them, of the Divine presence." Manichaeanism was rooted in materialism; Augustine's spirit, like his wit, was already taking wings.

Everyone in Milan called on Ambrose, and Augustine was not long in calling upon the bishop who already bore the character of a saint. "He received me," wrote Augustine, "like a father, and was pleased enough at my coming in a bishoply fashion." Ambrose was held in honor; Augustine evidently envied the aura of dignity surrounding him. Also, Ambrose was noted for his style in delivering sermons—another cause for envy. Milan was gay and splendid, the Imperial capital, the residence of the boy Emperor Valentinian II. In this brilliant court Augustine hoped to find a sinecure. His earnings already made him comparatively wealthy: he could afford to pay for the passage of his Carthaginian mistress and her son, Adeodatus. He was popular. He had a villa, and there were a number of friends from Carthage to make him feel at home: his brother Navigius, two cousins Rusticus and Lastidianus, Alypius, a few others. Soon he invited Monnica, and Monnica decided the time had come for her son to marry, or put his mistress aside. She advanced arguments to show that it was evil to live in sin with a girl. There was another, holier alternative. He could keep the boy, but the girl must go. For some reason Augustine consented. "When they took from my side her with whom I had slept for so long, my heart was torn at the place where it stuck to hers (*cor ubi adhaerebat*), and the wound was bleeding."

There followed what may have been the most painful period of his life. Monnica prayed, hoping against hope that he would alter his ways, becoming a Christian, living a life of the purest chastity, and surrender to the will of God, putting no trust in the two opposing wills of the Manichees.

The crisis, long expected and long prayed for, came in July 386. The two wills struggled for a decisive victory, and as often happens neither will succeeded, but both were defeated and replaced by a third will, or rather by a mode of being which was altogether beyond the will, by a sense of the perpetual immanence of holiness and a quite indefinable sweetness. For Augustine the crisis became miracle. It was a miracle never to be repeated again, even when Monnica lay dying and he felt such a kinship for her that it passed beyond the love of created things into something else, and then once again he found no name for this love, except that it was God's will that they should be separated and at the same time together, and yet it was not will. When he came to speak about this strangeness which came to him, he could find no better description than that it possessed the quality of a steady, perfect light. "At such times," he wrote, "I am conscious of something within me that plays before my soul and is light dancing in front of it; were this brought into steadiness and perfection in me, it would surely be eternal life." But there were not many times when he was aware of this light, and all his life by his own account he was fully aware of it only once— in a garden, on a hot summer's day, in the shade of a fig tree, listening to a child singing nonsense somewhere beyond the high walls, while the sun dazzled him and his heart pounded with the violent repetitive rhythms of his colloquy with his own soul, and then was suddenly quietened.

As Augustine tells the story, the day began ordinarily enough. He was staying in the villa with Alypius and his mother. There came a visitor, an officer of the Imperial household called Pontitian, an African and a Christian, who had arrived from Treves. They sat down to talk, and suddenly Pontitian observed a book lying on the table, a table which had been marked out for a game of dominoes. Pontitian opened the book idly and was surprised to discover that it contained the Epistles of St. Paul. Delighted, he spoke of his own conversion, of Antony and the anchorites of Egypt, and then of the monasteries of Italy, and particularly of the monastery outside the walls of Milan where Ambrose officiated in the intervals of ruling over the archdiocese of Milan. He praised the ascetic life, and he told the story of how one afternoon when he was off duty, because the Emperor was attending the circus and there was nothing else to do, he strolled with three friends among the gardens along the city walls. Two of these friends went ahead. They came to a cottage, where a copy of *The Life of St. Antony* lay on a table. They opened it, and began reading and soon there came to them a sense that all their problems were solved. What am I doing on this earth? Whom do I serve? We pass through dangers only to confront an even greater danger. What is the use of this life if all we can attain to is a position as Imperial favorite? The answer to the problem lay in asceticism, the flesh and the spirit stripped of ornament, the utmost barrenness. There and then they were determined to follow the ascetic life, and when Pontitian returned and told them they must go on their way because it was getting dark, they informed him of their discovery and begged for Pontitian's prayers. Some days later Pontitian heard that the women to whom they were betrothed had also become Christians and were dedicated to virginity.

Augustine was more moved than he had ever been in his life. He had never heard of Antony before. The struggle within himself had reached a pitch of intensity where desperate solutions were necessary. Strangely, he seems to have been more moved by the thought of the young brides dedicating themselves to virginity than by the recital of the discovery of *The Life of St. Antony*. In his youth he had prayed: "Give me chastity, but not yet," and this came back to him, to torment him further, and even while Pontitian was talking the furious quarrel with himself went on, but it seemed to him at last that he was being turned toward himself, compelled to confront himself, seeing himself foul, crooked, and defiled with the habit of lechery, and now there must be an end to it. When Pontitian was gone, he turned to Alypius. "What is the matter with us?" he exclaimed. "Yes, what is it? Didn't you hear? Simple men take heaven by violence, but we, heartless and learned, see how we wallow in flesh and blood! Are we ashamed to follow because others have gone before, and not ashamed not even to follow?" His mind was on fire. Alypius could hardly recognize him, so changed was his expression, and when Augustine threw himself out of the house, Alypius followed him closely, perhaps afraid he would harm himself.

Resting in the garden Augustine found himself confronted again with the problem of the will. To what end does the mind will itself? The old confusions, the old intricate and formidable dialectic of the will, the old temptations returned, more cunning than ever, until he could bear the presence of Alypius no longer and flung himself weeping out of the garden and found solitude under a remote fig tree. There he babbled like a child: "How long, how long? Tomorrow and tomorrow? Why not now? Why should there not be an end to my uncleanness now?" Almost he expected to hear God summoning him out of the clouds, but the voice he heard came from an unknown child, chanting: *"Tolle, lege."* "Take up and read." He tried to think whether these words formed any part of a child's game, but he remembered none, and it did not occur to him that the child might have been chanting the command with which an instructor would begin the lessons in a Roman school: "Take up and read from the sixth book of the Aeneid," though it would have been perfectly natural for a child away from school on a hot summer's day to recite his instructor's words with a pleasurable and dreamy mockery.

For Augustine the words came like an angelic visitation. No longer weeping, he rose to his feet and ran to the place where Alypius was sitting with the Epistles of St. Paul beside him. At the age of nineteen St. Antony had opened the Bible at random and discovered the words: "Go, sell all thou hast, and give to the poor, and thou shalt have treasure in Heaven, and come and follow me." In the same way Augustine opened the Bible and his eyes fell on the verse from the Epistle to the Romans where St. Paul demands that the servant of Christ should renounce all voluptuous pleasures: "Not in rioting and drunkenness, not in chambering and wantonness, not in strife and envying, but put ye on the Lord Jesus Christ, and make not provision for the flesh, to fulfill the lusts thereof." He put his finger in the page, calm at last, and with Alypius beside him he went into the house to tell the story to Monnica. She was overjoyed, radiant with exultation, for the vision of her son converted had at last come true. In the garden Augustine had hoped and believed that his tears were an acceptable sacrifice; now he knew it was necessary to offer the sacrifice of praise.

But though Augustine was finally converted and was never again to lose his faith in God, the furious rages remained, providing the groundswell to the music he played for the rest of his life. He had loved "the perishable beauty of the body, the brightness of the light, the soft melody of the *cantilenae*, the delicious scent of flowers and the limbs made for the embracing of the flesh." His hot African blood was not stilled by the conversion: like many others he would have to wait until he was old before the fleshly demon was silenced: his senses remained keen, and the texture of his prose, urgent and demanding, mirrors his sensuality as it mirrors his violence. He was the least calm of the saints, the most impetuous, and even after his conversion he was able to talk about doubt as though he understood the matter well enough: he is not entirely convincing when he takes the part of the devil's advocate, pretending to be inventing false arguments. Yet he was sustained by the vision in the garden, the momentary brightness. What had he seen? He can only hint at it. There was a sense of blinding, tumultuous peace, of dedication, of superhuman relief, even of superhuman grace, but of this last he was never quite certain. All he could say was that "it was as though the light of salvation had been poured into my heart." Never again was he to be so close to God.

The great crisis in Augustine's conversion was now over, but there were other crises to come, to be fought with anguish and terror and a sense of brooding willful impatience, for if Augustine thought the heavenly grace had altogether destroyed his will, he was mistaken. He was ill and feverish. He had difficulty in breathing; his voice was muffled and thin; and he wondered whether there was blood in his lungs. Perhaps there was. The whole story of the crisis in the garden seems to speak of a simultaneous crisis with physical origins: and even when he came to write his account of the conversion thirteen years later a tubercular excitement is revealed in the long strained sentences with their curious repetitions, the same strange thudding music you find in the later works of D. H. Lawrence and in the letters of Keats.

The strain was beginning to tell: the struggle with the angel had concluded with a showering of gifts, and for a brief while Augustine contented himself quietly with assembling the gifts and observing them, holding them up to the light, remarking upon their holy shapes and the colors that shone through them. It was nearly the end of the semester. He decided to resign his professorship and disappear to some quiet place where he could think out his problems in seclusion. Verecundus, a grammarian at the university, offered him the use of a small country house not far from Lago Maggiore and under the shelter of Monte Rosa, among olives, vineyards, fields, and thick chestnuts, and there Augustine went with a few students including Licentius, the son of his patron Romanian. The classes that Augustine should have addressed were taken over by Nebridius; Romanian underwrote the expenses of the holiday; and the small company which spent the autumn months in the country house included Monnica, Alypius, Navigius, and Adeodatus, as well as two cousins Lastidianus and Rusticus, and another pupil called Trygetius. Licentius was something of a poet, and he became Augustine's chief confidant.

It was the period when Augustine might have been expected to retire into the desert, but he did not have—he was never to have—the anchorite's temper. He had put away his mistress, but he surrounded himself with a group of handsome boys, buried himself in the country, and disputed with them gently concerning the things of the spirit. It was the gentleness of exhaustion. He slept badly and prayed interminably. During the day he walked to the baths, and there, naked, they would discuss God, the good life, the order of the universe, the duties of the Christian, and there is almost no fever in Augustine's words, which were carefully copied down in shorthand by one of the pupils.

Augustine wrote to Ambrose, and asked for suggestions

about what book they should study. Ambrose suggested Isaiah. It was an excellent choice, but Augustine turned it down, admitting that the first chapter confused him. He preferred the Psalms and most of all he preferred Cicero's *Hortensius*, which he now used as a class-book for Licentius and Trygetius. So, disputing in the bathhouse and wandering in the country among the limes, the hazels, and the northern firs, his sexuality submerged in disputation, no young woman in sight, he would ask simple questions like: "What kind of person possesses God?" as though there were a special class of God-possessors. Licentius answered: "He possesses God who lives truly." Trygetius responded: "He possesses God who performs God's will." The reply of Adeodatus was more forthright, and it is possible that it was aimed at Augustine's sense of guilt, for the handsome boy of fifteen replied quietly: "He possesses God who has no unclean spirit." But on the whole there was little talk of unclean spirits, and instead they lost themselves in happy generalities that reflected their reading in the Greek skeptical philosophers. Listening to their quotations from Cicero, Monnica would intervene in her usual abrupt down-to-earth manner: "Weak-minded, that's what they are!" and saying this she would fling herself out of their company and disappear in the farmhouse, complaining a little at the thought of scrubbing and cleaning for eight disputatious boys.

The days passed quietly enough: at night the unclean spirits and the devils returned to plague him. He had a remarkable facility for summoning up images of the past: the very smells, the very textures of things he had touched returned to plague his dreams. There passed before his eyes the women he had known, and in the silence of the night he heard their clear music. Toothache, dreams, half-dreams, memories, none of these was so monstrous as "the infernal fire of lust" which burned to a white heat before his awakened senses were put to sleep, and when he slept the lust remained, and he saw himself performing like a lewd clown in the brightly lit chambers of his dreaming mind. "Am I not," he cries, "am I not in dreams the man I am, O Lord my God? Does my reason slumber as well as the senses of my body? Cannot Thy mighty hand purify the weakness of my soul, and with rich grace exterminate the guilt within my dreams?" But no, the lascivious dreams went on, and to avoid them he would try to lie awake beyond the point of exhaustion, taming himself by wakefulness, searching in his mind for some problem to solve, finding in argument the solvent for dreams and toothache alike.

One night when he was restless his attention was caught by the intermittent chugging sound of water flowing along a channel into the bathhouse. Licentius, who slept with him, was beating off the mice with a stick, and Trygetius, who also slept in the same room, was also for some reason awake. "Tell me, Licentius," said Augustine, "for I see that your muse has kindled a light for your lucubrations, what on earth makes the water sound like that?" Licentius said it was nothing new. He had heard it before. He had deliberately awakened earlier, because he wanted to know whether it was raining, and this would tell him whether the next day would be fine. "It was exactly the same then," he answered. Trygetius added that he too had noticed the strange phenomenon. It occurred to Augustine that perhaps someone was crossing the stream, or washing in it, but it was very late: unless one of the boys was playing a trick there was no conceivable explanation. It was Licentius who explained that the drift of autumn leaves had choked the channel, which remained choked until there was a head of water heavy enough to dislodge the leaves and sweep them away; then more leaves would drift into the channel, and then for a while the water would build up a head and dislodge them and the whole process was repeated.

"Then there is nothing to wonder at," Augustine said, pleased with the boy's intelligence, and a little while later he said: "Of course you were right not to wonder, and right too to stay at home with your muse."

"Yes," Licentius answered, "but the thing that puzzles me is that you were puzzled."

Augustine reflected for a moment. There were traps here, as elsewhere; and he could still hear the strange sound of the water.

"Surely I was right to wonder?" he asked. "What is wonder? Isn't wonder caused by something unusual, beyond the known order of causes?"

"I agree, as long as you put a special stress on the word 'known'. Nothing really happens outside the order of causes."

"Exactly," Augustine said, delighted, for the incident could now serve as the basis of a disputation, and besides he was more than ever pleased with his pupil and began to laud him with compliments, saying he had already progressed beyond the summits of Helicon, and was ready to storm the gates of Heaven. Augustine begged him to substantiate his opinion concerning "the order of causes," and was crestfallen when Licentius said: "Shut up! I am trying to think!"

Annoyed, more than a little querulous, Augustine launched into a discussion of Licentius's poetry and the long epic he was writing about Pyramus and Thisbe. The trouble about the epic, according to Augustine, was that it was building a wall between Licentius and God, which was a matter of considerably more importance than the wall built between Pyramus and Thisbe, for after all there was a chink in that wall, and through the chink the lovers spoke to each other. Augustine probably hoped he had stirred Licentius's mind to thoughts of the underlying order of the universe. He was mistaken. After a long pause Licentius said: "I'm in a worse fix than a mouse—I'll swear to that!" It was a line from the Roman poet Terence, and Licentius's sudden evocation of the words had something to do with the mice he was thwacking with his stick. He went on: "That's what I think about myself, but of course, when the poet goes on to say: 'I'm completely finished,' that's not true of me at all. You mustn't turn up your nose at mice, though I agree superstitious people do.

The mouse told you I was awake, and I told the mouse (by knocking with my stick) to be a good fellow and lie down quietly in his hole: and perhaps you are right—there was a tone in your voice which suggested I would be better engaged in philosophy than in poetry, for philosophy is, as you have begun to persuade me, our true and unshaken home. So ask me anything you like. I will defend the order of things. I will assert that nothing occurs which is outside that order, and if you convince me I am wrong, I will agree that even what is extraordinary occurs within the natural order of things."

At this point Trygetius said they were talking nonsense: the important thing was to behave in all these matters with a truly academic "suspension of belief," but Augustine paid no attention to him and launched immediately into a question which had been uppermost in his mind for some time. Surely, over large areas of existence, blind chance ruled. The falling leaves—wasn't it purely by chance that they fell in the channel?

"You really are a rather horrible questioner [*odiosus percunctor*]," Licentius replied. "Why blind chance? If you take into account the position of the trees and the branches, and the rate of fall of the leaves, and the air they fall in, then you have your explanation; and if you go on to ask why the trees were there in the first place, the answer is that there is always a cause—"

"What about the trees which produce no fruit?" Augustine asked sharply, smiling to himself in the dark. "Answer me that, you who called me a horrible questioner."

Trygetius said something about the question being irrelevant: the important thing was to keep a sense of proportion and to remember they were discussing how everything existed within an order of causes.

Suddenly Licentius jumped up excitedly. It occurred to him that there was order in all things: there was the mouse which had squeaked and waked him up, and then there was the thwacking with the stick, and then there was Augustine's voice, and then there was the irrelevant disputation, but all these things followed logically one after another, and somewhere behind them lay the falling leaves, and behind the falling leaves, remote, inaccessible, perfect, and eternal, lay the Platonic idea of order.

"Well then," asked Augustine, "if nothing happens without a cause, does the order of nature seem to you good or bad?"

"Neither good nor bad, but between the two."

"Then what is the contrary of order?"

"There is no contrary, for order prevails everywhere. What is contrary to order would of necessity be beyond order."

"Isn't evil contrary to order?" Trygetius demanded.

"Nonsense. There is always a cause to evil. It must be so, for one thing follows after another."

"Idiot," said Trygetius. "What you are saying is not only contrary to the truth, but definitely profane, for what you are saying amounts to the statement that evil is included within the natural order, and this order comes from God, and is the object of His love. Therefore evil comes from God and is the object of His love."

Augustine intended to interject some remark at this point, but wisely remained silent. The brain of young Licentius was searching among the mysteries which were to bemuse Augustine himself for the rest of his life. He waited in suspense, until finally there came a remarkable statement from the young African boy who searched in the dark for a solution to a problem he had never thought about until that moment; and when he spoke there was all the freshness of youth in his young words. Very gravely Licentius said: "No, God does not love evil! And this is so, because it is not within the realm of order that God should love evil. God loves order for the same reason that he cannot love evil, and evil remains within the realm of order precisely because God does not love it. The order of evil is the very fact that God does not love it. Evil therefore, which God does not love, is not beyond the order which God loves: for the order of things consists in his loving good and not loving evil. So evil is the contrary of good, but order is preserved."

"Yes," said Augustine, after Trygetius had interjected a few puerile complications, "and now the best thing is that we should go to sleep, for dawn will soon be coming, unless it is the moon throwing its light on the window."

Before they went to sleep, Augustine was moved to the depths of his soul by the sound of Licentius singing, not his interminable "Pyramus and Thisbe," but some lines from the Psalms: "Turn to us again, Thou God of Hosts: shew the light of Thy countenance and we shall be whole." Augustine was not always to be moved by the singing of those lines. There came a time when young Licentius sang the same verse interminably, all day and half the night, and once, when he was heard singing it in the lavatory, Monnica objected strongly. Augustine, of course, stoutly defended his pupil. He pointed out that it was as good a place as anywhere to sing the praises of God.

The next day was cloudy. Alypius went off to market, Monnica attended to the cooking, Augustine worked on his correspondence, and this may have been the day when he wrote to Romanian that "your son has become an almost perfect poet." He gave orders to the farm-laborers, read through half a book of Vergil, and wrote out or dictated the conversations of the previous night. The next day it was decided to continue the conversation on the subject of order. They went to the baths. On the way Augustine observed some cocks fighting. He was struck with admiration by the splendor of the conqueror. "Look at him!" he exclaimed. "He crows triumphantly. He struts and plumes himself in a proud sign of victory. And now look at the conquered one, without voice, his neck unfeathered, an expression of shame. All this has I know not what beauty in harmony with the laws of nature—"

He did not go on to describe the reasons why the survival of the fittest should be a law of nature, but he had acquired

another peg on which he could discuss the nature of order.
He asked Licentius to give him a definition of order. Licentius
wisely refused. "A definition is like being drenched with ice-
cold water," he replied; but a moment later he offered the
definition: "Order is that by which all things are wrought as
God determines," and at once difficulties began, and for the
whole of the day they tore the brilliant definition to pieces.
Did "all things" include evil? Did it include incurable idiots?
What did, or didn't it, include? They were still arguing when
Monnica came to announce that dinner was ready. Augustine
begged her to stay and help them resolve their problems, and
when he flattered her by saying he was her disciple, she answered briskly: "Stop it! You shouldn't tell such whopping
lies!"

So the arguments went on, while the leaves drifted down
and the snow thickened on the mountains, and sometimes there
were moments of pure terror, but mostly there was a peaceful autumnal calm. Toothache, nightmares, the processions of
naked women, the moment of horror when it suddenly occurred to him afresh that Adeodatus was growing into an
amazingly intelligent youth—what could one do with a son
when the whole of one's life should be spent in orderly adoration of God?—these moments passed, and in their place there
was all the quiet of renunciation, all the minute preparations
for the time when he would receive baptism from the hands
of Ambrose in Milan. The last flickering flames of Neoplatonism were dying out. On the verge of becoming a catechumen, he began to speak like a man about to renounce life
altogether, and there is a grave gentleness in some of his remarks at this time. At the end of a discussion with the boys,
he said: "Now the sun warns me to put the playthings I
brought for the children back into the basket." At another
time, shaking his head sadly, he told Licentius: "Go you,
meanwhile, and search for your muses." For himself, he had
put the pagan muses behind him at last.

As winter came on, Augustine began the writing of his *Soliloquies*. The word was invented by him, and he was a little ashamed of it, wondering whether it would be understood.[1] These *Soliloquies*, which cover only about forty pages in the Latin text, were evidently written with three or four purposes in mind. In them he crystalized many of his discussions with Licentius and Trygetius. They are lecture notes, diary entries, explorations of the spiritual landscape, and among them are to be found two moving prayers. At odd moments, sometimes when they were least expected, he was to include prayers in his works, but the first he ever wrote was among the greatest, and shows his sense of poetry as well as it demonstrates his continuing perplexity before the problems of beauty, order, and evil, which were to remain with him for the rest of his life:

O God, through whom all things which of themselves were not came to be,

O God, who permittest not to punish even that which destroys itself,

O God, who from nothing has created this world which all eyes know to be most beautiful,

O God, who dost not cause evil but dost cause it to become not most evil,

O God, who to those few who take refuge in the true and real dost show that evil is nought,

O God, through whom the universe, even that which is sinister in it, becomes perfection,

O God, through whom the utmost discord is as nothing, since worse things are brought into harmony with the better,

O God, who art loved knowingly or unknowingly by all those who know how to love,

[1] A number of other words were invented by Augustine, and since the words men invent are extraordinarily revealing of character, Augustine's inventions are given here: *anathemare, convictio, excommunicatio* (which he shares with St. Jerome), *imperfectio, perfruitio, ploratio, somnolentia, monstrositas, beatifico, extirpator, justificator, luminator, deificare.*

*O God, in whom are all things, yet the shame of every creature
    does not shame thee, nor does their wickedness harm
    thee, nor does their error deceive thee,*
**O God, who hast not willed that any save the pure should know
    the truth,*
*O Father of truth, Father of wisdom, Father of the true and
    supreme life, Father of blessedness, Father of the
    good and the true, Father of the intelligible life,
    Father of our vigils and our illuminations, Father
    of the covenant by which we are admonished to re-
    turn to thee.* (Augustine, *Soliloquia*, III.)

One of these statements, marked with an asterisk, he withdrew when he was very old and had developed a passion for correcting the mistakes of his youth. He often returned to the *Soliloquies*, reproducing their phrasing in his voluminous interpretations of texts. It is here that there occurs the passionate: "It is my guilt which causes Thy sufferings." But most remarkable of all, Christ plays almost no part in these strange outpourings, and indeed throughout his life Augustine was more concerned with God the Father than with God the Son.

The *Soliloquies* took the form of a continuing dialogue between reason and the soul. The soul is not always victorious. "I have nothing else but my will," Augustine admits at one point. "I love only God and the soul." Then he asks himself whether this means that he doesn't love his friends, and with exquisite sensibility and with a complete absence of Christian logic he answers: "I love the soul; how therefore should I not love my friends?" He is as always terribly concerned with himself. "God, who art always the same," he cries, "let me know myself, let me know Thee." Once or twice there are sudden desperate pleas for help. "Hear me, hear me, my God, my Lord, my King, my Father, my Creator, my hope, my possession, my glory, my home, my country, my salvation, my light, my life." Already he can say: "Thee only do I love, Thee only follow, Thee only seek, Thee only am I ready to serve." But it is essential to observe that in the *Solilo-*

quies Augustine occasionally finds himself talking a strange nonsense; and the "Thee only" language comes perilously near to a "me only" language, in which his heaven-storming pride asserts itself, and the inflamed will twists and turns in the hot prison of the body, his alarming sensitivity exasperated by its own brilliance, its fierce shining. As he said himself, in one of those amazing lines of poetry that occur more often than we suspect in the *Confessions*, a poetry which defies translation and therefore must be quoted in Latin: *Mens mea pervenit ad id quod est in ictu trepidantis aspectus.* "My mind reached that which is in the thrust of a trembling glance."

All through that winter Augustine lived two lives: the life of philosophical inquiry and the life of the impassioned mystic. There were jokes with Licentius and Trygetius, "a little man," said Augustine, "but a great eater," and there were the disputes lasting sometimes well into the night, so that a servant would be sent for and ordered to bring a torch under the great tree in the meadow or in the bathhouse. Essentially Augustine was preparing himself for the ordeals ahead. Slowly, effortlessly, almost quietly, he was stripping himself to become the naked "athlete of God."

In the spring he was baptized, together with Alypius and Adeodatus, by then a boy fifteen years old.

According to the Milan rite the candidate for baptism was prepared by a long examination. On the day of the actual baptism he fasted. He was led to the altar, stripped naked, anointed with oil by presbyters and deacons, asked whether he renounced the devil and the world, answered: "I renounce," accompanying the words with a dramatic spitting into the face of the devil, and was then immersed in the waters of the baptismal basin. Afterwards he was dried with linen cloths, anointed again on the head with chrysm, and then "signed." Later the bishop washed his feet, whereupon the newly baptized person was robed in white, emblematic of innocence and joy. Augustine, his friend, and his son were baptized by Ambrose on Easter Eve, April 24, 387.

When Easter had passed Augustine decided to return to Africa. There were many reasons. His mother was growing old, and she had long ago expressed the wish to die in her own country. He was also determined to return to Carthage for reasons of charity: he would convert the heathen among whom he had lived. Accompanied by his mother, his son, his brother, Alypius, and another friend, he journeyed to Ostia. By that time Monnica was ill. One day when she had strength enough to stand with him by the window overlooking the garden of the lodginghouse, they found themselves talking of spiritual things. They were talking about the truth, which was God, and the eternal lives of the saints, and suddenly a hush fell between them. To Augustine it was as though God had spoken, and suddenly Augustine found himself speaking about the quality of that silence:

So if to any person the tumult of the flesh were hushed, hushed the images of earth, and waters, and air, hushed also the poles of Heaven, yea, the very soul be hushed to herself, and by not thinking on self surmount self, hushed all dreams and imaginary revelations, every tongue and every sign, and whatsoever exists only in transition, since if any could hear, all these say, We made not ourselves, but He made us that abideth forever—if then, having uttered this, they too should be hushed, having roused only our ears to Him who made them, and He alone speak, not by them, but by Himself, that we may hear His word, not through any tone of flesh, nor angel's voice, nor sound of thunder, nor in the dark riddle of a similitude, but, might hear Whom in these things we love, might hear His Very Self without these (as we two now strained ourselves, and in swift thought touched on that Eternal Wisdom, which abideth over all);—could this be continued on, and other visions of kind far unlike be withdrawn, and this one ravish, and absorb, and wrap up its beholder amid these inward joys, so that life might be forever like that one moment of understanding which now we sighed after; were not this, Enter into thy Master's joy? And when shall that be? When we shall rise again, though we shall not all be changed? (Augustine, *Confessions*, IX, 10.)

It was a moment of mystery and revelation such as Augustine had not experienced before, and it continued long after he thought it was over. Monnica had seen the vision, and was now prepared to die. She said quietly:

My son, for my part I no longer take delight in anything in this life. I know not why I am still here, now that my hope in this world is accomplished. I wished to live for one thing, that I might see you a Catholic Christian before I died. My God has granted me this, and more—even that I should see you despising earthly happiness and devoted to His service. What do I linger here? (Augustine, *Confessiones*, IX, 10).

Augustine did not remember whether he made a suitable reply. Five days afterwards Monnica took to her bed and fell into a delirium, from which she awoke to say: "Here you shall bury your mother." They were appalled, but she went on: "Lay this body anywhere; let you not be disquieted in caring for it; all I ask is that you should remember me at the Lord's altar, wherever you are." A little while before, when someone asked whether she was afraid of dying far from her own city, she answered: "Nothing is far from God, and I have no fear that He will not know where to find me." She died when she was fifty-six and Augustine was thirty-three.

After the burial Augustine went to the bathhouse. He remembered the Greek proverb: "The bath drives away sorrow," but he discovered that the proverb lied, and though the sweat flowed out of him and the attendants covered him with hot towels, the weight on his heart showed no signs of leaving him in peace. At last he fell asleep. When he awoke the grief had disappeared, and in its place there flowed through his mind the most famous of Ambrose's songs:

> *Creator of the earth and sky*
> *Ruling the firmament on high,*
> *Clothing the day with robes of light,*
> *Blessing with gracious sleep the night.*

That rest may comfort weary men
To face their useful toil again,
And soothe awhile the harassed mind,
And sorrow's heavy load unbind—

But at the word "sorrow" the thought of his dead mother returned to him, and then he flung himself down on the bed, all his pent-up tears flowing for her who had for so many years wept for him.

Now that he was alone, he was once again plagued with himself, his own domineering will, his desire for fame, his terrible unrelenting quest for God. He did not go to Carthage, perhaps because he wanted to be near his dead mother. Instead he returned to Milan and then went to Rome, where he set about writing his book, *The Free Choice of the Will*, which he finished later in Africa. It is a supremely brilliant book. It attempts to solve the problem whether God is the author of evil, and all the passion of his quarrel with the Manichaeans recurs in the long argument which is supposed to take place between himself and his friend Evodius. There are moments where Augustine exalts the human will, other moments when he debases it. Is the will good? Perhaps; he is never sure. Or else there is only the will of God. Evodius says everything springs from necessity, not the will of God: Augustine determines to prove the contrary by an astonishing display of brilliant syllogisms and by an appeal to the necessity of God's mercy. Yet, in spite of its admitted brilliance, the book leaves a curiously dry taste in the mouth. We are not aware that the problem is solved. Pride keeps rearing its head: for no reason except that he suffered from the sin, Augustine must constantly rebuke the presence of pride. There is, however, a foretaste of things to come, and Augustine was never so Augustinian as when he came to his conclusion: "For better is one day in Thy courts over thousands, for the term of that day may be called the immutability of eternity [*unius autem diei nomine incommutabilitas aeternitatis vocetur*]."

He wrote other books during that last year in Italy, including a sketch of *Manichaean Morality*, which complemented a comparatively short study of *The Morals of the Christian Church*. He returned to Africa, and after a brief stay in Carthage went back to his native town. There, remembering how he had been brought into the Church, he decided to devote his life to meditation in Thagaste, imitating St. Antony. He formed a community. The first members were his son Adeodatus, Alypius, and Evodius, but soon many of his old friends joined. They lived in a small house surrounded by small meadows. They gave themselves to the reading of the Scriptures and long colloquies with the master, and obeyed him in all things, and watched untiringly so that he should not be tired. Augustine had sold his possessions for the upkeep of the monastery, and for three years, as he wrote voluminously, now a book on communication in language, now a commentary on Genesis, now a textbook for the understanding of music, he was perfectly content with himself. He had been the monastic scholar ever since he could remember, or rather one part of his mind had always been concerned with inquiry into the nature of things: now he could devote his whole nature to his professed studies.

The idyllic life, hardly to be distinguished from the months spent in the garden at Milan, was not to continue. Adeodatus died in the first year of their seclusion at Thagaste. Not a word remains to describe Augustine's grief, but there is some evidence that he worked harder after his son's death and that he considered the death a punishment for his own sins. Two years later Valerius, Bishop of Hippo, asked Augustine's aid in administering the diocese and ordained him priest, urging him to occupy the pulpit. This Augustine did. Later he regretted that he had ever been so foolish as to become a priest, for his old knowledge of rhetoric returned, and he spoke so convincingly that his popularity rivaled that of the bishop. Four years later, alleging his age, Valerius called upon the people to elect a new bishop. The cry for Augustine was unanimous, and he was forced to accept. From that moment he was never to know any real leisure, and sometimes, in his desire to punish those who molested him with demands for attention, he would snap: *"Discedite a me, maligni!* Go far from me, ye wicked ones! Let me study in peace the commandments of my God."

If he did not study those commandments in peace, at least he wrote about them. Before he died, he had composed two hundred and thirty books on subjects ranging through the whole gamut of knowledge. Some of his works are worthless. His excessive subtlety found pleasure in learned disquisitions on the meanings of words, customs, even letters of the alphabet. He will stumble among small points of grammar which weary the attention. He defines a single dogma through a thousand pages, and will write a commentary thirty pages long on a single sentence of the Bible. But those are small faults when set against the inordinate brilliance and penetration of his mind. An earthiness remained with him, and it was characteristic of the man who wrote so much that he confessed he preferred reading to writing.

The collected works of Augustine fill fifty huge volumes. It is to be doubted that anyone has read them all, or ever will. But lost in the huge volumes are many things that should be remembered, for hardly anyone else has possessed in a single mind a superb gift for poetry and a singular skill in dialectics. There are times when he could say difficult things with ease, other times when easy things are wrapped in endless difficulties of his own making, but nearly always he was crystal clear. Often, as when he said: "You are not to suppose, brethren, that heresies are produced by small minds; on the contrary, only great minds can produce them," he says what needed to be said with exemplary precision. He wrote of "humility raised to the heights, drunkenness sober," and it was in this temper that he wrote his books, in a divine drunkenness and a divine pride. Sometimes he can be willfully aphoristic, as when he said in his famous book *On the Trinity:* "God always is, nor has He been and is not, nor is but has not been, but as He never will not be; so He never was not." The ideas disentangle themselves in the end, but the complexities remain.

Some of his lesser-known passages should be quoted here, because they give the measure of the man, his poetry, his melancholy, the settled joy and the pervading sense of an attainable peace. He liked to write of the joy in God, and he liked to declare the goodness of the earth which was created by God:

In creation I find the sky good, the sun good, the moon good, the stars good, the earth good, the things which are brought forth from the earth and are rooted there, all good; and all that walks and moves is good, and all that flies in the air and swims in the waters is good; and I say that man is good, for "the good man out of the good treasure of his heart bringeth forth good." I say, too, that the angels are good, if they have not fallen by reason of their pride and become devils—they are good if they remain obedient to Him who made them. I say all these things are good, and when I turn towards God I think I can describe Him in no other way than by saying He is good, and I remember that the Lord Jesus said: "No one is good, save God alone." (Augustine, *Ennarationes in Psalmos*, CXXXXIX, 4.)

But though for Augustine there was perpetual joy in the world, there was also perpetual sorrow, the knowledge that time was slipping away, that the enemies were at the gates, that only grief was left when the lover has gone away; and some of his most moving passages concern the landscape of grief. He wrote often about the waters of Babylon. Here, for example, is a passage from his sermon on Psalm CXXXVI:

And then there are those other citizens of the Holy Jerusalem who have knowledge of their imprisonment: they know how human desires and the various lusts harry them, dragging them hither and thither, so driving them into the sea. But they are aware of what is happening, and so they do not throw themselves into the waters of Babylon, but they sit down beside the waters of Babylon, and beside the waters of Babylon they weep, either for those who have been carried away in the waters or to find themselves in such a place. So they sit and humble themselves. "By the waters of Babylon we sat down and wept when we remembered Sion." O holy Sion, where all is firm and nothing ever flows! Who has thrown us headlong in these waters? Why have we come away from the Founder of all things and his community? Behold, where all things are flowing and gliding away, there is scarce one who can snatch at a tree and escape. Therefore we humble ourselves in our captivity, taking our places beside the waters of Babylon; and let us not dare to plunge into these waters, or be proud and uplifted in the evil and sorrow of our imprisonment, but let us sit and so weep. (Augustine, *Ennarationes in Psalmos*, CXXXVI, 3, 4.)

Or else, as often, he will allow himself to remember that Christ came into the world at a time when one world was perishing and another was being born:

Christ came when all things were growing old: He made them new. As something fashioned, created, perishable, the world was declining to its fall. And so it was inevitable that there should be miseries. He came to console thee in present troubles and to promise an everlasting rest. Choose, therefore, not to cleave unto this ancient world, nor be unwilling to grow young in Christ, who said to thee: The world is perishing, the world is growing old, the world is failing, the world has the labored breathing of old age. Fear not. "Thy youth shall be renewed as an eagle's." (Augustine, *Sermones de Scripturas*, LXXXI, 8.)

The imperious claim to an eternal youth in Christ is constant in Augustine; so, too, at odd moments, and often unexpectedly, are those paeans of joy which occur throughout his work. Here is one from the *Confessions*:

All the things of the earth do shew that thou art to be praised. What things? The dragons, and all the abysses; fire, hail, snow, ice, stormy winds, they fulfill Thy word; mountains and all hills and fruitful trees and cedars; the beasts and all the cattle; all creeping things and all flying fowl whatsoever; all the kings of the earth and all the peoples; all the princes and all the judges of the land; all young men and maidens, old men and children; let them praise Thy name. Seeing also these in Heaven praise Thee, praise Thee, O our God, in the heights, thine angels and all thy hosts, sun, moon, stars and light, the very heaven of heavens and all the waters that are above the heavens, seeing that they praise Thy name, I do not desire better than to praise Thee. (Augustine, *Confessiones*, VII, 13.)

But it is not enough that he should praise: he must find a hundred ways to describe, as it were, the texture of his love of God:

What do I love when I love Thee? Not beauty of bodies, nor the fair harmony of time, nor the brightness of the light, so lovely to the eye, nor the soft melodies of many songs, nor the sweet smell of flowers and ointments and spices, nor manna and honey, nor the limbs acceptable to embraces by the flesh. None of these I love when I love my God. Yet I love a kind of light and melody and fragrance and meat and embracement, when I love my God, and these are the light, melody, fragrance, meat and embracement of my inner man: where there shineth unto my soul, what space cannot contain, and there soundeth, what time beareth not away, and there smelleth, what breathing disperseth not, and there tasteth, what eating diminisheth not, and there clingeth, what satiety divorceth not, when I love my God. (Augustine, *Confessiones*.)

What is magnificent in Augustine is that he speaks a language that is immediately perceived by the senses; and some of his power evidently comes from the earthiness of his spiritual quality. He is not ashamed to talk about eating God. He will use rough Punic words where he can. He shows a novelist's knowledge of the world around him. Occasionally, the bright images darken and are lost in confusion and at such times he reminds you of an autumn bonfire. The damp leaves send up great curtains of smoke, the eyes smart, the wits are fuddled, but every now and then a flame flashes out, all the brighter for the surrounding obscurity. Then the gardener puts on more leaves, and all is again darkness.

He has the novelist's power of making past things over-whelmingly present. He remembered his childhood under the African sun with peculiar precision; he remembered smells, the wine stain on his mother's dress, the dusty roads; he could summon them back at will. He was appalled by the accuracy of these visions of the past. "Thus my childhood, which now is not, is in time past, which now is not: but now when I recall its image and tell of it, I behold it in the present, be-cause it is present in my memory." But was it? He was never quite sure. There are mirages in Africa; and sometimes as he watches how his childhood recedes and then draws nearer to confront him everywhere, we are suddenly made aware that the hard definition in his writings may be a disguise for uncer-tainty, and the shining in his writings is like the shuddering brightness of an African noon sky. In *The City of God*, as in all his works, there are some passages of great lucidity, but in others the lucidity has the feverish quality that comes to men who live on a sunburned land. Dostoevski received his illumination on a winter day when he was led out before a firing squad in St. Petersburg: Augustine received his illumina-tion on a hot afternoon in Milan when he had thrown himself weeping under the branches of a fig tree. Both were athletes of God with surprisingly similar tempers.

The City of God is many things, for Augustine was divinely incapable of writing simply about any one thing. It has over-tones which suggest Dmitri Karamazov, a terrible sexual vio-lence, a delight in curses and anathemas: he rains down curses upon Rome as though he had just come up from its sewers, and Cotton Mather was right in his very great work, the *Magnalia Christi*, when he said: "Alas, alas, how much of Babylon is there in his best book, *De Civitate Dei*." It is all of Augustine, his memories, his hopes, his passions; and though the City of God provides the major theme, the minor theme is man's progress through the comedy of the world. Dante, in a famous letter to Can Grande, explained that his subject was man—*subjectum est homo*—and so it is here, though

Augustine is not interested in man in general so much as in himself. As he travels back through all past history and shows with considerable skill that history is simply a road which leads to the Heavenly City, he seems to be peering into the faces of the ancients in the hope of finding himself. Over that immense and haphazard book there looms the giant figure of Memory.

The City of God is as shapeless as any work by Dostoevski or Proust. He could not avoid it. The book was his diary, into which he poured his daily thoughts, shaping them a little under chapter headings, without the advantages that occurred to Gregory when, commenting on the separate lines of the Book of Job, he could allow any stray thoughts to enter his head and regard them as part of an inevitable commentary. For Augustine there had to be some form, if only because the book was divided up among chapters which demanded that he should for the most part stick to the point. Yet he rarely does; his mind leaps from one thing to the next. In the eighth book, for example, there are twenty-seven chapters, covering in the Everyman edition twenty-seven pages: in them he discusses Plato, the logic of Socrates, Apuleius's doctrine concerning the airy spirits, the wickedness of black magic, the opinions of Hermes Trismegistus, the customs of the opinionated Egyptians, and the glory of the Christian martyrs. It is all grist to his mill. He will go on to the end, until all problems are solved, until the whole of the past has been placed under review.

He argues about the meanings of words, triumphantly asserts the superiority of Rome to all other civilizations (though Rome is and always has been "a decaying corpse"), relates his dreams, introduces incidents from his childhood, battles with the problems of the will, denounces the Manichaeans, furiously opposes the Arians and the Donatists, bitterly attacks the gods, and, far from finding any glory in the earthly city, hates it with the passion of Marx, who similarly denounced the city-dwellers, the *bourgeoisie*. "The world," says Augustine, "is a sea in which men devour one another like fish." The *pax civica* is based on naked fear, and it is pure heresy to put one's trust in cities, for Rome was founded by a murderer and Babylon by a brigand, and the existence of the city is a cause for wars. His horror of the bourgeoisie sounds strangely in our modern ears, which hear the same horror broadcast over the Moscow radio. Yet in fact the basic theories of Communism and Augustine's City of God have this in common, that both regard the state as the cause of all evils, and the state must eventually wither away.

Just as Augustine laid the basis for the strong and permanent establishment of the Catholic Church, which arose to power with all the sanction of his theories, so the Communists, detesting the state and looking forward to an "inevitable" anarchy, only made the state more secure in its powers. For Augustine the state, far from being a source of security, was a source of insecurity. "If the household, the common refuge from the evils of human life, affords but imperfect security, how much more so the state which, the larger it is, the more full of civil suits and crimes, even when for a moment it earns a respite from turbulent, often bloody seditions and civil wars, from the occurrence of which states are rarely free, from the apprehension of them never." What then? There is no solution, he says, except to put one's faith in God like the psalmist, who declares: "O Lord, remove me from my troubles." And so he envisages a theocratic state, ruled by holy men whose power derives directly from God, monks and anchorites on the thrones.

It is here, in the bitter denunciations of the *pax civica*, that Augustine speaks with the keenest energy and the most blinding contempt; and he is disturbing precisely because he is so often just, and also because he sees no hope of renovation from within the city itself, though it is precisely by renovation that the cities have lasted down the centuries. For him only by Christian love may all things be made new. As they stand the cities repose on falsehoods—at least a quarter of the book may be regarded as an examination of the various forms of illusion embodied in popular ideology; the illusions of peoples, poets, philosophers, and statesmen. From what strange beliefs, he says, do people derive a sense of security! Why, there are people who derive security from the demon goddess of the doorhinge! It is all arrant nonsense. There is only love, there is only God's mercy, which is another name for love. And so he goes on, jotting notes in his diary, mining the city from underground, and sometimes he will make statements concerning the nature of the city which are still relevant today:

It is the peculiarity of secularism that it worships a god or gods, by whose aid it may reign victorious in temporal peace, animated with the love of wise counsel but with the lust of possession. For the good use this world in order that they may enjoy God; but the evil use God in order that they may enjoy this world. (Augustine, *De Civitate Dei,* XV, 7.)

Against the law of lust he set the law of love, which he described best in one of his letters:

The law of love comprehends all the discussions and writings of all the philosophers, all the laws of all states. It is embodied in two precepts upon which, in the words of Christ, hang all the laws and the prophets: *Thou shalt love the Lord thy God with all thy heart and with all thy soul and with all thy mind; and thy neighbor as thyself.*

Here your physic, here your ethic, here your logic: here also salvation for the state which deserves to be praised. (Augustine, *Epistola* CXXXVII, ch. V, 17.)

But to lay down the law of love in opposition to the law of the state was to demand, as he must have known, a general holiness and an absence of willfulness rare at all times, and he made no effort to solve the practical problems that face the people who attempt to love and at the same time attempt to live in the state. He seemed to believe that the City of God could be brought into being at once, in the time taken for a lightning-flash to illuminate a landscape, brought into existence by a single grace from God or by a single act of the prophetical will; and in this, as history proved, he was mistaken. The state did not wither away, and the City of God has never existed on earth.

All through the book Augustine gives the impression of a man deliberately swimming against the current, deriving a harsh pleasure from the conflict. There are moments when he rages easily or laughs uproariously. His blood boils before the hecatombs ordered by emperors. He attacks imperialism, suggests the advantages of living in a small state, paying a surprising tribute to Athens, "mother and nurse of liberal learning, home of so many great philosophers, the glory and distinction of Hellas," though Athens was herself a colonial power; and he inveighs continually, with memories of the Roman fivefold destruction of Carthage, against the madness in their souls which led the Romans to conquests overseas. There is an astonishing vigor in his denunciations of the evil of the state, but sometimes there were moods of terrible acquiescence, and at such moments there comes from him a grave poetry. Rome was Babylon, doomed to destruction. The empires would perish, the barbarians would come over the frontiers, and the sword would rule where previously there ruled the threat of the sword held in the power of the state. What should be done? He does not know. Rome falls; Christ rises; but the sadness remains.

There is a theory, often repeated, that Augustine envisaged the City of God as a universal church like the medieval papacy, but the theory is mistaken. The Church had no need of Augustine's sanctions; and for himself he had no real belief in any earthly city even when ruled by a theocracy. The true city, *beatissima civitas Dei*, was built of faith and love, inhabited by pilgrims, owing its strength to the Christian fortitude of the human heart. The pilgrim of this city obeyed no ruler except God. The ultimate effect of the City of God is the elimination of the state and the church, and the enthronement of divine charity. At the very end of the book he equates Jerusalem, the city of peace, with the phrase from the Psalms: "Be still, and know that I am God," and in the final peroration, half prayer, half statement of a divine vision, he wrote:

Then being freed from toil we shall see that He is God, which we ourselves wanted to be when we fell from Him, hearing from the seducer: "Ye shall be as gods," and departing from the true God, by whose means we should be as gods by participation of Him, not by forsaking Him. For what have we done without Him, but that we have fallen from Him and gone back by His anger? But by Him being restored and perfected with a greater grace we shall rest forever, seeing that He is God, with whom we shall be replenished, when He shall be all in all. . . . This seventh day shall be our sabbath, whose end shall not be the evening, but the Lord's day, as the eighth eternal day, which is sanctified and made holy by the resurrection of Christ, pre-figuring not only the eternal rest of the spirit, but also of the body. There we shall rest and see, we shall see and love, we shall love and we shall praise! (Augustine, *De Civitate Dei*, XXII, 30.)

When he wrote these words the candle of his life was already running low. He was seventy-two. His hair was white. There were conspiracies among his flock, and a great scandal which shook Hippo to its foundations, and always there were threat-ened invasions. He had written the funeral oration on the Roman Empire, passed all theologies under review, and now at last there was no longer any room for doubt. He thought for a while of writing a huge *Mirror of the World*, where once more he would attempt to grapple with the problems of the soul, but he was already growing weary. Now, knowing that death was near, he went back to his earliest writings and wrote his *Retractions*, stating simply and firmly the mistakes he had made. His generation was passing. Alypius was still alive, but Marcellinus, who was once his closest friend, was dead, and this hurt him like a hard and prolonged physical blow. He had wanted to dedicate *The City of God* to him, and most of all he wanted the comfort of his presence. He knew there were not many more months left to him and, shortly after *The City*

178 THE FATHERS OF THE WESTERN CHURCH

of God was completed, he walked in state to the basilica and addressed his flock, urging upon them that they should accept Heraclius as their priest. He had received formally from the people the promise that for five days a week he should not be disturbed, so that he could continue his scholarly labors, but the promise was continually broken, and he half knew it would continue to be broken until he died. The noisy Africans applauded him, shouted "Thanks be to Christ! Preserve us, Augustine!" their voices echoing and re-echoing against the roof of the basilica, but he was too weary to care. He had been an awkward administrator; he wanted to put administration behind him. It was the autumn of 426, and he may have been thinking of another autumn forty years before when a small group of careless and devoted young men had gathered on a country estate near Milan. There had been no rest since then.

There was no peace until his death. He had hardly finished writing *The City of God* when there came the first rumors that the Moors of the Atlas and the Kabylian mountaineers were preparing to ravage the coast. They had heard that the Vandals and the Alani in Spain were preparing to invade North Africa under Genseric, for they came like a horde of locusts in advance of the main tide of armies. Augustine rejoiced when Rome fell, and even now, so little faith had he in the *civitas terrena*, he hardly cared when he learned that the barbarians were burning the harvest and destroying barns and grainhouses. "Countries lately prosperous and populated have been changed into solitudes," he said.

In the spring of 429 the Vandals were at the gates of Hippo. A strange calm descended upon Augustine, and he said: "Why should those who are steadfast in heart grieve to see the falling roof-beams and the dying children?" They accused him of being callous, but they did not understand him. Christ had said: "When they persecute you in this city, flee ye into another," but he was too old to move, and besides he had duties to perform in Hippo. He helped where he could. He was seventy-five, but his brain was still clear, and he still sent out letters appealing for help to all those who might listen; and when the Vandals were so close that their hammering could be heard within the besieged city, he said: "I ask God to deliver this city from its enemies, or if that may not be, that He may give us strength to bear His will, or at least that He take me from the world and receive me into His bosom." It has been suggested that he was faint-hearted when he said these words, but it is unlikely that he was ever faint-hearted: the words were a simple prayer for delivery from evil.

In the third month of the siege he fell ill. He had rarely been ill before except in his youth, and this illness was strange to those who knew him, so strange indeed that it was immediately assumed that he could now perform miracles. A man was brought to him to be healed. Augustine smiled. "You see, my son, what a state I am in. If I could cure the sick, I would begin by curing myself." As he lay dying he ordered that someone should write and put up against the wall where he could see them the words: "Man goeth forth unto his work and to his labor until the evening." It comforted him to remember that the trials of his youth had only brought him nearer to God. For forty years he had praised God, and he knew that God would eternally nourish the Church he had celebrated. "*Non tollit Gothus quod custodit Christus*. The Goth cannot capture what Christ protects." The sufferings of the present time would not endure; the Goths would roll back; the City of God would remain. It was observed that he called often for Monnica, Adeodatus, and the woman who had given birth to his son. Then, quite suddenly, the strong body began to fail. He died at the age of seventy-six on August 28, 430, the greatest of the Fathers and the one whose fame outshone the rest from the day of his death. He had said once: "Thou hast made us for Thyself, and our heart is restless until it finds repose in Thee," and perhaps of all his writings these were the words closest to his heart.

VII. ✵ BENEDICT:
THE SCHOOLMASTER

ALL THROUGH THE HISTORY OF THE WORLD, AT times when the empires are crumbling, there are men who disappear into the wilderness. They gather the shreds of a failing civilization, surround themselves with acolytes, and with minute care set the young monks to copying the writings of the forefathers, in the hope that they will survive the cataclysm. They are men who scent danger long before it falls. So, during the Han dynasty in China and toward the end of the T'ang dynasty, small scattered groups of monks disappeared into the remote temples, taking their books with them, and dedicated themselves to the task of keeping the past alive. Most of our knowledge of medieval China and medieval Europe comes from these monkish scholars: without them the history and poetry of whole epochs would remain a blank.

When Benedict was born in 480, men still remembered the tragic days when Attila, an Altaic chieftain from central Asia, threatened to conquer Rome, and marched with his hordes right up to its gates. He had retired, baffled by the Pope, who had walked into his camp, showing that there was at least one fearless man left in Rome. Thereafter Attila returned to France, only to be defeated at the battle of Châlons. When he died, he left almost no trace of his coming. Yet the Empire was disintegrating. There was no Emperor in Rome, nor was there to be until the end of the century. The Vandals, from their capital in Toulouse, were extending their power northward over France. The northern coast of Africa was in the

hands of the barbarians, who had swept down across Europe
and fashioned a long sickle as they marched along the southern
littoral of the Mediterranean, their progress to be repeated
later in a reverse direction by the Mohammedans: and still the
pressure came from the tribes of Germany and from the melt-
ing pot of nations north of the Bosphorus. Meanwhile Rome
was half in ruins, the countryside was depopulated, and the
scent of death hung in the air. Christendom was to recover
from the invasions, but slowly. It would not recover through
the fervor of the Christians so much as through their patience;
and with Benedict a Christian patience comes onto the scene
for the first time. Quietly, against all the odds, he was to marry
the Roman *gravitas* with the Christian joy. By a miracle of
coincidence, he founded the first Benedictine monastery in the
same year that the Academy in Athens, which had sheltered
Plato, closed its doors.

Through the Benedictine monasteries the tradition which
we know as the Western tradition survived. Without Benedict
the tradition of scholarship might have collapsed: there might
even have been no universities: certainly they would have
come about in a different form: and it is oddly disturbing that
we know so little about him. Only the famous rule, the *Ben-
edicti regula monachorum*, and a short account of his life by
Gregory the Great remain to suggest what manner of man he
was.

That he was born of noble parents in the Sabine hills; that
he studied the seven liberal arts in Rome; that at the age of
fifteen he wandered in search of a desert where he could practice austerities; that he came to found the monastery at Monte
Cassino and fifteen years later, in an odor of sanctity, ascended
to heaven—all this we may surmise from the accounts which
have been handed down the centuries, but how much of it is
true? With Benedict legend and the hard core of fact are in-
timately connected, and not even the great Benedictine scholars have been able to disentangle truth from legendary fiction.

But here and there, walking through this brushwood of

clinging legend, one can form some kind of picture of him. Not all the legends are to be set aside. There are moments when the man who wrote the *regula*, that masterly summary of monkish devotions, comes springing to life: a slight, bearded man with a high forehead and immense eyes, walking with a curious hovering stride; half mystic, half scholar, born in the same year as Boethius and Cassiodorus, and like them determined to impose his own order on a disorderly universe. Like so many of the Fathers, in the short space of a lifetime he raced through the whole gamut of Christian experience, beginning as a hermit in the wilderness and ending as the acknowledged master of whole cities of monks.

It began with a lovers' quarrel. In Rome, when he was hardly more than a boy, he fell in love with a Roman girl. He seems to have been spurned. In the delirium of his lover's grief he decided "to please God alone," and wandered eastward across the hills, accompanied only by his nurse, in search of a place where he could worship God "in utter peace." He was untaught. Gregory says of him, "he was full of ignorant learning and wise where he was not taught [*scienter nescius et sapienter indoctus*]," but the phrase is a little too Gregorian to be wholly credible. The strange pair came to a small village called Enfide among the mountains about forty miles from Rome. The name of the village, which could be interpreted to mean "here is the faith," may have pleased him. He was content to live there quietly, learning the art of prayer, his bodily needs cared for by the aged nurse. But if he had thought to lose himself completely and to pass unnoticed, he was mistaken. Miracles enter the story. One day Benedict came back to his hut and found his foolish old housekeeper in a flood of tears over a broken sieve. It must be mended immediately, for there was no money to pay for a new one; it had been borrowed to sift the grain for his bread and untold harm would result if it was not returned. Benedict prayed, the sieve was magically refashioned, and so great was the miracle that for centuries the sieve could be seen hanging from the church tower, evidence of Benedict's divine powers. Soon afterwards Benedict fled from Enfide, leaving the nurse behind, since he desired a greater solitude.

He came to Subiaco, originally called Sublaqueum, meaning "below the lakes." These were three artificial lakes in a steep valley among the hills. Nero had ordered them to be made, but he never went there again after he barely missed being struck by lightning in this place. By the time Benedict arrived, the villa and the gardens were abandoned, the paths were overgrown, even the lakes had drained away; it was a wild, desolate place, with a small struggling river leaping over rocks and with precipitous cliffs, small grottoes, barrenness everywhere. Benedict lived in a cave. A young monk called Romanus fed him, letting down every day a cord on which there was attached a little bell and a loaf of bread. The deed was one of sincere charity, though irregular; most of the time Benedict must have starved. Also, the bell attracted the attention of the devil, who had long since incurred Benedict's displeasure. One day the devil dislodged a rock on the bell and smashed it forever. Romanus must have thought Benedict had perished in the cave, for no more food came down on the string.

Benedict, however, did not starve to death. It was Easter; and in some place far away, no one knows where, another athlete of God was piously preparing to sit down to a succulent dinner, which he had cooked himself. Suddenly he paused in his ministrations over the food, and he heard a voice saying: "You are preparing to feast deliciously, while my servant is starving to death over there." At once he made his way toward Benedict, plodding across ditches and streams, climbing mountains and groping through valleys, till he came to Benedict in his retreat. At once they fell to prayer.

"Come, let us eat," said the stranger. "Today is Easter Day."

Benedict answered: "Surely it is Easter, since you have come to me," meaning that it was a day of great joy to see another saint.

But the stranger cut him short. "It really is Easter," he said, "and no one should fast on Easter Day. Myself, I have been sent to give you these gifts of the Almighty Lord." Then they said grace and set to eating. Soon the stranger went away, and once more Benedict was left to his loneliness and the misery of the cave.

He did not always stay in the cave. Sometimes he went down to the valley, not to wash himself, for such a thing would hardly have occurred to him, but to gather herbs. Some shepherds wandering through the valley came upon him moving about in his shaggy dress of hides among the bushes. They thought he was an animal until he stood up, and then, realizing that he was a saint, they knelt before him, accepted his blessings, offered him food, and later brought others to share their tidings. From that time the country folk came crowding to the cave.

For some years he continued his austerities, fighting off the perpetual inroads of the devil, who appeared to him in the form of a nagging raven or a beautiful girl. The raven was easily dismissed; Benedict made the sign of the cross after enduring its presence too long; then it vanished. The girl was less easily dismissed; she came often in his dreams and waking visions; at last, unable to endure her presence any longer, Benedict threw off his dress of skins and rolled into a clump of briers and nettles. The physical pain shocked him free of any belief in the pleasures of the body, and "from that time," he said, "I was entirely free from the temptations of the flesh." Many years later, when Francis came to the cave and saw the briers still growing luxuriantly, he prayed over them until they became roses. Today there are still two rose trees beside the sacred cave.

Benedict desired to live alone with God, but the monks came forward with their arguments. They said one could live alone with God and still be surrounded by monks. The abbot of the monastery of Vicovaro twelve miles away had recently died. Benedict was asked to take his place. He had no desire to go there, believing the monks were lax in their devotions.

He refused, and then for some reason accepted the position. His hand was evidently heavy on the monks. One day a drop of poison was put in the cup of blessing which he lifted to his lips at the beginning of the monastic meal. The moment Benedict made the sign of the cross over the cup it smashed into a thousand pieces, and the wine splashed on the table. Benedict said quietly: "The Lord Almighty have mercy on you, my brethren. Why have you thus dealt with me? Did I not tell you before that there was nothing in common between my manner of life and yours? Go ye all and seek a father after your own heart; for no longer can you have me."

It is the first recorded speech of any length by him, the first time the accent of the *regula* is heard. Henceforward the theme of *gravitas*, of austerity and power, emerges. A new Benedict is revealed. There are a few more stories of miracles, but he has grown beyond the need of them. When Florentius, a monk of Vicovaro, became jealous of the communities Benedict was establishing in the valley, he sent a gift of poisoned bread. Benedict threw the bread to a raven and commanded: "In the name of Christ our Lord take up this bread and remove it to some hidden place where none shall know." When the raven croaked and fluttered round, desperately appealing to the saint and warning Benedict of the poison, he answered: "Have no fear." Three hours later the raven returned from its mysterious errand to "the place where none shall know," content with itself, ready to receive its dinner. The story is left there, the devilish poison removed offstage. When seven naked dancing girls came to torment Benedict's monks he performed no miracle over them, did not even run them out of the valley, did not turn them into creeping toads, uttered no *anathemas*, but quietly decided to go elsewhere. There was however one small final miracle. As Benedict departed with twelve disciples Florentius watched him in triumph, but even as he was watching, his house fell down on him, burying him in the ruins. When the monk Maurus, whom he loved dearly, came running after Benedict with the joyful news that Florentius lay destroyed beneath the house beams, Benedict rebuked him. "It is not seemly to rejoice over such an end," he said, and marched toward the boundaries of Campania.

Subiaco was famous for Nero's pleasure grounds; Cassinum, where Benedict founded his monastery, was famous for the revels of Mark Antony. It was as though Benedict needed the ruins of ancient Rome for his own pleasure grounds.

Cassinum had none of the ruggedness of Subiaco. The town lay at the foot of an immense isolated hill which looked down on a valley known as "the home of the nymphs." There were no precipices, no grottoes, no dark tangled valleys. Here all was light, immense sweeps of light, and at the very top of the mountain, surrounded by pine trees, lay a temple dedicated to Apollo, the god of light. The thirteen monks toiled up the mountain, set light to the pines, threw down the temple, and began to build an oratory dedicated to St. Martin of Tours.[1] Close by rose the monastery, the mother house of monks, and soon enough, beyond the great walls there appeared gardens and orchards and wheatfields shining in the sun. The mountain became a workshop, and the monastery at the summit became another Pisgah.

Stern, implacable, no longer a John the Baptist alone in the

[1] St. Martin of Tours (316-397?) was the logical choice, if only because he was the first to found a monastic settlement in the West. He was, however, strangely unlike Benedict: there is a purely French gentleness in the stories which Sulpicius Severus relates about him. Once when the devil appeared to him in the form of Christ wearing the purple and the diadems of an earthly emperor, St. Martin rebuked the devil: "If thou wast Christ, thou wouldst come naked and bleeding from thy wounds." The most famous of his adventures occurred on an ice-cold day in January 354. St. Martin was then a cavalry officer stationed at Amiens. Seeing a shivering beggar near the gate, he seized his short sword and cut his own wool-lined cape in half, giving one half to the beggar. That night he dreamed Christ had come to him wearing the beggar's half of the cape. Christ was surrounded by a multitude of angels to whom He said: "Martin, who is still but a catechumen, gave me his cloak." Some time later Martin left the army and established himself in a wattle hut on the edge of the Loire, near Poitiers, where he gave himself up to a life of continual mortifications. His fame rests on the impulse he gave to monasticism and on his visions, and though he is counted among the Fathers of the Church, he in no way affected doctrine.

wilderness but a Moses, Benedict ruled his community. According to the *regula* the abbot is in the place of God; he rules by the force of his authority, not by his example, a mysterious remote figure, rarely approached, whose word is law. The most minute details of the monks' lives were ordered; every moment of the day had its appointed task. He who once lived the life of a lonely hermit now lived as emperor; and still he performed miracles. They were very small ones. A servant entered his presence, a bottle of wine under his habit and another in his hand. By magic Benedict saw inside the hidden bottle. "Take care, my son," he said. "Be sure you do not drink of the flagon you have concealed on yourself. Turn it over very carefully, and you will see what is inside." The servant obeyed, removed the bottle from its hiding place, tilted it gently, and was surprised to see a deadly serpent crawling out. Benedict was a mindreader as well as conjuror. A young nobleman was thinking himself a fool to be a servant to so demanding an abbot, for one of his tasks was to hold a candle over the abbot at meals. "Why should I hold this candle?" he thought. "Have a care, my son, put down the candle," Benedict murmured. "Go away a little space and think of your sins." He could practice levitation. A huge awkward Goth was working at cutting down the briers in a monastery garden. He worked with great sweeps of his arms, and suddenly the billhook snapped in two and the iron blade fell into a pool. The Goth had no idea what to do. He wept at the thought he would no longer be able to cut briers. A message was sent to Benedict, who came hurrying into the garden, to find the Goth with the stave still in his hand. Gently Benedict removed the stave from his hand and threw it into the water. Then the iron blade rose from the muddy depths, joined itself to the stave, and swam tranquilly to the edge of the pool. "There, go on with your work," said Benedict, "and don't cry your eyes out."

Toward the end of Benedict's life Belisarius was making his raids on Italy, and when Ravenna had fallen, the Gothic King

Totila was made the leader of the Goths to resist the invaders. Coming to Monte Cassino, he thought of playing a trick on the abbot. One of his bodyguards, named Riccho, was sent ahead in disguise. He wore the royal shoes and all the royal emblems. Benedict, now nearly sixty, was sitting in front of the monastery. He saw the procession advancing, and long before Riccho had arrived in his presence, Benedict was heard saying: "Take care, my son, take off those clothes which are not yours." When Totila arrived at last, Benedict thought to give him a lesson in manners, accused the king of cruelty, prophesied that he would indeed capture Rome, and would then cross the sea. He concluded: "You shall reign for nine years, and in the tenth you shall die." The chroniclers are at pains to point out the accuracy of the prophecy.

All these stories hint at the man, but we see him dimly. We learn more when he speaks in the *regula* of the role of the abbot in a monastery, when he recounts the twelve rungs of humility and the seventy-two spiritual tools, when he goes into the minute details of monastic ritual. The legends are playful, and seem to have been invented to give color to the disciplinarian, to the august figure who remains concealed like Kafka's judge somewhere in the depths of the monastery; but there is one story in which he reveals himself. His twin sister Scholastica had become a nun, living in the convent of Plumbariola a mile and a half away. Once a year at sunrise she paid a visit to her brother. Then they would spend the day together in prayer in a secluded house within the monastery grounds, not far from the main gate. They were both old, they must have known they were dying and would never see each other again, but there was an unchangeable rule that Scholastica must return after evening prayers. But that evening, while they were sitting at table, Scholastica said: "Please do not leave me tonight, let us talk till morning of the joys of heaven." Benedict demurred. Such a request had never been made to him before. "Sister," he declared, "what is this you are saying? How can I stay away from the monastery?" There were no clouds in the sky. Suddenly Scholastica clasped her hands on the table, bowed her head and prayed for rain, the thicker the better. When she lifted her head the thunder was pealing on the mountain and flashes of lightning could be seen through the windows, and the thickest rain ever known to the monastery began to fall. Benedict realized he had been outwitted. He cried: "Good God, Sister, what on earth have you done?" Scholastica answered demurely: "Well, I asked you and you wouldn't listen, so I asked God, and He did. I don't mind if you do go back to your monastery—" Gregory, who wrote the story, observed that Scholastica was entitled to pray for thunder and lightning on the ground that her love was larger than her brother's authority, and he adds sententiously: "for God is love." Peter the Deacon, to whom Gregory told the story, was less sententious. He remarked: "I think that's a very nice story indeed."

According to tradition Benedict died on March 21, 543, a restless man who only in his death received the ultimate peace, *summa quies*, which he had striven for all his life.

His monument lies in the *regula* and in all the monasteries of the West. He has left his trace on each. Yet the *regula* is one of the most baffling of all medieval works. The imprint of Benedict's character is there: his justice, his sense of largeness and dedication, a distinct voice which moves through the heavy and often legal phrases; yet in the whole work there is hardly an original sentence or an original thought. It is a compilation of all the works of previous monks. From the days of the Twelve Tables the Roman mind had moved without difficulty toward the reign of law, a hard law, where all the penalties were clearly prescribed and all the rewards were stated. When the rule was being written, Justinian had recently compiled his great Code. The time had come for a code which would put law and order into the profession of the monks; and though the code is barren of any ornament, deliberately dry, content to measure out areas of responsibility, it remains an extraordinarily thrilling document: for it provided the blueprint for building the dykes against the barbarians. With some such rule, if our own civilization perishes, we may in time be able to restore our traditions.

With the rule Benedict developed St. Antony's monasticism into the most powerful cultural institution of the West. He seems to have done this deliberately, observing how all over Italy there crept the shadow of resignation and defeat. The weight of responsibility hangs heavy on Benedict; and in those taut paragraphs, which were written to provide a single rule for all Western monasteries,[1] we are conscious that Benedict is drawing up the blueprint for the capture of an empire, at the same time that he is drawing up plans for keeping the barbarians at bay. The rule is hard, but it is supremely civilized: and if at times it resembles a form of totalitarian communism, with the abbot as a benevolent autocrat at the head, the conclusion can hardly be avoided that monasteries cannot be managed democratically, and there were at least three ways in which the abbot could be replaced.

Yet the Benedictine monastery *is* based upon a form of totalitarianism. The abbot is the supreme ruler, implicit obedience is demanded, every detail of the day is carefully worked out in advance, and all necessary food and clothing are distributed equally. Poverty, obedience, and hard work are demanded of the monks. The work, however, was carefully trimmed to suit the monks' capabilities. Fanaticism was to be avoided at all costs. The rule of St. Columban in the seventh century said: "Let the monks go to their repose broken with weariness, and let them sleep upon their feet." By the Columban rule every normal human impulse was to be thwarted and the body made obedient to the will. Benedict was wiser. He knew, or he had read in the works of St. Gregory of Nyssa, that sleep is neces-

[1] This is the view of Dom John Chapman in his *St. Benedict and the Sixth Century*, (New York: Longmans Green, 1929). He believes that the rule was drawn up as an official code, and though it has been objected that St. Benedict's power extended only over Monte Cassino and one other monastery, it is difficult to avoid Dom Chapman's conclusion.

sary for digestion, and so he included in the rule the statement: "They may rest a little more than half the night and rise when they have digested." As for the labors of the monks he says: "Let all things be done with moderation, on account of the faint-hearted."

Here and there, through this strange legal code, there occurs this outpouring of the milk of human sympathy: Benedict trembles with love for the wayward children of men, and like Gregory later, he will hold the rod in one hand while beating time to the singing of the children with the other. In a sense, of course, it is paternalism gone rampant; and he seems to have been the first to use the word "abbot," meaning "father," from the Aramaic *abba*, the same word as the Arabic *abu*. But it is a paternalism unlike anything that had gone before: it was profoundly complex. The key word is rest: the peace of the soul. "The abbot," said Benedict, "shall strive rather to be loved than feared. He shall not be troubled and anxious; he shall also not be too obstinate; he shall not be jealous, and too suspicious; for then he will have no rest."

The whole edifice of the Benedictine monastery revolves around the abbot. He represents Christ. From him all powers flow. He is the supreme ruler who bears the responsibility for all the actions of all the monks. He is Christ's representative, called by Christ's name, for Benedict points out that the word "abbot" derives from the words of the apostle: "Ye have received the spirit of adoption of sons, wherefor we call Abba, Father." At one moment Benedict even prescribes the punishment of death for those who have scorned the word of God, but immediately afterwards he grows more humane, though the hard core of doctrinal punishment remains. "Reprove, rebuke, exhort," he says, quoting St. Paul, and he goes on to say that "seasons must be mixed with seasons, blandishments with terrors." Certainly, Benedict never concealed the awful majesty which lay in the representative of Christ on earth.

In the cloistered Benedictine monasteries, where the cowled

monks walk with heads bowed in silence, their eyes fixed upon the ground, something of the ancient Roman rituals has survived. It is not only the large gravity of the monks, whose faces, like the faces of the Roman augurs, are concealed: there is also the Roman sense of order, and the Roman desire for peace, and the Roman conception that idleness is the greatest of curses. Yet here again mercy must be shown to the fainthearted: "On feeble or delicate brothers such a labor or art is to be imposed that they shall neither be idle nor shall they be so oppressed by the violence of labor as to be driven to take to flight. Their weakness is to be taken into consideration by the abbot." So it was that when a monk fell ill, all the established rules were set aside: he was allowed to read such books as he demanded, he could eat meat (which was never given to the other monks), and every possible care was given to his body—that body which he had severely mortified in the monastery.

The monks lived their lives in a perpetual Lent, with the result that Benedict finds it difficult to discover how they should behave themselves when Lent arrives: there must be even greater care, greater solemnity, greater awareness of their sins, fasting even more, offering of their own will something more to God. "They shall restrict their bodies in food, drink, sleep, talkativeness and merrymaking, and with the joy of a spiritual desire they shall await the holy Easter." It is a grim picture, and Benedict does not make it any the less grim when he observes, at the conclusion of the paragraph concerning the perpetual Lent of the monks: "All things are to be done according to the will of the abbot."

But here and there in those rules an occasional tenderness emerges. When guests come, all is holiday. True, the holiday has little enough of merrymaking; but there is a sense of the blessedness of all strangers, all arrivals and departures. When he speaks of the coming of the guest, Benedict forgets the rigid rules, for is not each guest the pattern of Christ:

All guests who come shall be received as though they were Christ: for He Himself said: "I was a stranger and ye took me in." To all guests fitting honor shall be shown, but most of all to servants of the faith and to pilgrims. When, therefore, a guest is announced, the prior or the brothers shall run to meet him, with every office of love. And first they shall pray together, and thus they shall be joined together in peace. Which kiss of peace shall not first be offered, unless a prayer have preceded; on account of the wiles of the devil. In the salutation itself, moreover, all humility shall be exhibited. In the case of all guests arriving or departing: with inclined head or prostrating of the whole body upon the ground, Christ, who is also received in them, shall be adored. (Benedict, *Regula*, 3.)

And so Benedict goes on to discuss the quiet adoration of the guest, how water is pressed into his hand, for he must be tired after the journey, and his feet are washed by the monks and by the abbot in congregation with the words: "We have received, O Lord, Thy loving-kindness in the midst of Thy temple." Even the fasts may be broken on the arrival of the guest, and if the guests are poor, then all the more worthily must they be attended, "for in them Christ is the more." Special kitchens are, of course, set aside for the guests far from the places where the monks might ordinarily be found, yet if a monk should pass them, he "shall salute them humbly, and ask a blessing of them, and say he is not allowed to speak with them."

Benedict was determined that the monks should live hard, and perhaps there is no way of obtaining that inner peace he demanded except by a stern asceticism. Since everything was provided for the monks, it could be expected of them that they should worship God with all their strength; and implicit throughout Benedict's account of them is their strenuous worship. As for their asceticism, they are to live almost as Benedict lived at Subiaco. Their beds must be hard. They were to possess only two gowns, a fur-lined cowl in winter and a plain one for summer. Apparently, they were to be naked under their gowns, for Benedict says that they shall be provided with suitable loin-clothes when they go on a journey, and says nothing of loin-clothes worn in the monastery: all he mentions is a loin-binder, which may have been no more than a wide strip of cloth, rather like those which are worn by boxers and ballet dancers. They were to have shoes, the cheapest available, a handkerchief, a needle, a pen, a knife, a tablet to write on. "All excuse of necessity shall be removed," says Benedict ominously, and he quotes the Pauline injunction, which was borrowed by Karl Marx with surprising effect: "For there is given unto each man according to his need." Benedict seems to have recognized the alarming plenitude of most men's needs, and suggests that the beds be carefully examined for hidden property.

The ceremony of initiation was strangely homespun. When a son is presented by a noble to the monastery, he makes a petition with his own hand in the name of the saint whose relics lie within the altar, and then the petition is placed in the hand of the boy and the altar cloth is wrapped over the hand. This is the sign that he has offered himself to the monastery. From that moment, says Benedict, "let him know that he shall not have power even over his own body." The same ritual, with slight changes, occurred at the initiation of poor monks. Thereafter the boy must be wholly obedient to the abbot: he may not travel an inch outside the territory of the monastery without the abbot's permission; every hour of the day he is at the beck and call of the abbot, whom he must "obey willingly and with decorum."

Benedict lived at a time of incredible strain, when the Empire was ruled by the wise Theodoric, but seemed incapable of meeting the attacks of Belisarius. There was danger everywhere. The whole of the Mediterranean was in ferment. The Vandals were established in North Africa and brigands were everywhere in Italy. When Benedict said:

"There is no need for the monks to wander about outside: it is not at all good for their souls," he might have added: "It is also extremely dangerous." In that time, so extraordinarily like our own, danger had become a commonplace, it was something men tasted in their food and breathed in the air. So he ruled strictly. The monks might drink their half liter of wine a day, but even this might be taken from them if they were late for supper. Wine was the only solace. The rest was hardness: the children were whipped if they made the slightest mistake in singing the psalms, the monks rebuked if they paused in their labors, and if they paused too often they too were whipped. For the crime of possessing any object other than those specifically laid down by the abbot, the monk might be cursed with *anathemas* and made to lie prostrate at the abbot's pleasure.

The Benedictine tradition of learning seems not to have existed in Benedict's day: for the most part the monks were farmers, builders, beekeepers, architects, or men at prayer. There are times in the rule when Benedict seems to share Francis's horror of learning, and it is possible that the last words of the rule were added at a later time. They read: "Thou who dost hasten to the celestial fatherland, perform with Christ's aid this rule written out as the least of beginnings, and then at length under God's protection thou wilt come to the greater things: the summits of learning and virtue." It was uncharacteristic of Benedict that he should have invoked learning; it was characteristic of him that he should have regarded the rule as "the least of beginnings," very much as Thomas Aquinas regarded the *Summa Theologica* as a kind of introductory lecture for babies. It was not the least of beginnings; and Gregory the Great, who considered that the rule was divinely inspired, who followed it through his life and gave it the impetus by which it spread through all Christendom, poured scorn on those who believed the rule was hard, if only because Hell offered a harder punishment. The rule remained. The monasteries were to grow; and the learning, which Benedict half despised, was to become a characteristic of the Benedictine monks in the future, until their black cowls became as familiar as the black ink of medieval manuscripts. More than any other orders, they determined the shape of the Catholic future; and the monasteries with their august doorkeepers, the hosts of boys who addressed their superiors as "*nonni*," which means "father," and who continually tripped over their gowns and slept in beds near their masters, who thus kept a watchful eye on them, the abbot who was rarely seen and who emerged only at moments of majesty, the psalms sung almost perpetually, and the gardens and farmyards kept clean as new pins—it was through these monasteries that the Western tradition was kept alive; and if once again our traditions should fail, only the return to the monasteries is likely to save us.

Perhaps it was the very hardness of the rule interpreted humanly that allowed it to survive. The triple vow of *stabilitas*, perpetual adherence to the order, *conversio morum*, monastic observance, and *obedientia coram Deo et sanctis ejus*, obedience to the abbot as representative of God, ensured its survival. Yet in a sense such vows were not hard to make, and when Gregory wrote of divine servitude being at once the least and the hardest of all servitudes, he was perhaps repeating the words of Benedict, who had no love for hardness for its own sake. Once, when he came upon a hermit with an exaggerated sense of asceticism chaining himself to a rock, Benedict said: "Break your chains. The true servant of Christ is chained not to rocks by iron, but by righteousness to Christ."

Benedict began his life like a raging hermit: he was to end his life like a king, ruling over thousands of men. But throughout his life there ran a common thread: the unchanging belief that men should be allowed to live in peace, the desire to find a machine which would give them this blessing. The Benedictine monastery was such a machine. There, with learning and labor, a man could live out his life in that *summa quies* which is the greatest of all blessings. The Archbishop of Salerno, who was trained at Monte Cassino, gave him the title of *"Fundator placidae quietis,"* the founder of a placid peace. It was a deserved title. Cardinal Newman spoke of the Benedictines with a dying fall in his cadences. He spoke of the monks as "having neither hope nor fear of anything below; in daily prayer, daily bread, and daily work, one day being just like another, except that it was one step nearer than the day before it to that great Day which would swallow up all days, the day of everlasting rest." In this he was wrong. There were no dying cadences in the lives of the Benedictines. They lived for a perfect peace, but strenuously, as we must.

VIII. ❦ GREGORY:
THE PROUD WARRIOR

THE PATTERN OF THE CHRISTIAN FATHERS CON-
tinually repeats itself. Jerome derives from Ignatius;
Augustine from Tertullian; Gregory from Ambrose;
Francis from Bernard. Ambrose towers, but he lacks
the weight of Gregory, who spoke with an even greater authority. They are so strangely similar that sometimes when
reading the life of Gregory we remember that we have read
it all before, in a book dealing with another age, another dis-
pensation of providence: only, as we read on, the figure of
Ambrose grows dimmer, until he seems to be contained in
the massive figure of his successor. Both were patricians, both
lost their fathers when they were young, both grew up at a
time of desperate wars, both were hot-tempered and vigorous
and steeped in the Roman tradition, and both were proud and
delighted in their power, and they wrote like angels, and
were restless, and could see no hope of rest in their lives. In
any age they would have placed their mark on their times.
There was, however, one important difference. Ambrose was
fundamentally humble in spite of his show of pride; Gregory
was proud, and knew it and wrestled with pride, like Jacob
wrestling with the angel.

It is one of the characteristics of the Fathers of the Church
that nearly all of them lost their own fathers when they were
young. On Gregory in his teens the shadow of his dead father
weighed heavily. The old senator, who had suffered in the
wars against Totila, was a man with an imposing presence,
with a long face and a tall forehead. He seems to have been

enormously wealthy, with large estates in Sicily which descended to the son, and a palace on the Caelian Hill, and he was deeply respected for the soundness of his judgment and his cautiousness. He bore the imperial name of Gordianus, and John the Deacon, who saw a painting of him in the ninth century, speaks of his air of nobility and the honesty of his expression as he stood in his chestnut-colored gown. Gregory was made in the image of his father. He had small yellow-brown eyes, with long arched eyebrows so delicate that they seemed to have been painted on; a long nose with open nostrils; full lips; and a prominent chin which bore a tawny beard. His expression was usually one of intense concentration, the eyes flickering and alive. He became bald early, though a thick fringe of yellowish hair hung over his ears. People remembered the intelligence of the domed forehead, the flickering eyes, and the beauty of the long hands. He bore himself with a deep sense of dignity, as befitted the descendant of many senators.

He could hardly have been born at a more angry time. In his childhood Rome changed hands over and over again, now falling to Totila, now to Belisarius. He was fourteen in the year 554 when Narses became viceroy of Italy under the Emperor Justinian, who ruled the Empire from Constantinople. Then at last, with the Gothic dominion over Italy destroyed, there followed a few brief years of peace. But Rome was no longer the Rome that Ambrose and Augustine had known. The pagan temples were closed and falling into ruin. The city of the Caesars was in process of becoming the city of the Popes; and it was Gregory's fate to be born at the time of transition. From this he drew much of his strength and many of his weaknesses. He seems to have had little schooling, except at home, and even if he studied at college, he would have learned little, for scholarship was in full decay. Gregory never learned Greek. Except for Vergil, he knew little about Roman poets. According to Paul the Deacon he was well versed in grammar, rhetoric, and dialectics: but his grammar is often shocking, his knowledge of dialectics faulty: only in rhetoric was he superb, and this he learned from his reading of Augustine and Ambrose, his favorite authors until the end of his life. Of science he knew nothing: when he asked himself why the sea did not rise and overflow the land, since the rivers were always filling them, he appealed not to Aristotle but to Clement, who in turn appealed to King Solomon. One of his biographers called him *arte philosophus*, but it would have been more accurate to call him *arte monasticus*. But in one learned study he was proficient: he knew law; yet even here he showed no more knowledge than is necessary to the son of a great landowner perpetually drawing up accounts of mortgages and entails. Grave in speech and prematurely old, bearing one of the greatest names in Rome, he began to climb in the *ordo honorum*, being remarked for the clarity of his mind and his determination to get things done. Suddenly, at the age of 33, he found himself appointed Prefect, or mayor, of Rome.

No one knows why he was given this high office. Like Ambrose, who became governor of a province at a comparably early age, Gregory may have owed his appointment to high connections. The Prefect of Rome wore the purple cloak of the *triumphator* and rode in a chariot drawn by four snow-white horses. The whole economy of Rome depended upon his will: the grain supplies, the free doles for the poor, the construction of new buildings, baths, sewers, and riverbanks, all these had to be decided by the Prefect. He worked in close contact with the Pope. His appointment, which occurred in the year 573, coincided with another Lombard invasion, the death of a Pope, and the death of Narses. The road to Constantinople was cut. On Gregory's shoulders there fell some of the burdens of the dead Pope and the dead Viceroy.

At some time in his youth Gregory came in contact with disciples of Benedict. The character of the old abbot pleased him. Later, he decided to model himself after the stern master of monasteries. As soon as his tenure of the prefecture expired, he spent the greater part of his fortune in founding seven monasteries, distributed the rest in alms for the poor, then laid aside all vestiges of rank and transformed his palace in the Caelian Hill into a monastery dedicated to St. Andrew. He exchanged the purple toga for the coarse robe of a monk and began to live with extraordinary asceticism, eating only raw fruit and vegetables, praying most of the night, wearing a hairshirt, throwing himself into the manifold duties of an abbot. He had never been strong, and now unceasing fasting ruined his digestion and played havoc with his heart. The only emblem of his former wealth which he continued to prize was a silver serving dish: on this his mother sent him daily a few shreds of raw vegetables.

In the end he gave the dish away to a shipwrecked sailor begging alms. The sailor, as he might have expected, was an angel in disguise. That was the first miracle. Other miracles were not slow in coming. One day a monk called Merulus lay dying in the monastery of St. Andrew. Gregory loved him and kept watch over him. Then Merulus said he saw a crown of white flowers descending from heaven and falling on his head: shortly afterwards the monk died. Some time later, when his body was exhumed, there came from it, says Gregory, "the odor of all flowers blended together." For the rest of his life Gregory was determined that "the odor of all flowers" should be associated with his name.

In later years Gregory looked back on the three years he spent in the monastery as the happiest of his life. He had no desire to leave the monastery, and probably would not have left it if the times had not been so dangerous. There were more threats of invasion, this time from the Franks. The Pope, Benedict I, sorely needed an assistant with knowledge of public affairs, and Gregory found himself appointed "seventh deacon," which meant that he was in ecclesiastical charge of one of the seven districts of Rome. In the same year there was a plague, followed by a tremendous rainfall which suggested that the Day of the Flood was about to return, or perhaps it was the Day of Judgment. In the hot Roman summer Benedict died. His successor, Pelagius II, realized that Rome could survive only with reinforcements. An embassy was sent to Constantinople, with no success. A second embassy was sent, with Gregory as *apocrisiarius* or permanent ambassador to the Court of Byzantium. He had been Prefect, monk, seventh deacon, and ambassador in the space of five years.

In Constantinople Gregory was in his element. He admired the Emperor Tiberius, a tall, deeply religious man whose gray eyes stare down from many mosaics, but he was unable to gather reinforcements for the defense of Rome. The Eastern Empire was fighting against Persia, and military reserves were needed in the capital to put down the perpetual revolts of the Byzantine aristocracy. Gregory petitioned repeatedly, with no success. The courtiers flattered him. He paid no attention to them, but searched out some of the people close to the Emperor. It was the time of Santa Sophia, great pageants, week-long feasts, prolonged theological disputes. Tiberius died and was succeeded by Maurice, a short bandy-legged and bald general of the armies, who was raised to the purple only because he was known to be honest. Still the feasts and pageants went on, but gradually Gregory found himself more and more removed from Court circles. He still petitioned for reinforcements, but none came. Altogether, he spent nearly seven years in Constantinople, never learning a word of Greek, writing studiously, never tiring of wandering round the city which shone with a splendor Rome had long ago forgotten; and if he had nothing to show for the experience, he had at least gained a knowledge of the world and its chicanery. He was recalled to Rome in 586. The parting gift of the Emperor Maurice to the ambassador was the head of St. Luke and the arm of St. Andrew, and these Gregory placed in his own monastery on the Caelian Hill.

In Rome he resumed control of the monastery. He was now over forty and his habits were fixed: an ascetic, with the man-

ners of an aristocrat, suffering horribly from diarrhea and
skin eruptions, often having to spend the whole day in bed,
in love with the Book of Job, whose hero he resembled. There
was a hardness in his soul, and he was beginning to write
those stern, thundering letters that characterized his later
years, letters of a prodigious violence. Perhaps it was the
change of atmosphere, the sickness in the air which hung
over Rome. "I am all honey and stings," he said once: it was
true enough, not of any particular period, but throughout
his life. He does not change. He is the same vitriolic and
peaceful person when he goes as legate to the Court of Constantinople as when he sits in a corner of his palace in Rome,
peering up at the window for a sight of the Uncircumscribed
Light. He talks often of "the chink of contemplation, through
which we see the glory of angelic brightness," but there is no
blaze. Birds, too, he describes at length, and enviously, and
never is he so tender as when he speaks of "the hinds in the
high hills." He was a man of fierce passions which he tamed
with the utmost difficulty; and something of that explosive-
ness is visible in the long diary known as the *Moralia* which
he began at Constantinople and completed in Rome.

It is a pity that the *Moralia* is not more widely read. The
patient reader prepared to wade through the two thousand
pages of the magnificent translation in the Oxford *Library of
the Fathers* published a hundred years ago is amply rewarded.
No one else could be as dull as Gregory when he was determined to be dull. The number of the hobby-horses is
legion; there are moments when Gregory seems to be riding
all of them at once. Theoretically, the book is an extended
sermon on the Book of Job. Every sentence, almost every
word, is analyzed, weighed, compared with neighboring
words or with remote texts. He is convinced that Job is a
prophetical book; and all that distinguishes Job from Christ
or the Church is carefully wished away. But as the work
progresses, changing temper, growing sterner and more inflexible toward the end until it bursts in a crackling fire of

indignation with the final summary of the character of Leviathan, who is the devil and the proud man caught in the devil's toils, we see that he has put into it, subtly disguised, his most intimate passing thoughts; it is the day-book of his own toils, his own pride, his griefs, his sorrows, and his struggles with words.

Gregory is said to write Latin badly. It is true enough. He had the greatest contempt for classical authors, he never quotes them, and even when he abuses them, he does not mention them by name or give any indication of what it is he most objects to in them. But against his will he absorbed them, for they came to him in the very rhythms of Jerome's Vulgate, which he read assiduously, with the result that he writes a more sensuous prose than any of the Fathers when he is at his best, without the lushness of Augustine or the rhetoric of Jerome. Here and there in the *Moralia*, perhaps thirty or forty times altogether, there are long passages where he speaks gloriously. There are innumerable odd phrases that glitter and flash, as when he says: "In this golden cup of Babylon Eve was the first who was made drunken of her own accord," or "The alleviation of our darkness lies in the just and incomprehensible power of the Creator being called to mind, which both never leaves the wicked without taking vengeance, and surpasses the righteousness of the just by the boundlessness of its incomprehensibility." But it is in the longer passages, where he can take breath, where the breath itself takes the words under its wing, that he reaches astonishing heights, speaking with a pure voice, all the stumbling blocks removed. More than halfway through this interminable book he comes upon the text of Job: "He heareth not the cry of the exactor." It is not a very rewarding text, and for some reason which he hardly troubles to explain, the memory of Gideon's war occurs to him at the same time as the thought of the holy martyrs; and quite suddenly, without any excuse, he launches into one of the most beautiful of all the fragments that can be extracted from the *Moralia*:

Our Martyrs came armed under their Leader to battle, but armed with trumpets, with pitchers, with lamps. And they sounded with their trumpets, when preaching; they broke their pitchers, when exposing their bodies to dissolution by the swords of the enemy in their suffering; they shone forth with lamps, when after the dissolution of their bodies they flashed forth with miracles. And their enemies were presently put to flight, because when they beheld the bodies of dead Martyrs glittering with miracles, they were overpowered by the light of truth, and believed that which they had impugned. They sounded therefore with the trumpets, that the pitchers might be broken; the pitchers were broken, that the lamps might appear; the lamps appeared, that the enemies might be put to flight. That is, the Martyrs preached, till their bodies were dissolved in death; their bodies were dissolved in death, that they might shine forth with miracles; they shone forth with miracles, that they might overthrow their enemies with divine light; so that they might no longer stand up and resist God, but submit to, and be afraid of, Him. (Gregory, *Moralia*, XXX, 76.)

This is surely one of the great passages of declamation, and though the logic of it is shaped like an hourglass, and the Martyrs are almost drowned in the glow of a miraculous shining, and what he says is hardly more than: "The martyrs shine in glory," the organ notes sound with implicit purity, and a host of other musical instruments can be heard in the distance. He is not always so complex, or so symphonic. On the text; "Which doeth great things and unsearchable, marvelous things without number," Gregory writes of the most marvelous of all things—the resurrection of the flesh. He is now simple, studied, and urgent. He is not so much attempting to convince as pointing to the daily miracle of existence, yet here too his music takes the form of successive choruses, so that we begin to believe that the songs attributed to Gregory may well have been written by him:

Who may see to the bottom of the marvellous works of God, how He made all things of nothing, how the very framework of the world is arranged with a marvellous mightiness of power, and the heaven hung above the atmosphere and the earth balanced above the abyss, how this whole universe consists of things visible and invisible, how He created man, so to say, gathering together in a small compass another world, yet a world of reason; how constituting this world of soul and flesh, He mixed the breath and the clay by an unsearchable disposal of His might? A part, then, of these things we know, and a part we even are. Yet we omit to admire them, because those things which are full of marvels for an investigation deeper than we can reach, have become cheap from custom in the eyes of men.

Hence it comes to pass that if a dead man is raised to life, all men spring up in astonishment. Yet every day one that had no being is born, and no man wonders, though it is plain to all, without doubt, that it is a greater thing for that to be created, which was without being, than for a man to be restored. Because the dry rod of Aaron budded, all men were in astonishment; every day a tree is produced from the dry earth, and the virtue residing in dust is turned into wood, and no man wonders. Because five thousand men were filled with five loaves, all men were in astonishment that the food should be multiplied in their teeth; every day the grains of seed that are sown are multiplied in a fulness of ears, and no man wonders. All men wondered to see water once turned into wine. Every day the earth's moisture being drawn into the roots of the vine, is turned by the grape into wine, and no man wonders. Full of wonder then are all the things that men never think to wonder at, because, as we have before said, they are by habit become dull to the consideration of them; but when he said, *which doeth great things*, he did well in immediately adding, *and unsearchable*. (Gregory, *Moralia*, VI, 18.)

It is possible, and very likely, that Milton, who read deeply in Gregory's *Moralia*, remembered these lines when he came to write the last chorus of *Samson Agonistes*.

But we have not yet done with Gregory on the subject of the resurrection of the flesh. It was a subject so close to Gregory's heart that he repeats the theme twice in the *Moralia*, almost in the same words; and one of his most famous controversies is concerned with the subject. When Gregory was in Constantinople as papal legate, he met the aged Patriarch of Constantinople, Eutychius, who had written a book maintaining that the body of our resurrection would be impalpable to the touch. Gregory stoutly denied this. As Gregory relates the incident in the *Moralia*, his own reasoning was perfectly clear, for "how can there be a true resurrection, if there may not be true flesh? so that plain reason suggests, that if it shall not be true flesh, assuredly it will not be a true resurrection." So he pressed Eutychius with the words of Jesus, *Handle me and see; for a spirit hath not flesh and bones, as ye see Me have.* The Patriarch, already nearly on his deathbed, replied that Jesus did this in order to remove all doubt from the minds of the disciples. "What!" cried Gregory. "Are we then to doubt of the very thing which cured the doubt of the disciples?" There followed a battle of texts. Eutychius quoted: *Flesh and blood shall not inherit the kingdom of God.* Gregory thereupon pointed out that the word "flesh" has two senses, meaning either "according to nature" or "according to sin and corruption." He was exceptionally good at discovering differing meanings in words—about a tenth of the *Moralia* is a monument to his resourcefulness in that direction —but Eutychius did not wholly concur. The quarrel reached the ears of the Emperor Tiberius, who summoned the disputants into his presence. They argued their opinions before the Emperor, who inclined to Gregory's opinion and ordered the Patriarch's book to be burned. Shortly afterwards the old Patriarch died, but in the brief interval before his death he was visited by the friends of Gregory, who told a strange story. Lying in bed the Patriarch would pluck a little fold of skin on his hand before their eyes, saying: "I confess that we shall all rise again in the flesh." Gregory quotes the story, and evidently approves of the old man's admission of defeat; but it is just as likely that there was a malicious gleam in his eyes as he plucked up a fold of aged skin. He may have been saying to himself: "This is old worn-out flesh I shall be appareled in, and what use is that to me?" As in so many of the doctrinal quarrels of that age, a deep seriousness informed the contestants, for the stakes were high: the stakes were the bodies of men in the kingdom of heaven.

There is a quiet passion in Gregory's determination to believe, even in what was against all belief. The child born from the invisible seed, the dead becoming invisible dust—these arguments offered him comfort, and when he writes of them the prose flows smoothly and with an assurance rare at other times. "Where is the evidence of the resurrection?" he asks, and answers that it is everywhere, in all the seasons, at every moment, each day proclaiming the event:

What does the universe every day, but imitate in its elements our resurrection? Thus by the lapse of the minutes of the day the temporal light itself as it were dies, when, the shade of night coming on, that light which was beheld is withdrawn from sight, and it daily rises again as it were, when the light that was withdrawn from our eyes, upon the night being suppressed is renewed afresh. For the progress of the seasons too, we see the shrubs lose the greenness of their foliage, and cease from putting forth fruit; and of a sudden as if from dried up wood, by a kind of resurrection coming we see the leaves burst forth, the fruit grow big, and the whole tree clothed with renewed beauty; we unceasingly behold the small seeds of trees committed to the moistness of the ground, wherefrom not long afterwards we behold large trees arise, and bring forth leaves and fruit.

Let us then consider the little seed of any tree whatever which is thrown into the ground, for a tree to be produced therefrom, and let us take in, if we are capable of it, where in that exceeding littleness of the seed that most enormous tree was buried, which proceeded from it? where was the wood? where the bark? where the verdure of the foliage? where the abundance of the fruit? Was there anything of the kind perceived in the seed, when it was thrown into the ground? And yet by the secret Artificer of all things ordering all in a wonderful manner, both in the softness of the seed there lay buried the roughness of the bark, and in its tenderness there lay hidden the strength of its timber, and in its dryness fertility of productiveness. What wonder, then, if that finest dust, which to our eyes is resolved into the elements, He, when He is minded, fashioneth again into the human being, Who from the finest seeds resuscitates the largest trees? And so, seeing that we have been created reasoning beings, we ought to collect the hope of our own resurrection from the mere aspect and contemplation of the objects of nature. (Gregory, *Moralia*, XIV, 70.)

Much earlier in the book, when Gregory presented the same arguments, he admitted that the resurrection of the flesh can never be comprehended by the reason, and he admits too that "when the dust of the human flesh is thought on, the mind of some is shaken and despairs of the time when dust shall return to flesh." He was not among them; yet despair moves through his prose, and no one can be certain he believed himself among the Elect. As always, there is a hint of violence in his argument: which is not surprising, since he was a violent, tempestuous man. He was as violent in action as he was in thought. Once, shortly after his return from Constantinople, when he was living as abbot in the monastery formed of the ancestral palace on the Caelian Hill, one of the monks, called Justus, confessed on his deathbed that against all the rules of the Benedictine Order he had hoarded three gold coins. The monk was closely attached to Gregory. He was a doctor and had cared with great devotion for Gregory during the saint's bouts of sickness. When the story of the hoarding was told to Gregory, he gave summary orders that the monk should be left to die alone. None were to comfort him, not even his own brother: and if he should ask as he lay dying why none came to him, he should be told that he was held in utter detestation by the monks. When he died, his body was to be thrown into a ditch or dunghill, and the three gold coins were to be thrown after him, while the monks cried in chorus: "Thy money perish with thee!"

Though the story has a hideous violence about it, Gregory regarded his own actions as merciful. He hoped that punishment in this world would bring redemption in the next. As he tells the story in the *Dialogues*, there is a formidable sequel. For a month the monks, alarmed by the fate of Justus, came creeping to the abbot begging to be allowed to perform acts of penance, for they too had kept a few trifles against the law of the monastery. Gregory found himself continually thinking about the fate of Justus. He summoned one of the monks and said: "For some time Justus has been in the fiery torment, and now I believe we should show some charity, and so I command that for the next thirty days the Sacrifice should be offered for him." This was accordingly done, and Gregory gradually forgot the incident altogether. Then one day the monk Coposius, the brother of Justus, came running to Gregory, saying he had seen his brother in a dream, and Justus said: "Hitherto I have been miserable, but now all is well with me, for today I received Communion." It was only then that Gregory realized it was exactly thirty days since he had ordered the offering of the Sacrifice. Gregory was content. The sorrow of the monk's dying hours had saved him from a sorrow which would have been eternal; and Peter the Deacon, who had listened to the story carefully, said: "What a wonderful and pretty tale!"

The violence of Gregory overflows into the *Moralia*. It could hardly be otherwise, for Gregory's character was formed when he was young. In one of those disconnected sayings which Bettina von Arnim heard from the lips of the poet Hölderlin, then in his dotage, there occurs the sentence: "Murder flows from the divine." The words would have been clearly comprehended by Gregory; and he would have added that after the murder the wounds are healed by a divine mercy, and the dead Hamlet arises at last, to run laughing off the stage.

What can one say of Gregory's violence? It was something innate in the man. It was his strength and his weakness: he is the athlete of God throwing thunderbolts rather than javelins. Though part of him talks softly of the windows of the soul, another part is obsessed with armor, breastplates, all the accouterments of the ancient Hebrew warriors, the great wrestlers. He seems always to be wrestling, always exerting main force. Only when he talks of the Fathers, the patriarchs of the past ages, does a kind of quiet fall on him; but even then he must exert his muscles a little, and when he comes to describe them we are aware that he has forced the issues; yet the description of them contemplating the Creator only to turn their faces away is one of the greatest sentences he wrote:

Thus it was that the old Fathers, who as far as the frailty of human nature permitted it, contemplated the sight of the Creator with uplifted soul, but foreseeing Him destined to become incarnate at the end of the world, they as it were turned away their eyes to the ground from gazing at the rays of the sun; and they as it were descend from highest to lowest, whilst they see Him to be God above all things, and Man among all things; and whilst they behold Him, Who was to suffer and die for mankind, by which same death they know that they are themselves restored and fashioned anew to life, as it were like the eagle, after gazing at the rays of the sun, they seek their food upon the dead Body. (Gregory, *Moralia*, XI, 48.)

Again and again, reading Gregory, we remember that we have heard that note before: it is the same note that we find in Milton's prose. The muscles ripple under the skin; the tremendous contest is perpetually engaged; and this long sentence, which moves forward under the impulse of a wonderful tenderness, comes to its conclusion like a ship which crosses the ocean and slides exactly into port. It is magnificent prose, but it is also magnificent poetry.

The temper of the times demanded that theologians should also be poets. Since the Old Testament was regarded as a continuing series of prophecies of the coming of Christ, every sentence had to be searched for an improbable Christian meaning, sometimes with strange results. When Gregory came upon the text in Ezekiel: *One among them was clothed in linen, with a writer's ink-horn at his reins*, it was perfectly clear to him that "the one clothed in linen" was Christ, but how explain the ink-horn at the reins? Gregory is clearly puzzled. He dodges the issue for a while, and then suddenly leaps upon the solution. The word "reins" means "backside," therefore "something coming after," therefore the phrase refers to "the writings of the New Testament which He, having departed, carried in an ink-horn behind him." Nothing could be easier, and Gregory's whoop of enjoyment at the success of discovery can almost be heard over the ages.

But the method Gregory followed—a method that continued to be followed throughout the Middle Ages—has much to commend it. The Old Testament provided a fruitful source of metaphors. By quoting from the Old Testament, by attempting to discover the link between the old and the new, by seeing mysteries where everything was plain, by coloring the New Testament with the richer colors of the Old Testament, drama and depth were gained. Just as a modern poet like William Butler Yeats will describe his own time with amazing accuracy by conjuring up a vision of Byzantium, so the Church Fathers brought Christ closer to themselves when setting him against the background of the Old Testament. A phrase from the Book of Job could be detached from its setting, impregnated with new meanings, and be all the richer, for the poetic process was at work and the final product possessed an authenticity of its own. Here are three examples of Gregory's extraordinary poetic improvisations on the Old Testament:

The stars of rain

Did not Moses appear in heaven as a star of rain? Did he not shine above and water the hearts of sinners? Did not Isaiah appear in heaven as a star of rain? Did he not hold up the light of truth and water the thirst of the unbelieving with his prophecies? Were not Jeremiah, and the other prophets, placed as it were in heaven like stars of rain, who, when exalted on the high eminence of preaching, while they dared boldly to reprove the depravity of sinners, kept down as it were the dust of human blindness, by watering it with the drops of their words? But since the judgments of heaven take away from this present life the souls of these persons, enclosed in this corruptible flesh, the stars of rain are withdrawn as it were from the face of heaven. And the stars return into their hidden places, when the souls of the Saints, having completed their courses, are laid up in the treasuries of the Inner Disposal. (Gregory, *Moralia*, XXVII, 12.)

Scarlet and blue, and fine linen

Moses was commanded by the voice of God to weave curtains of fine linen, and scarlet, and blue, for the covering of the Holy of Holies within. And he was ordered to spread, for the covering of the tabernacle, curtains of goats' hair, and skins, to sustain the rain, and wind, and dust. What then do we understand by the skins and goats' hair, with which the tabernacle is covered, but the gross minds of men, which are sometimes, hard though they be, placed on high in the Church by the secret judgment of God? What is signified by the blue, scarlet, and fine linen, but the life of holy men, delicate, but brilliant? And while it is carefully concealed in the tabernacle under goats' hair and skins, its beauty is preserved entire. For in order that the fine linen may shine, the scarlet glitter, and the blue be resplendent with azure brilliance, the skins and goats' hair endure the rains, and the winds, and the dust from above. . . . What splendor or brightness would the scarlet and blue displace should the dust light on, and defile them? Let the strong texture of the goats' hair, then, be placed above, to resist dust; the brightness of the blue, fitted for ornament, be placed beneath. . . . Let not him who now gleams with spiritual brightness within Holy Church, murmur against his superior, who is employed in worldly business. For if thou glitterest securely within, like scarlet, why dost thou blame the goats' hair with which thou art protected? (Gregory, *Moralia*, XXV, 39.)

Out of whose womb came the ice

Abraham was heaven, Isaac was heaven, Jacob was heaven. But because the persecutors of the Lord, the high priests of the Jews, who were frozen with the torpor of unbelief, sprang from the race of those ancestors, the frost came, as it were, from heaven, because the frozen herd of unbelievers came forth from the lofty offspring of the Saints. For when Caiaphas was born from Abraham, what else was it, but that ice came forth from heaven? Satan also came forth as if ice from the womb of God, because the teacher of iniquity came forth, frozen with the torpor of sin, from the warmth of His mysteries. (Gregory, *Moralia*, XXIX, 55.)

There are times, of course, when the attempt to pour the new wine into old bottles becomes intolerably dull: he will translate the Biblical names, make them mean anything he wants them to mean, and go humming happily after butterflies. But surprisingly often he hits the mark. It is all a prodigious improvisation. Coming by chance on the word "leaves," he announces: "What is man but a leaf which fell in Paradise from the tree?" It is a blinding flash, soon over, for there is another quarry to be hunted, a page to be turned, the scribes are waiting to take down the words hurriedly dictated. He is like an artist who absorbs his sitter, devours him whole, to disgorge him on canvas; and the face on the canvas is at once a portrait of the artist and a portrait of the sitter. Everything becomes Gregory.

The danger lay there: pride dogged him. He was very conscious of his sin, for he speaks about pride so often that he was clearly obsessed with it. He sees pride in all its moods. There are so many references to it in the *Moralia* that one derives the impression that he is examining it from all sides. "When pride reaches up her arms," he says, "then is she truly abased." He watches pride carefully. He knows the glint in the eyes, the inward laughter, the way the proud smile before they speak. He wrote: "It is peculiar to the arrogant, even before they speak, that they always believe they are going to say some wonderful thing, and they anticipate their own words by their own admiration, because with all their acuteness they are not sensible how great a folly is their very pride." There are a hundred similar observations, but the greatest statement on pride, and one of the most magnificent things Gregory ever wrote, occurs when he came to comment on the text: *He is king over all the sons of pride.* It is as though Gregory had hoarded his deeper knowledge until he had come to a text fit for the occasion:

Pride, which we have called the root of vices, far from being satisfied with the extinction of one virtue, raises itself up against all the members of the soul, and as an universal and deadly disease corrupts the whole body. When pride assaults the mind, a kind of tyrant closely invests, as it were, a besieged city: and the wealthier is anyone he has seized, the more harshly does he rise up in his authority; because the more largely is the business of virtue transacted without humility, the more widely does pride exercise its sway. But whoever has with enslaved mind admitted its tyranny within, suffers this loss first of all, that from the eye of his heart being closed, he loses the equitableness of judgment. For even all the good doings of others are displeasing to him, and the things which he has done, even amiss, alone please him. He always looks down on the doings of others, he always admires his own doings; because whatever he has done, he believes that he has done with singular skill; and for that which he performs through desire of glory, he favors himself in his thought; and when he thinks that he surpasses others in all things, he walks with himself along the broad spaces of his thought and silently utters his own praises. (Gregory, *Moralia*, XXXIV, 48.)

The portrait of the proud man walking along the broad spaces of his thought, silently uttering his own praises (*per lata cogitationum spatia secum deambulans, alaudes suas tacitus clamat*) is fixed forever. Like so much of Gregory's work, it is strangely modern. The medieval theologians were to describe the proud man at length, but never with such terror or such an adequate knowledge. Here for the first time we encounter Hamlet on the ramparts of Elsinore. It is clear that Gregory himself suffered from the disease. All his frenzy, the continual urgent letters sent all over Christendom, the determination never to rest for a moment, all these seem to spring from his knowledge of his own pride, from his desperate desire to face the evil and vanquish it. It was not given to him to see God face to face. He had hoped it would be possible, prayed incessantly, examined himself carefully to see whether he was worthy, but at the most there is the crack of light, a faint gleam somewhere. Once, however, in brief and imperfect contemplation, he saw the one face he desired to see. Listen to him as he describes, with what yearning, what helpless desire, the vision of God:

The fire of tribulation is first darted into our mind, from a consideration of our own blindness, in order that all rust of sins may be burnt away. And when the eyes of our heart are purged from sin, that joy of our heavenly home is disclosed to them, that we may first wash away by sorrow that we have done, and afterwards gain in our transports a clearer view of what we are seeking after. For the intervening mist of sin is first wiped away from the eye of the mind, by burning sorrow; and it is then enlightened by the bright coruscations of the boundless light swiftly flashing upon it. At which sight, seen after its measure, it is absorbed in a kind of rapturous security; and carried beyond itself, as though the present life had ceased to be, it is refreshed in a manner by a kind of new being. The mind is then besprinkled with an infusion of heavenly dews from an inexhaustible fountain. It there discerns that it is not sufficient for that enjoyment, to which it has been hurried, and from feeling the Truth, it sees that it does not discern how great that Truth is. And it counts itself to be further removed from this truth, the nearer it approaches it, because unless it beheld it in a certain degree, it would never feel that it was unable really to behold it.

The effort therefore of the mind is driven back, when directed toward it, by the bright encircling of its boundless nature. For filling all things with itself, it encircles all things; and our mind does not expand itself to comprehend that boundless object which encircles it, because the imperfection of its own circumscribed state keeps it within narrow bounds. It accordingly falls back at once to itself, and having seen as it were some traces of truth before it, is recalled to a sense of its own lowliness. But yet this unsubstantial and hasty vision, which results from contemplation, or rather, so to speak, this semblance of a vision, is called the face of God. (Gregory, *Moralia*, XXIV, 11.)

Gregory's powers were large, but he could not see the face of God, however much he desired to. His account stumbles toward the end: he is like a warrior beaten back from the citadel. The splendors of the flashing lights coming from the Boundless Light in sudden rays (*resplendente raptim coruscatione incircumscripti liminis illustratur*) are convincing enough, but nowhere else is he so convincing: and even the infusion of heavenly dew is described according to St. Augustine. Like Benedict, whom he regarded with a devotion he offered to no one except God, he knew that the soul increased in its powers of comprehension according to the harshness of the trials endured. "One must go on, and further," he said, but at the farthest reaches he is always lost.

That strenuous athlete could not fight along all planes at once. "The wild deer on the lofty mountains" escaped the man who was perpetually at odds with the world. His mind was like "the flames of torches which burn and are dark." He wrote as though the earth was shaking in the trumpet blasts which announce the Last Judgment. To the Emperor Maurice, who ordered from Constantinople that no ex-soldiers and no civil servants should become monks, because he was afraid they would then owe their only loyalty to Gregory, he wrote: "Amid heavens ablaze and earth ablaze, and elements flashing and crackling with flames: with Angels and Archangels, with Thrones and Dominations, with Principalities and with Powers the tremendous Judge will appear! If when He is forgiving the sins of men, He accuses you of opposing His will therein, what excuse, I beg, will you find?" There was, of course, no excuse; and Gregory simply dispatched a decree *urbe et orbi* countermanding the law of the Emperor. The crackling flames which he saw as he approached the Godhead, and which he saw again rising above Maurice's misdeeds, were ever present. He is always summoning people to remember the Last Judgment with grief and terror. The barbarian invasions had left a foretaste of the Last Judgment, and had not Benedict said to the Bishop of Canossa: "Rome shall never be destroyed by the Gentiles, but shall be shaken by tempests and lightnings, by earthquakes and whirlwinds, and will decay of itself"? Gregory comments: "The mysteries of this prophecy we now behold as clear as day, for in this city we see the walls demolished, houses overturned, churches destroyed by tempestuous winds, and buildings rotten with old age decaying and fallen into ruin." "Perfect fear draws the soul to love," he wrote at another time; and he seems to have been often afraid.

If the *Moralia* is a great work full of willfulness and a strenuous beauty, the *Dialogues* which were to become so famous that he became known as "Gregory of the *Dialogues*" show a loosening of the fibers, a sudden abandonment of strenuous exercise. The *Dialogues* contain the famous account of the life of St. Benedict, from which we derive almost all our knowledge of the monk, but they also contain the most fabulous hodgepodge of miraculous fables ever invented. When writing the *Moralia* he was the pure athlete; when writing the *Dialogues* he is suddenly transformed into an old crone stirring a witches' brew. Something had snapped. Or perhaps nothing had snapped: perhaps he was simply amusing himself seriously with those tales of unauthenticated miracles, impossible terrors, because there were greater miracles and greater terrors in his own soul, and the music of one drowned the music of the other. There was a nun of Portus who lived a chaste life, but was given to relating scandal. When she died she was buried within the church, and the same night the sacristan was honored with a revelation of her dead body lying before the high altar. The body was cut in two, and half of it burned to ashes. The next morning there were the smears of burning on the altar steps. A priest of Valeria, named Stephen, returned one day from a journey, and said carelessly to his servant: "Come, you devil, take off my stockings." Immediately invisible hands began to loosen his garters. The priest, in mortal terror, cried: "Away, foul spirit, away! I spoke not to thee, but to my servant." The devil departed, but the priest saw that his garters were already half untied. The authentic shudder is there; but such stories are normally told by crones, not by pontiffs.

Some of the stories Gregory relates with great glee are as pointless as the stories told by Zen Buddhists; it is conceivable that monks listening to the stories found depths of meaning in pure pointlessness. Some of the stories are brutal, others gay. And it was characteristic of Gregory, who was all stings and honey, that he should have enjoyed them equally. He says that he liked to listen to these stories from old men, and faithfully recorded them in the intervals of attending to the duties of his pontificate, but it is at least as likely that many of them were invented by himself: and some of them suggest the strange flame-lit corners of his own mind. He relates, for example, that Boniface, Bishop of Ferenti, was invited by a certain nobleman to dinner after Mass on the Feast of St. Proculus Martyr. The bishop was about to chant a pontifical grace when, to his complete astonishment, a strolling player with an ape appeared at the door. Worse still, the man was clashing his cymbals together. The bishop was furious at the noise, and cursed the poor player: "Alas, alas, the wretch is dead, the wretch is dead!" the bishop shouted in the uproar. "Here I have come to dinner! Not a word have I yet uttered for the praise of the Lord, and then this fellow comes in with his ape and clashes his cymbals! Go of your charity and give him to eat and drink; but know he is a dead man!" The bishop continued to say grace, and sat down at table, while the strolling player was entertained with food elsewhere. But the next day, as the bishop had prophesied, he was dead—a boulder had fallen off a roof and cracked his skull. The same bishop was once plagued with a swarm of caterpillars in his garden, but he said a prayer over them, gently requested them to depart, and watched them trooping out in formation through the gates.

As Gregory tells these stories, running breathlessly to a conclusion, all the measured terror of the voice which thundered through the *Moralia* is dissolved in a soft holy laughter.

He is tense with excitement when the phantasms of the night appear; he laughs childishly when the devil's blandishments are reproved; his finger wags in rebuke. He notes that the great saint, Isaac the Syrian, who performed many miracles, was as crafty as any faun in the hills, and did so many nonsensical things they were past counting. Then there was the Abbot of Sora, who was murdered by bandits, whereupon the mountains came crashing down over the place where his body lay, "for God could not suffer that the earth should allow the weight of so much holiness." The *tremendum* moved in him; and the same tremendous chords which Ambrose uttered only in grief Gregory uttered in his joy.

Perhaps it was partly fear. There was never any stability in Rome during his life; and the wit of the supreme pontiff was tempered by the knowledge of the leaping flames. Privately, he speaks with utter grief as often as he speaks with composure. "I have lost the deep joy of my quiet," he wrote to the Emperor's sister, "and while I seem outwardly to have risen, I am inwardly debased. Wherefore I grieve that I am driven from the face of my Creator." The same organ note is struck in the sermon he delivered when Rome was ravaged by the plague and in fear of Lombard invasions. He ordered solemn processions to march from one church of Rome to another, and from the pulpit of St. Peter's he thundered:

Fiery swords, which reddened with the blood of mankind, and soon after flowed in streams, were seen in the heavens before Italy became the prey of the Lombards. Be watchful and alert! Those who love God should shout for joy at the end of the world. Those who mourn are they whose hearts are rooted in love for the world, and who neither long for the future life, nor have any foretaste of it within themselves. Every day the earth is visited by fresh calamities. You see how few remain of the ancient population: each day sees us chastened by new afflictions, and unforeseen blows strike us to the ground. The world grows old and hoary, and through a sea of troubles hastens to approaching death. (Gregory, *Homillae in Ezechielem*, II, 8.)

He had said such things before the coming of the Lombards; he would say them again later; and the grief, exploding from the savage words, can still be heard across the centuries, reminding us of our own griefs as we survey a similar age of devastation. "Where is the Senate?" he cried. "Where are the people? The bones are dissolved, the flesh consumed: all the pomp and dignities of the world are gone. The whole mass is boiled away." It is significant that he grieved over the disappearing pomps: like Ambrose—for he resembled in so many ways a fiercer Ambrose—he regretted the ancient symbols, but still adored them; and he was half a Roman senator until the end.

But the somber mood was not continual. Somberness was characteristic of him, and the peculiar quality of it he expressed best of all in the words: "To him who sees the Creator all creation is small indeed." But there were moments when the holy mordant laughter became a smile; and few things in his life are better attested than his quiet remarks to the slaveowner who was offering three young English boys for sale on the Roman marketplace. Gregory saw them, shortly before he became Pope, and was immediately attracted to them. "Alas! alas!" he exclaimed, "that such bright faces should be the slaves of an inward darkness. So beautiful they are, and yet their minds are sick and without God's grace." He asked what nation they came from. "They are Angles," answered the slaveowner. "Yes, indeed," Gregory went on, "they have the appearance of angels and they should be co-heirs of the angels in Heaven. What province do they come from?"

"From Deira," said the slaveowner, mentioning the ancient name for what is now Northumberland.

"From Deira? Then indeed they should be saved from God's anger (*dei ira*) and called to the mercy of Christ. Who is their King?"

"Aella."

"Then," said Gregory, "must Alleluia be sung in Aella's land."

That was not quite the end of the punning. Some time later,

Gregory himself decided to make the journey to England, to convert the heathen. He went to the Pope, Pelagius II, who at first refused his consent and afterwards relented. Gregory gathered some of his monks around and then set out from Rome. On the third day, when they were sitting by the wayside, he opened a book and a locust settled on the page. "*Locusta!*" Gregory exclaimed; then it occurred to him that this was some kind of divine warning. He translated "*locusta*" into "*loco sta*," meaning "stay in place," and decided that he had been enjoined to journey no farther.

During all this time Gregory was no more than an abbot in the monastery he had founded. He was perfectly content to be an abbot, and he would probably have continued in this position if the plague had not once more swept through Rome. It was perhaps the most terrible of all the plagues which visited the city. Men felt hardly more than a little soreness of the throat: afterwards came the black eruptions and a swift death. The carts were piled with corpses. People went insane. Rome became a desert, and the Pope himself died, screaming in agony. For six months no Pope reigned from the throne in the basilica of St. Peter's. It was decided to elect Gregory. He refused the office and even, like Ambrose, took to flight, hiding in the forest, until he was found and dragged back to Rome. He was consecrated on September 3, 590.

He was now fifty, very bald and very ill. He had no desire for office. He complained that he was "so stricken with sorrow that he could scarcely speak"; he regarded his elevation as a punishment; but once in power, he threw himself into activity. From now on there was no time for the long meditations he had practiced while abbot. He wrote urgent letters to the managers of his estates in Sicily ("You sent me a sorry nag and five good asses: the nag is too wretched to ride, and I simply can't ride the asses because they are asses"); he began a vast correspondence with his bishops ("You evidently paid no attention to my last letter"); wrote a *Pastoral Rule*; reformed the Papal household; gave vastly to the poor and kept a ledger in which the names, sexes, ages, and professions of the poor people to whom he had given money were entered; preached on the Gospels or dictated sermons which were spoken for him; reclaimed the Arian churches; allegorized, punned, told stories, and discovered profound mysteries in numbers. He decided, for example, that the one hundred and fifty-three fishes netted in a miracle contained the Ten Commandments plus the seven gifts of the Holy Spirit. That made seventeen, and this was necessarily multiplied by the Three Persons of the Holy Trinity in whom we work, making fifty-one; and inevitably this sum must be multiplied by the Three Persons of the Holy Trinity in whom we rest, making one hundred and fifty-three. There was never such a symbolic mathematician. Strange marvels continued to plague, amuse, and delight him. Once he discovered an old church falling into ruin, and decided to hold a service in it. A huge crowd followed the pontiff. While the service was progressing a pig went running through the church. No one saw it, but they all felt it, and they knew by the way it ran among them that it was making for the door. Then, on the same night, the rafters roared, as though someone of immense weight was running over them; finally there was a crash, as the devil exploded of his own evil. A few days later, though the sky was cloudless, a cloud came and settled over the altar like a veil, filling the church with an odor so strange and sweet that no one dared to enter, though the doors were wide open. On another day the unlit lamps suddenly kindled into a flame, and still later the sacristan one evening turned out the lamps, only to discover, when he passed the church some while later, that they were all burning. The moral of all this was that the church had passed from darkness into light. This was the story as Gregory told it in his letters; and if we accuse him of credulity, there is always the possibility that these things happened, for Gregory speaks about them with quite extraordinary authority.

Many of the things that Gregory is supposed to have done he did not do: he did not compose the Missal, and the Gregorian chant probably derives from another Gregory. He lived in strange visions of miracles, but at the same time he was eminently practical. He administered the church wisely and sternly. He suppressed simony and concubinage among the clergy, restored discipline to the monasteries, and continued to give money to the poor. Under his pontifical robes he remained faithful to the asceticism of the Benedictine monks. When he heard that a Roman beggar had died of hunger, he insisted that it was his own fault and chastised himself. He called himself *servus servorum Dei*, "the servant of the servants of God": and he attempted to live up to this proud title which he was the first to invent. "Please do not keep on writing 'your handmaiden,'" he wrote in a letter to a virgin. "Once would be quite enough. As Pope I am the servant of all." "Your poor servant," he signs himself in a letter to the Emperor Maurice; but in this he was rather like an English civil servant who signs a letter "Your most obedient servant" after uttering threats.

There were many miracles in Gregory's life, but perhaps the most miraculous of his miracles was the way he could lead a double life. He was both the organizer and the fabulist: he lived in a real world surrounded by fables. The man who more than anyone else gave an organization to the Church, demanding that the priests live by a stern discipline, was an endless dreamer. He loved marvelous stories and he also loved marvels. Ambrose collected dead martyrs; Gregory collected relics, more relics than have ever been counted. He encouraged relic worship, and would send to his closest friends scrapings from the iron chain which had once bound SS. Peter and Paul, with instructions that they should pour the scrapings in water and bathe the wound with the mixture. "I have found such scrapings marvellously efficacious," he wrote. When the Empress wrote from Constantinople, asking that a portion of the bodies of SS. Peter and Paul be sent to her, he answered in alarm, saying that a divine power existed within those bodies. Instead he offered to send her some scrapings.

He dominated the end of the sixth century as Justinian had dominated its beginning, but he was essentially the child of his times. Like the earlier Fathers, he could see no reason why classical writings should be allowed to exercise power over the minds of men; and if he did not destroy classical writings, he at least opposed their circulation. His credulity was typical of his period, that nightmarish period in the history of Rome which saw invasions followed by plague, and plague followed by more invasions: when he spoke of his belief that the end of the world was at hand, he was speaking his most intimate thoughts. Yet though the world was about to perish he was determined to broaden the foundations of the Church. Head of a strong central organization, he aimed at and nearly succeeded in establishing his authority throughout France; he did succeed in establishing his authority over the Visigothic Kingdom in Spain; he fought the Emperor continually on the basis that the Pope was above the Exarch, the Church above the State. He would not have been able to do this unless he had exerted an unusual personal ascendancy and possessed immense vigor. The vigor of the man bursts through his human dress. He is always stripped for action, always in command, always warning, always in peril—the Lombards are coming closer, the Church is in decay because the bishops refuse to obey him, sin is triumphant, thievery rampant, and meanwhile the flames are coming closer, and he is lying on a couch, crippled with rheumatism, gout, and indigestion, fires burn in his body, pride vexes him, everyone is shameless, no one listens, he must write hurriedly against the clock, against the time of the Last Judgment, and all the time he gives the impression of being as inflexible as rock, as young as Jesus. When he died, overburdened with the weight of his sorrows, in the year 604, having ruled for thirteen years and six months, his epitaph proclaimed him to be "God's Consul." It was a singularly appropriate description of the man who had exerted himself to the uttermost, like a Roman statesman, the last of his line.

IX. ❦ BERNARD: THE SINGER

IN ONE OF THE FIERCE LETTERS WHICH BERNARD addressed to the Pope, urging him to examine his conscience and ask himself whether he was worthy of his throne, he quoted a child's song:

> There's an ape upon the housetop,
> And a silly king on a throne.

Through most of his life Bernard showed an abundant saintly childishness: and he possessed a child's temper and a child's waywardness. Like a child he saw through the worldly motives of others, and like a child he hated, claimed attention to himself, practiced terrible austerities, conjured up dreadful demons, refused to eat the food that was given to him, and smiled angelically whenever it suited his purpose. He was a great saint, and he differed from other saints in the depth of his love for the Virgin, the clarity of his vision, and his impulsive childishness.

Perhaps it was inevitable that he should be born in a family of aristocrats: for the aristocracy of Europe are by nature childish, though their childishness takes many forms. Thomas Aquinas was related to half the kings of Europe: he was the severe child, forever playing with his spiritual bricks. Bernard did not play. He wept and screamed and adored and loved with singular effrontery: he was still weeping and screaming and adoring and loving when he died. He loved the Virgin so passionately that, we are told in his legend, one evening when he was reciting the *Ave Maris Stella*, and came to the words

Monstra te esse Matrem, the Virgin bared her breast, and there flowed into Bernard's mouth a stream of holy milk. In the life of a saint like Bernard such a miracle seems congruous, as it would not have been in the life of Thomas Aquinas.

His father, Tescelin, was descended from the Counts of Châtillon; he was a soldier, a large landowner, and sometime an officer at the court of the Duke of Burgundy, into whose family he married. His wife Aletta was deeply religious, devoted to her family, and in the habit of doing the most menial tasks in the house because she believed that it was the duty of châtelaine to be the "servant of all." She bore six sons and one daughter. Bernard was the third child and, like the others, he was breast fed by his mother, though few noblewomen of the time nursed their children. Bernard seems to have been a sickly child, small and slender, with thin pale yellow hair and enormous soft blue eyes, helplessly in love with his mother, who ruled the household with mingled affection and stern discipline. "She ruled her house in the fear of God," said Guillaume de St. Thierry. "She was urgent in works of mercy and brought up her sons in perfect discipline [*enutriens filios in omni disciplina*]." It is at least possible that the stern discipline at home led to the extraordinarily undisciplined character of Bernard's mind.

The large castle near Dijon known as the Château de Fontaines where Bernard was brought up was surrounded with rolling wheatfields. There was a broad hill called the Côte d'Or which took its name from the golden wheat on its slopes. Along the main highway to Paris, in 1096, when Bernard was five, came Peter the Hermit calling upon all Christians to take part in the First Crusade. Bernard may have seen the processions led by the gaunt crusader: it is certain that he saw the funeral procession which brought the body of Hugh, lord of Burgundy, to its resting place in the Abbey of Citeaux, and the procession itself, with the black plumes waving and the black-ribboned standards bowing over the coffin of the feudal monarch—for the lords of Burgundy owed almost no allegiance to the French King—left ineffaceable traces on his mind. Henceforward he was determined that the West should be avenged upon the East, and he thought in terms of great processions making their way across Europe toward Palestine. He was quiet, unnaturally self-assured, given to long periods of contemplation, rarely playing, and it was observed that at a very early age he had dedicated himself to the religious life.

He was eleven when the huge procession accompanying Hugh of Burgundy passed near his father's castle. He mingled with the duke's servants who accompanied the body and learned from them about the wars, and his passion for oriental color seems to date from that time. The Abbey of Citeaux, which had been founded only a few years earlier by the saintly Robert de Molesme, became the center of his life. He was determined to become a monk there, and in complete simplicity worship the Virgin, living under a sky full of the Virgin and the hierarchies of the blessed.

The strange wayward youth with the pale face, modeling himself upon Hugh of Burgundy, who had once prayed in the oratory of the obscure monastery and had given orders that he should be buried there after his death, was haunted by the thought of the great prince. To understand Bernard's life we must remember the pride of these Burgundian dukes who ruled from Dijon, and were crowned there, and were offered the holy ring and the purple robe by the abbot of St. Benignus. Citeaux was a mean hovel of a monastery, and that Hugh should have desired to be buried there at all must have seemed an inexplicable verdict on the sanctity of the place.

Bernard's mother and father both died when he was fifteen or sixteen, and the boy was left alone with his dreams of the great prince. Because his father was related to the counts of Châtillon, Bernard and his brothers were admitted to the cathedral school at Châtillon. He was a good pupil, though perhaps not so good as his biographers contend, for every kind of virtue at this period is heaped upon his head. There is the usual story of the beautiful woman who made advances to him: to escape her embraces, and to avoid the sin of concupiscence, Bernard jumped into an ice-cold lake and stayed there until she tired of waiting on the bank and went on her way. He was lonely and moody, and talked often of retiring to a monastery. His brothers disapproved, though once when Bernard was imploring his younger brother Andreas to devote himself to the religious life—they would go off together into some hermitage—Andreas, wild-eyed with horror, exclaimed: "I see my Mother." In the vision she seemed to be smiling with joy and congratulating her son on his resolution. Bernard said he also saw Aletta. Later, when he rode with his brothers to war, he saw the vision again, and this time the face of his mother reproved him. He retired to a church by the roadside to pray, and when he rose from his knees his mind was made up: he would not go to war, he would pray to the living God until the day he died, and he would bring his brothers and cousins to a hermitage with him. Surprisingly, since his brothers were soldiers, they obeyed him, and even his distant cousin Nivard, hardly more than a boy playing in the castle gardens, was brought into their community. Told that all their possessions would be left him because they were entering a sacred order, the boy answered: "So you shall have the heavens, and I shall have the earth? It's not a fair division between us." Thereupon he joined them.

The year was 1113, the same year in which the wonderful carvings on the west portal of Chartres were made, and all over France small bands of young nobles were making their way to the monasteries, but they went if possible to the richer and more comfortable monasteries like Cluny and St. Denis. Yet asceticism was in the air, and Bernard's journey to the poor Abbey of Citeaux, where the only glory lay in the tomb of the Burgundian prince, was no different from those of many other young noblemen. Bernard had long meditated flight from the world. In the cell of the novices he spent his first year in relentless austerities, worshiping and praying with such abstraction, such watchfulness over his eyes, that at the end of the year he did not know whether the ceiling was vaulted or plain, or whether there were three windows or one. He worked like a peasant, slept in his habit, refused even the meager Cistercian fare, and prolonged his prayers and watches "beyond what was human." At the end of the year his health broke down, an inevitable consequence of his desire to keep awake day and night. He made his final profession of faith in 1114, and seems to have spent part of the next year on a sickbed.

When Robert de Molesme founded the Cistercian order, he deliberately sought out a wasteland where the monks could live in complete detachment from the world. He had thought of peopling the lonely places of the earth with monks and of reviving an ascetic form of the Benedictine rule. There were to be no ornaments in the monasteries of the Cistercian order, no embroidered vestments, no lace, no cloth of gold: only the wooden altar, a brass crucifix, a single iron chandelier in the church, a single silver-gilt chalice for the wine of the Eucharist. The monks would work hard. They would eat only one meal a day between September and Easter. Once again there were to be athletes of God.

In 1115, when the order had been in existence a bare seventeen years, the Abbey at Citeaux was already overcrowded. In that year three parties of young monks were sent out to found new monasteries. Together with twelve young monks representing the twelve apostles, Bernard marched out in search of undiscovered territories to conquer.

Carrying the cross above his head and singing hymns, Bernard with the other monks made his way past Dijon, where his mother was buried, and the Château de Fontaine, where he had passed his childhood, and then to Châtillon, where he had studied and where his father's relatives were living. It was as though he was sternly passing in review the whole of his past life, eager to divest himself of all earthly attachments. He was thin as a scarecrow, but his voice was rich and deep. He was twenty-four and looked thirty. He had a reddish beard and wore the rough white woollen habit of the Cistercian monks. A hundred miles beyond Citeaux, in a valley along the river Aube, he came to what he was searching for: a place of tangled briers called in Latin *vallis absinthialis*, or Valley of Wormwood. This name was exchanged for another when the briers were cleared, *clara vallis*. By this Bernard presumably meant that the clear light of God now flooded the valley.

The early months were heartrendingly difficult. They had little money. They had to clear the undergrowth; work on upland and meadow; plant, reap, and divide the stream; plot out the shape of things to come. There would be an immense stone monastery, fruit orchards, vineyards on the slopes, a tannery, meadows, fish-ponds, a spring of sparkling water. But all this came later: for the present there were only the small wattle huts where they lived beside the stream, and later a rough-hewn house which contained under one roof a chapel, a refectory, a dormitory, and a workshop. Their floor was the earth, and their pillows were logs. For many months their only food was barley bread, with broth made from boiled beech leaves. Once Bernard said: "What I know of the divine sciences and holy scriptures I learned in woods and fields. I have no other master than the beeches and the oaks." It was, of course, pure exaggeration, but there is in his prose a peculiar rhythm that suggests the waving of branches and the trembling of leaves, and when he shouts—he shouts surprisingly often—you hear the shuddering branches and the crackling of timber: with the result that one of the most exquisite pleasures is to read his *Sermons on the Canticles* while listening to the music of the Pastoral Symphony.

Slowly the work of clearing the valley went on. They had come in July, too late for planting, and winter came unexpectedly early that year. When winter came there was no more barley and they were reduced to living on beechnuts and the roots of herbs. Following the Benedictine rule, they took no meat, no chickens or eggs. Salt ran out. They were in despair until Bernard bade one of the monks go to a neighboring village. The monks were unpopular in the village, and there seemed no hope that the salt would be provided by the villagers. All this the monk charged with the mission of finding the salt explained at great length. Bernard said: "Be not afraid. He who has the treasure will be with thee." And so it was: providence, as so often in the annals of the monks, worked necessary miracles.

It was two years before the stone buildings went up and the desert began to flower. Then, as he says, "the place once known as the valley of bitter wormwood began to distill sweetness, and the fields, barren before, blossomed and grew fat under the divine benediction." A great deal of the burden of the work fell on Bernard's shoulders. He behaved like a Benedictine abbot, a permanent overseer of men's souls and actions, but unlike the Benedictine abbots he refused to place himself in a position of priority. He preached a daily sermon, but he also went about preparing the dinners and washing the kitchen plates and vessels, he numbered the pigs and counted the poultry and greased his own sandals. One day, according to the legend, the devil disguised as a black monk came upon him suddenly when he was rubbing them with grease.

"Well, abbot, what are you up to?" the devil said. "I have come a long way to see you, and there you are greasing your shoes. Isn't it strange that an abbot should behave like that?"

Rather sententiously, Bernard took it upon himself to reprove the devil, saying: "I have no servants, and do not wish to have them, imitating the Lord my God, and for love of Him performing the most menial actions." The devil was abashed and fled.

There was purpose in Bernard's madness. If the Benedictine rule was hard, he would drive his monks harder, and himself be the most driven. The enemies were all about, and above all there was the enemy of pride. "A solitary man is either a beast or an angel," says an Italian proverb, and these solitaries living in community were at the mercy of temptations unless they worked feverishly. As Bernard observed to a young novice found empty-handed in the kitchen: "If you neglect to wash the pots and pans, you will neglect to worship God."

In time Clairvaux flourished, becoming famous for its wines, its scriptorium, where the manuscripts were carefully copied on vellum, and the prodigious numbers of young aristocrats who came there, to wear rough woolen gowns and lose completely the habits of aristocracy. Above all it was famous for the presence of Bernard, living in a small wattle hut apart from the monks, austere and gentle, forever planning new Cistercian abbeys—in his lifetime one hundred and sixty colonies of monks were sent out by him, including Fountains Abbey in Yorkshire, named after Bernard's birthplace. The monks came and went, were blessed by Bernard, and something of his gentleness as well as his austerity seems to have passed to them, for all the stories of the early Cistercians speak of them as smiling men, quiet, reserved, glorying in the knowledge that Bernard would counsel them; not until Francis arose in Italy was there to be such joyful faith in simple things.

About this time a young novice, Peter de Roya, wrote an account of Clairvaux:

Although the place is in a valley, yet its foundations are upon the holy mountain of God, which the Lord loveth more than all the dwellings of Jacob. Glorious things are spoken of it, for a glorious and wonderful God works glorious wonders here. Those who have been long insane return to reason; though the outer man perishes, the inner is renewed. Here the proud are humbled and the rich become poor. Here the poor hear the gospel and the terrors of sin are exchanged for light. Here come great multitudes of the blessed poor from all the ends of the earth, having one spirit and one mind.

Here the monks have found a Jacob's ladder, and some of the angels are descending to provide for the bodies of the monks who do not faint by the wayside, and some ascend to heaven gathering the souls of the monks that they may be glorified. The more attentively I watch these poor people in their happy life, the more convinced I am that they follow Christ in all things and shew themselves true ministers of God. When I watch them singing hymns and in their nightly vigils which last from midnight until the dawn with only the briefest intervals, so holily and unweariedly do they sing that it seems to me they are a little less than angels and much more than men.

I have heard that some of them were bishops, others princes, while others were full of dignities or learned men; still others have lived illustriously in their youths. Now, by God's grace, all degrees of rank have been removed from them, and those who thought themselves high in the world, now think themselves lowly. It seems to me that I am hardly looking on men when I see them in the gardens with hoes, in the fields with forks and rakes and sickles, in the woods with axes, clad in rough homespun garments: they look like fools, without speech or sense, but my reason assures me their life is concealed with Christ in the heavens.

It is hardly surprising that Peter de Roya should have ended his long letter with the words: "Farewell! God willing, on the next Sunday after Ascension Day I shall put on the armor of my profession as a monk."

The sweetness of those times was typically French, and exactly the same music is to be heard among the Victorines—the scholars of the Abbey of St. Victor in Paris—with whom Bernard was in continual correspondence. Something was happening in the very air of France. It was the time of the Cathedrals, the sun was shining brighter than ever, and a religious fervor moved the peasants. Once Bernard wrote to Heinrich of Murdach, who later became Archbishop of York: "But surely it is possible to suck honey from stones and oil from the flinty rock? Do you not see the mountains dripping with sweetness, the hills flowing with milk and honey and the valleys abounding with corn? [*An non montes stillant dulcedinem, et colles fluunt lac et mel, et valles abundant frumento?*]" Even in Latin the words move with a peculiarly French intonation.

But though an almost incredible peace descended upon Clairvaux, Bernard was perpetually restless. His nerves were finespun; he was the prey of "the great storms of tears" which afflict the mystics. He had "poured forth his heart like water" on the day when he prayed in the wayside church and came at last to believe that he must dissuade his brothers from going to war. He poured them out again when his favorite brother Gérard died, speaking with such violence of grief that he seemed to doubt his faith, doubt God, doubt everything. He had been giving his sermons on the Song of Solomon. Suddenly he could go on no more, and broke off: "What have I to do with this Canticle?" he declared. "I am overwhelmed with the bitterness of grief." That was the beginning; the rage mounted:

I have dissembled to you all, lest it should appear that faith was overcome by feeling. The others wept when his body was taken to the grave. My eyes were unmoistened. I stood there quietly. Not a tear fell from my eyes until the earth covered over my brother. Those who watched me wept, and wondered why I did not weep, and their pity was less for him than for me who had lost him. Today I am no longer able to conceal my grief or hide my anguish. It is contrary to justice that I who have been wounded should call back one who has wounded me. I am despised, and I must seek after the one who despised me. I have suffered injury, and I must offer satisfaction to him who injured me.

Oh, but grief does not deliberate, grief knows no shame, grief has no recourse in the courts of reason, never fears to lose its dignity, never conforms to rule, never submits to sound judgment. Grief ignores method and rule. The mind suffering from grief is wholly occupied with grief. Gérard, I am wretched because I miss thee, because I do not see thee, because I live without thee. To die for thee would give me life: to live without thee is to die. Only come back; then I shall have peace. Return; then I shall have rest. Return, I say, return! Then I shall sing joyfully: "He who was dead is now living." It was my fault that you died. I was too severe with thy delicate youth; my harshness wounded thy tenderness. And I say this, not to confound thee, but to admonish thee, my most dear boy, for though thou mayest have many teachers in Christ, thou hast not enjoyed many fathers. And though I am thy brother, I was like a father unto thee, leading along the road to Christ. O brother by blood, but more brother in Christ! Have mercy on me! But thou knowest, dearest one, that a multitude of angels flock around thee, and instead of me thou hast Christ Himself. Because thou hast put on God, thou hast not altogether put aside all care for us: *He also careth for us.* Thou hast discarded thy infirmities, but not thine affections. Thou lovest us still. Therefore we are grateful to thee! (Bernard, *Epistola ad Robertum*, I.)

It is an extraordinary *oraison funèbre*, the first of the long line of great sermons on the departed which were to be produced by French priests, and perhaps the greatest. Bossuet dressed the dead in silk, placed crowns on their heads, surrounded them with baroque angels, then sung them softly to sleep. With Bernard, the wound is still naked, the nerve-ends wildly lamenting. In later years the monks embroidered upon the telling of the grief-stricken sermon. They said he spoke in the open, and though a shower of rain fell, none fell on the parchment where a monk was busily taking down the sermon, for the words were hot with love and kept the rain away. In the collection of his works they placed this sermon first, as though all of Bernard was contained in his song of grief, as indeed it was. He had lost his parents when he was young, and he was to lose two more brothers later, and he never reconciled himself to his losses.

Bernard was a tangle of contradictions, now gentle, now harsh, now proud, now humble, and always French. The monkish commentators love to recount his fury, but they are not always credible. Exaggeration seeps in. The fury of Bernard and the fury of his antagonists are always resolved in Bernard's favor. Most furious of all Bernard's antagonists was William, Duke of Aquitaine, the grandfather of Richard Coeur de Lion, who inherited William's strength and his gift for poetry. William was a huge man, who cared nothing for God or women, whom he seduced and murdered at leisure, an unprincipled tyrant who wrote some of the greatest poetry of his time. The Bishop of Poitiers had thundered from his throne that William would be stricken with the wrath of God unless he mended his manners, and William ordered him out of Aquitaine. The bishop refused. Other bishops were removed from their sees. The Pope was alarmed and sent Geoffroi, Bishop of Chartres, as papal legate to put an end to the quarrel, and Geoffroi very sensibly agreed to go only if he was accompanied by Bernard, whose reputation for sanctity had now spread over the whole of France. When they reached William's court, they were told that the duke had sworn on oath that he would never return the bishops to their thrones; useless to attempt to convince him. Bernard and Geoffroi then quietly proceeded to the church to celebrate Mass. For some reason William followed them, perhaps made curious by their ominous silence, only to be told that he must not enter the church because he was under Papal censure. He stood in the doorway, shouting derision at them. When the host had been consecrated, Bernard lifted his arms and marched toward the doorway with the paten in his hands, his face flashing and eyes alight (*ignea facie et flammeis oculis*), and in tones of terrible authority addressed the duke:

We have besought you, and you have spurned us. The congregation of the servants of God, meeting you elsewhere, have entreated you and you have despised them. Behold, here cometh to you the Virgin's Son, Head and Lord of the Church you persecute! Your Judge is here, at whose Name every knee shall bow, of things in Heaven, and things on Earth, and things under the earth! Your Judge is here, into Whose hands your soul will come at last! Will you spurn Him also? Will you despise Him, as you have despised his servants? (Bernard, *Vita Prima*, II.)

The chroniclers say that there was a long silence weighted with dread, and then the duke reeled over and fell groveling at the feet of the saint. It may be true; it is more likely that William simply knelt. They say, too, that he was lifted up in the arms of his knights, foam raging round his lips, the huge red face suddenly turned pale, the eyes closed and the mouth speechless with horror over the crimes he had committed, and all his limbs loosened and nerveless. This also may be true, but it is conceivable that he continued to kneel open-mouthed at the audacity of the small red-bearded Jack who came to beard the Giant in his den. At last Bernard bade him rise, and the duke was compelled to listen to a singularly detailed summary of his crimes. Then the Bishop of Poitiers was pushed forward. Bernard commanded the duke to give the bishop the kiss of peace, and restore him to his throne. Finally, the monkish chroniclers say that William died shortly afterwards on a penitential journey to the shrine of St. James at Compostella; but this is untrue, for William remained many more years on earth, and he was whoring and murdering and writing exquisite poetry until the day he died.

Partly, the fear of Bernard arose from his power to perform miracles. Many of his miracles are recorded in great detail by capable and learned men; and Bernard himself made the quiet claim that he could perform them when he desired to, or rather when God desired him to. When he was present, the mute spoke, the lame walked, and the blind received their sight. Sometimes he laid a hand on the patient, sometimes he made the sign of the cross, sometimes he offered prayer, and sometimes he used the consecrated wafer or sprinkled holy water on the sick. When the church at Foigny was being dedicated, the congregation was plagued with flies. Bernard simply pronounced the words of excommunication, the flies perished and next morning were shoveled out with spades. He could miraculously manipulate dice according to the *Gesta Romanorum*, which is not an infallible witness to the truth. The story goes that a gambler offered to throw dice for Bernard's horse. Bernard replied that he was prepared to gamble on one condition: if the gambler failed, he would award his soul to Christ. When the gambler agreed, Bernard heartily entered into the proposition and won. From such

stories as these, and from his continual rebukes to the dukes
and emperors of the world, Bernard acquired his fame.

He had humbled the Duke of Aquitaine: he had still to
humble the King and the Pope. The Pope was to be humbled
last of all, but the King was humbled the moment he invaded
the territory of Champagne and began to lay it waste. Bernard
hurriedly wrote out a letter of denunciation, and even now
the fire can be heard crackling:

> What devilish impulse has made thee perpetrate this crime?
> Art thou a King or a murderer? I say, only the devil can have
> aided thee to pour fire on fire, murder on murder, while the
> cries of the poor, the groans of the chained and the blood of the
> slain sound in the ears of Him who is the Father of the father-
> less and the Judge of poor widows. So does the devil, the ancient
> enemy of our race, laugh to know of thy success: for was not
> the devil a murderer from the beginning? (Bernard, *Epistolae*,
> CCXXI.)

Against the *anathemas* of Bernard, Louis the Fat was weap-
onless; and he wisely retreated, made terms with Theobald,
Duke of Champagne, and some time afterward married Theobald's daughter. Bernard employed a different strategy with
the King of England. When Henry II refused to recognize
Innocent III as supreme pontiff, Bernard wrote to him: "Know
that for your other sins you shall give account to God. As for
this one, I take it on my own shoulders: the whole sin shall rest
upon myself." Henry II thereupon accepted Innocent III
as Pope, trusting a saint where he could not trust himself,
and happy to be rid of sin.

More and more Bernard was coming to the stage where his
word was law in the chancelleries of Europe. In 1128 at the
Council of Troyes he had helped to bring about the Order of
Templars. Himself the son of a soldier, he was determined to
avenge the defeat of the First Crusade. He admired the
Templars, for their lives were as hard as the lives of the
Cistercian monks. Like the monks they lived in community,

without women or children, dedicated to poverty and obedience, never laughing or raising their voices or singing bawdy
songs, their heads shaven, their beards shaggy and untrimmed,
rarely washing—as he describes them he draws a portrait of
himself. They were the bronzed soldiers of Christ prepared to
offer their lives beneath the walls of Jerusalem, and some years
later Bernard wrote an eloquent treatise on their perfections.
He called the treatise *In Praise of the New Army*, and made
clear from the beginning that it was an army which differed
from all other armies in being blessed by God:

What intolerable madness it is to fight at great cost and labor
for no other wages except sin and death! You deck your horses
with silken trappings, you put on I know not what hanging cloaks
above your corslets, you paint your shields, your spears and your
saddles; you ornament your bridles with spurs and gold, with
silver and precious stones; and so in pomp, in evil rage and shameless insensibility you rush upon death! Are these the signs of
soldiers, or is it not that these badges you wear are decorations of
dishonor? . . .
Nothing moves you to battle except the impulse of unreason-
able anger, or an empty thirst for glory, or the greed for earthly
gain! For such reasons, surely, it is neither safe to kill nor safe
to die. O, but the soldiers of Christ fight safely the battles of
their Lord, neither fearing sin when they kill their enemies nor
dreading the danger of death: since death for Christ, whether
borne on oneself or inflicted on others, has no crime in it, but
indeed deserves the highest glory. I say the soldier of Christ is
safe when he kills and when he dies he is safer. When he kills,
he profits Christ. When he dies, he profits himself. Not without
cause do such soldiers bear their swords. (Bernard, *De Laude
Novae Militiae*.)

Like Tertullian, Bernard rejoices over the deaths of the martyrs even before they have died: there is a hard, dispassionate
French pride in his utterance. He delighted in war, and he
delighted only a little more in peace. As though to take the
chill from his words, he added: "It is not necessary that the
pagans should be killed if in any other way they can be re-

strained from their hostility and oppression toward the faithful." Most of all, I think, he delighted in the panoply of the Crusades and the Templars, those rough-bearded men whose errand on earth was to fence with lances the places where the Saviour trod.

His dominant position in ecclesiastical councils was already manifest at the Council of Troyes. Two years later, when Pope Honorius II died—Bernard had detested him, and characteristically dismissed him with the pun: "The honor of the Church was wounded by Honorius"—two rival popes claimed the succession, one a cardinal of St. Angelo, the other the grandson of a Jewish banker known as Peter Leonis. The first called himself Innocent II, the second Anacletus II. They had already engaged in war; both were powerful; both had friends in high places; and both were known to Bernard. To avoid the disaster of a war between two Popes which would shake Christendom to its foundations, Louis VI called a council at Etampes. To the council Bernard was summoned. He was not yet forty, though he looked older. On his way to the council Bernard had a vision of the heavenly choirs singing *alleluias*, and interpreted the vision to mean that the whole congregation of the church was at last united. Like so many of his visions, it occurred at night, and may well have been a dream. But when he reached Etampes there was no unity, the bishops argued at cross purposes, and in the end Bernard was asked to make the choice himself. This he did. He drew a little apart, prayed for a while, and then announced that the choice of God had fallen on Innocent. Never before or afterward did an abbot choose a Sovereign Pontiff. But though Innocent was acclaimed in Etampes, Anacletus was still in Rome, and it was seven years before the schism was finally quelled.

Meanwhile there were triumphant processions through France. Innocent stayed with the court of the King at St. Denis, traveled everywhere in state, and even visited Clairvaux, where Bernard arranged that he should receive a necessary lesson. No pomp was shown to him. The walls were left undecorated, the monks did not lift their eyes when the Pope entered their church. No banquets were held. "Plain bread of unbolted flour took the place of wheat loaves, the juice of herbs was offered rather than sweet wine, vegetables in the place of rare fish, beans and pease instead of delicate meats." The Pope was not abashed; it was what he had expected.

There followed for Bernard three years of wild traveling. Lothaire, Emperor of Germany, had refused to accept Innocent. Bernard was sent to convince him. He traveled back and forth across Europe, performing miracles, chastising monarchs and worshiping God. He even made the devil useful. Once, when he was crossing the Alps in a carriage, one of the wheels was broken. Bernard gazed at the splintered wheel for a moment, and it occurred to him that so great an evil could only have been accomplished by the devil. He summoned the devil to his presence and ordered him to take on the shape of a wheel. Thus equipped, Bernard's carriage rolled down pleasantly into the plains of Piedmont.

The superb passion which moved Bernard in his dealings with kings appears in his sermons and his books. He wrote a book on the degrees of humility and pride. There were three degrees of pride, and one of them he described as "thoughtless mirth." "Such proud men," he wrote, "hide their faces in shame, close their lips and grind their teeth. They find themselves laughing involuntarily, giggling when they have no desire to giggle, and even when they cram their fists in their mouths to hide their laughter, still their laughter goes on and they can be heard snorting through their nostrils." There is power behind these descriptions, a fiercer power than that which moves Jerome in his portraits of the dissolute priests of Rome, almost as great a power as Gregory's. Nearly always when Bernard opens his mouth there is a sound like thunder. In his sermon on Christ's passion he wrote: "The Passion of the Lord is here, this very day, shaking the earth, rending the rocks and opening the tombs." When it pleased him, he could be extraordinarily illuminating, and even terrifying. He wrote of the last moments of Christ on the Cross:

He was offered because He willed. He not only willed and was offered, but it was because He willed. He alone had the power of laying down His soul; none took it from Him; he voluntarily offered it. When He had received the vinegar, He said: "It is finished." Nothing remains to be fulfilled: now there is nothing for which I have to wait. And bowing His head, being made obedient unto death, He gave up the ghost. *Who could so easily fall asleep on willing it?*[1]

In the last line he shatters all accepted interpretations of the Crucifixion. All this is dangerous ground. Like so many French writers, he is at first convincing, then profoundly disturbing, then unconvincing; and his own will enters abundantly into the dialogue with God, as Pascal's will enters into the *Mystère de Jésus*. Yet he can be convincing when he is simple and still more convincing when he is complex: it is only when he is neither one nor the other that there is heard the strange false note of mock heroics, the voice pitched a little too high. He refused to allow his monks to write poetry or decorate the church at Clairvaux: yet here and there in his work there are signs of decoration, and there is always poetry. He despised all the arts except music, but this he loved so much that they said of him he was always singing. He ordered his disciple Guy de Cherlieu to write a treatise on song for the use of the order: he told the monks to sing "purely and strenuously, not sparing their voices, virile, as needs be, full-

---

[1] In the Middle Ages Christ's sufferings on the Cross were often regarded with an astonishing calm, as though Christ Himself had been calm during the Passion. Anselm in his *Meditation on the Passion* describes the final inclination of Christ's head during the Crucifixion as a gesture which looks forward to an embrace: "Christ bends His head, since He wishes to kiss us; He stretches out His arms to embrace us, and He seems to say, 'Come unto me, ye who suffer.'"

But though Bernard could regard the crucified Christ as one who quietly sleeps, and Anselm regards Him as one making the gesture of the lover, the tradition of the extreme torture suffered by Christ remained. Significantly the torture was emphasized in Germany, Italy, and Spain; in England and France it was rarely emphasized.

throated and deeply sensitive [*pure et strenue, non parcentes vocibus, sed virili, ut dignum est, et sonitu et affectu*]." And all these qualities appear in his own writings. He loved the word *ordo*, but was himself the most disorderly of men. It was not an accident that the medieval story of the tumbler who offered his gift of tumbling to the Virgin was placed in a Cistercian monastery.

As a contemplative writing upon contemplation, Bernard is supreme. He writes with a strange gentleness concerning the mystical union with God, and with such conviction that it is impossible not to believe that he has, in his own words, "kissed God's mouth and known the joy of entering within." He uses sexual terms freely, as did many of the mystics: he even speaks openly of a "carnal love for Christ." An ascetic, he is sometimes extraordinarily forgiving of sexual sins; there are even moments when he exalts the flesh, as when he says: "For my part I believe the chief reason which prompted the invisible God to become visible in the flesh and to hold converse with men was to lead carnal men, who are only able to love carnally, to the healthful love of the flesh, and afterwards, little by little, to spiritual love." In his *Sermons on the Canticles* he employs the whole vocabulary of sexual union to suggest union with God. Altogether he wrote over a long period eighty-six sermons on this theme, and he was still writing the last of them when he lay dying; but so slow was his progress, with so much attention did he survey every word in the Song of Songs, that he never progressed further than the first verse of the third chapter.

The study of his sermons is immensely revealing of the temper of the man. Here nothing is held back. He walks with complex abandon along the knife-edge. God is there: to be adored, to be kissed, even to be caressed with the hands, and though every movement made by the lover has a mystical meaning, we are never entirely certain how much of it concerns pure mysticism and how much of it derives from a sublimation of sexual experience. "How is God to be adored?" he asks, and answers that He must be adored with kisses. There are three kinds of kisses. There is the kiss of the feet of God, meaning that the soul embraces God's mercy and truth in an act of adoration. There is the kiss of the hands, from which the lover derives divine strength. There is the kiss of the mouth, from which the lover derives an ecstatic union with God. Sometimes he speaks of this union in a strange vocabulary of his own, half sexual, half intellectual, as though he was describing a landscape on the borderland between the flesh and the spirit. Of his own union with God he wrote:

I confess in my foolishness that the Word has visited me, springing up in me, and this has happened more than once. But although He has frequently entered my soul, He has come in such a way that I have never been sensible of the precise moment of His coming. I have felt Him in me; I remember He has been within me; I have sometimes known a presentiment of his coming into me. By what means he has made entrance or departure, I confess I know not to this day. . . . He did not enter through my eyes, for He is not a color; nor through my ears, for He is not a sound; nor through my nostrils, for He mingles not with the air but with the spirit of man; nor again does He enter through the mouth, for He cannot be eaten or sipped on the tongue; nor may He be touched, for He is intangible.

By what way, then, did He enter? Perhaps He did not enter, for He does not come from without like an exterior thing. Nor does He come from within, since sanctity, I know, is not in me. How did I know he was present, since there is no way of describing his coming? I knew He was there, because He was living and full of energy, and as soon as He entered within me He quickened my sleeping soul, He aroused and softened and pricked my heart, until then in a state of stupor, hard as a stone. Thereupon He began to pluck and destroy, to plant and to build, to water the dry places and illuminate the dark corners, opening all that was closed, warming all that was cold, straightening the crooked paths and making the rough places smooth, so that my soul blessed the Lord and all that was within me praised His Holy Name.

So I mounted to the higher part of my soul, and higher still

reigned the Word. Strange exploration. I entered into the depths
of my soul, and perceived Him in still lower depths. I looked
outside: I saw He was beyond all. I looked within: He was more
close to me than my soul. . . . So I have been filled in some
degree with the loveliness of His beauty, and marveled at the
immensity of His power, as I meditated upon these things.

But when the Word withdrew Himself, all these spiritual
powers and faculties began to droop and languish, as if the fire
had been withdrawn from the bubbling pot: and this is to me
the sign of His departure. Then my soul necessarily falls into a
melancholy until the time comes when He returns and my heart
grows warm within me. . . . As often as He leaves me, so often
do I call Him back with my voice; nor shall I ever cease crying
to Him when he departs from me, in the ardour of my heart,
that He shall restore my salvation to me, restore to me Himself.
I confess to you, my children, that I take pleasure in nothing
when He has departed, and when He returns He is my only joy.
(Bernard, *Sermo LXXIV in Cantica.*)

In these frontiers of the spirit, where words have almost
no meanings and new vocabularies have to be invented at
every moment, Bernard is at home. He is prepared to invent
words—one of his most successful is the "Bridegroom-Word,"
which is God entering into the bride who is the soul. He invented the "waking sleep," the sleep of the soul in the arms
of God, a deep sleep, alive and wakeful, not dulling the senses
but entirely ravishing them, and like St. John of the Cross
he knows "the dark night of the soul," when all is torment
and unfulfilled desire. When he speaks of the highest form
of contemplation, he says simply: "thus one becomes God."
Or else he speaks of "a most sweet sleep and tranquil mar-
veling." He is wine slowly dissolving in the pure water of
God, an iron bar in the fire taking on the color of the surrounding flames, or the air growing luminous in sunlight. He
is all these things, but most of all he is the bride receiving the
bridegroom. In the most enchanting way Bernard is prepared
to speak of this love in terms of the physical body, like the
Persian *sufis*. He comments on the breasts of the bride:

Suddenly the Bridegroom is present and gives assent to her demand. He gives her the kiss she asks for, of which the fullness of her breasts is the witness. So great is the power of this holy kiss that the bride on receiving it conceives, and the evidence lies in the swelling breasts bursting with milk. Those who have prayed long know that what I say is true. Often we approach the altar and gives ourselves to prayer, but our hearts remain dry and lukewarm: but should we persist, then the flood of grace suddenly overwhelms us, our breasts swell and love fills our inward heart, and should we press on the milk of sweetness conceived within us spreads everywhere in a pure flood. The Bridegroom will say: Thou hast, O my Spouse, now received what thou prayedst for: and this is the sign: thy breasts have become better than wine. (Bernard, *Sermo IX in Cantica*.)

So in the same way he will comment upon her eyes, her forehead, her lips, and even the color of her skin. "I am black, but comely," says the Shulamite, and Bernard leaps to the defense of her darkness. Is not black hair beautiful? he asks, and there may be some irony in the question, for his own was flaxen. What is more beautiful than dark hair against white skin? But he evades the issue, remembering perhaps that devils in the Middle Ages were all described as having the appearance of Negroes, and says that if she was dark outside, she was white within, and if she was dark in the eyes of men, she was white in the eyes of the angels and of God. And was not St. Paul deformed and dark likewise, yet he was taken up into Paradise; and Jesus Christ was dark, without grace or beauty, dressed in rags, bleeding from a hundred wounds, with a mess of spittle on his face where men had spat on him, pale with the pallor of death, yet dark—surely he is dark. But ask the apostles how they found Him on the mountain, or ask the angels who it is they desire to contemplate, and then you will have no doubt about His beauty.

It is all strange, beautiful, explosive, the sense of every word twisted to suit his own purpose, which was the glorification of God and the Virgin. He speaks of "spiritual bleedings," and he likes to analyze the various possibilities of meaning in a phrase like "the skin, flesh and bones of the soul." Yet he could be amazingly childlike and simple, all the metaphysical poetry stripped from him. He declared once: "In those respects in which the soul is unlike God, it is also unlike itself," which is as good a definition of the medieval soul as you will find anywhere. Asked what God was, he answered: "I can think of no better answer than 'He who is.' Nothing is more appropriate to the eternity which is God. If you name God good or great or blessed or wise or anything else, it is all included in the words 'He who is.'" Yet there was one subject on which Bernard spoke best of all, with the utmost authority, and this was love. The *Sermon on the Passion* is strained. He allows himself to wander among bewildering mazes when he speaks of the Shulamite, but when he speaks of love he speaks with the poetry he had forsworn in his youth, quietly, passionately, and with complete conviction:

Love owes no reverence. Love takes its name from loving, not from honoring. Let those who are stricken with fear and trembling seek comfort in honor: but fear and trembling are absent from the lover. Love is filled with love; and where love is all other feelings are transcended, overcome. The loving soul loves, and attempts nothing else. Love seeks no cause or fruit beyond itself, it is its own fruit, its own cause. Of all the motions and affections of the soul, love is the only one by means of which the creature, though not on equal terms, may treat with the Creator and repay to Him what he has received. When God loves, He desires only to be loved, knowing that love will render all those who love Him blessed. . . . How could the Bride not love, she who is the Bride of Love? How could Love not be loved? (Bernard, *Sermo LXXXIII in Cantica.*)

But though Bernard wrote with such extraordinary sweetness on the nature of love and the divine union, he could curse and rage as well as any man. Almost he is Jerome's equal. Unlike Jerome, who attacks individuals, Bernard hated all who opposed him, as only the saints hate. These ferocious letters are so much a part of him that some passages should be quoted here. The first occurs in a letter to Guillaume de St. Thierry, the second in a declaration against the comfort-loving monks of Cluny:

Against the Worship of the Portraits of the Saints

So the lovely portrait of the saint is hung on the walls, and you account it holier according to the brightness of the colors. You rush to kiss it. You are inspired to offer gifts. You admire the painting, but you do not adore the saint. These portraits are placed in churches, not as jeweled crowns, but as great empty wheels of things, all set about with torches, glowing with a thousand jewels. As for candlesticks, no one thinks of employing ordinary ones: no, there must be great trees of massive bronze, cunningly fashioned, with inset jewels glittering brighter than the candles. What purpose is served? The contrition of the penitent? The wonder of the beholder? Vanity of vanities! The Church glistens on all its walls, but where are the poor? The stones are clothed with gold, but the children of the Church are clothed in nakedness! At the expense of the poor it feasts the eyes of the rich! The curious find what pleases them, but the wretched find nothing to give them succor. Certainly we do not show respect to the images of saints with which the very pavement swarms—those images which we tread underfoot. Often we come upon people spitting into an angel's mouth, or the face of some saint or other is beaten by the shoes of those who tread down on it. Why, therefore, do they decorate what must soon be defiled? Why these paintings, where the paint may be so soon scraped away? . . . And what help is this ridiculous nonsense for the brothers reading in the cloisters—that terrible twisted beauty, that appealing deformity? Why do they put up those filthy apes? Why those savage lions, those monstrous centaurs, those half-human figures? In such places you see one body under many heads, or many bodies under one head. Here is the tail of a serpent attached to some animal or other, there a fish with the face of a beast. You come upon animals whose front parts are horses and whose behinds are as those of goats. . . . For God's sake, surely they should be distressed by these monstrosities, and if they are not distressed by the awful things, at least they should be distressed by their expense! (Bernard, *Apologia ad Guillelmum*.)

Against the Intemperance of the Monks

I marvel at the extent of the intemperance now common among the monks. I marvel at their revelings, their garments, their comfortable chairs, their exercising of horses and the way they build their churches. Behold! economy is now thought to be avarice; sobriety is thought to be austerity; silence is thought to be melancholy. Let us go further. Laziness is now called discretion, profusion is called liberality, loquaciousness has become affability and laughter has become joy. As for the soft clothing and the trappings of horses, these are known as expressions of dignity. The too-great carefulness of the readers is rendered as elegance. . . . God help us, nothing is done about the Scriptures, nothing is done for the salvation of souls—it is all loose jests and jokes are banded about everywhere. At dinners their jaws are occupied with delicacies, as their ears are occupied with nonsensical trifles; and wholly preoccupied by eating, these monks show no moderation. Dish follows dish; and since they must abstain from meats, why, they simply have double the number of fish, and when they reach for their second helping, having stuffed themselves to overflowing with the first, they appear to have tasted nothing. . . .

I would ask you to count the number of ways the very eggs are tossed and tormented, how eagerly they are turned over and over, made soft or made hard, beaten up, fried, roasted, stuffed, minced with other delicacies or served alone. They pay very great care to the external appearance of things, and they see to it that the eye is charmed as well as the palate; and even when their stomachs by frequent belchings announce to the world that they are full up, these monks are still not satisfied. . . .

At these dinners I have seen three or four half-filled cups carried around, for the wine has been smelled rather than tasted; and if sometimes it was tasted, they did not possess the energy to drink to the dregs; and so they waited till the strongest and finest wine appeared. It is said that on feast days they have honey mixed with their wine, and they go so far as to sprinkle in their wine the powdered dust of many-colored spices. . . .

It is the same with clothes: they seek not that which is useful, but that which helps them to offer a fine appearance—not to keep out the cold, but to administer to their pride. And our customary habit, chosen because it represents our humility, is worn by them as a sign of their pride; and hardly can they find in the province clothes good enough for them to wear. Monks now wear the same clothes as soldiers; and neither the King nor the Emperor would disdain to wear the cloths they wear, though of course they must be shaped a little differently. (Bernard, *Epistolae*, CCCLXIII.)

Bernard's rage overflows when he discovers that the Germans, according to their practice, hated the Jews more than they hated the Saracens, their enemy in the East. At such moments he talks and writes like Isaiah:

Do you not understand that the Church triumphs more abundantly over the Jews in converting them than in putting them to the sword? Wherefore we utter our universal prayer for the unbelieving Jews, uttered incessantly in the Church from the rising of the sun to the going down of the sun, that God shall take away the veil from their hearts and lead them out of darkness that they may be led into the glorious light of the truth. Unless, therefore, the Church believes that they will enter the fold, though now unbelieving, how vain and superfluous it were to offer prayers for them. But to kill them—this is a monstrous doctrine, a foul counciling, contrary to the prophets, hostile to the apostles, destructive of piety and grace—a damned harlot of a doctrine impregnated with the very spirit of falsehood, conceiving anguish and bringing forth iniquity! (Bernard, *Epistolae*, XIX.)

Bernard talked to the Pope as he would talk to an inferior: he had no belief in Papal infallibility, nor did he believe in the Immaculate Conception of the Virgin or in justification by faith. All these were errors in the eyes of Bernard, to be attacked bitterly, with a furious fervor. He wrote to the Pope concerning the Papal legate:

This legate of yours has gone from country to country, and everywhere he goes he has left foul traces (*foeda et horrenda vestigia*). Advancing from the foot of the Alps through Germany and through the churches of France, he has proclaimed, not the Gospel, but sacrilege. Everywhere he went he committed crimes: he filled his pockets with spoils from the Church, and whereever he could he promoted pretty boys to high offices, and where he was unable to promote them, still he desired to give them honor. And everyone on earth detests him.

To Suger, Abbot of St. Denis, he wrote an even more thundering letter, calling him to renounce a life of monkish luxury:

Let the children of Babylon seek for themselves pleasant mothers, but pitiless, who will feed them with poisoned milk, and soothe them with caresses which will make them fit for everlasting flames; but those of the Church, fed at the breasts of her wisdom, having tasted the sweetness of a better milk, already begin to grow up in it unto salvation, and being fully satiated in it, they can cry: *Thy fulness hath become better than wine, Thy fragrance, than the sweetest ointments.* (Bernard, *Epistola ad Innocentium.*)

These strong tirades, all with their quotations from the Song of Solomon, continue throughout Bernard's works. Whatever he hates, he hates violently: the ferocity of his passionate indignation was unequaled at a time when passionate indignation was a commonplace. "These are damnable days [*his diebus damnatissimis*]," said the Englishman Adam Marsh in a letter to Grosseteste; and Bernard seemed to agree with him.

Surprisingly, when Bernard came face to face with the greatest and most dangerous of the heretics of his age, he cursed softly or not at all.

Peter Abélard was everything that Bernard detested. The mystical love of God had no place in him. He was no ascetic, though during his stay in the oratory of the Paraclete he lived like Bernard in a wattle hut beside a stream and contemplated the Trinity. From Abélard, Peter Lombard derived his *Sentences*, which so profoundly influenced Thomas Aquinas, and therefore Abélard is among the ancestors of the modern Catholic dogmatic tradition; yet he was the pure rationalist and, like Descartes, who also came from Britanny, he was intoxicated with logic. "A doctrine is not to be believed," he said, "because God has said it, but because we are convinced by reason that it is true." Such a statement was heretical. Abélard chose to arrange conflicting passages from the Church Fathers side by side to show the impossibility of accepting two contrary statements. With his high forehead, long aquiline nose, and clean-cut jaw, he looked like a young cardinal, and he was as graceful and carefully dressed and negligent as any cardinal of the Middle Ages could be. Like Bernard he was descended from the nobility, but there the resemblance ended. There was all the fire of pride in Abélard. Had he not taken Héloïse in his arms? Had he not stormed the gates of heaven, like a young Prometheus, not waiting for an answer, but driving in?

Bernard could forgive the seduction of Héloïse, but he could not forgive the heaven-storming pride. He was younger by twelve years, had known Abélard casually, and for many years had been too busy to pay much attention to the schoolmen in Paris, and he half hated Paris. But gradually the rumors went around that Abélard was not a minor heretic, but one who threatened to disrupt the Church. He had said: "Crime is not in the act, but in the intention." He said, too: "Those who crucified the Lord, without knowing He was the Saviour, did not sin." He had revived the ancient Platonic saying: "Know thyself"—a statement which Bernard could only regard with distaste, for what else was there to know except God? As Bernard wrote in one of his letters to the cardinals, Abélard was talking as one talks with women and boys; he was not approaching, like Moses, the cloudy darkness in which God dwelt. He asked too many questions. There was no need to ask questions: there was only a great need to know the answers. "He lifts his head to Heaven," says Bernard, "examines the lofty things of God and returns to report to us the ineffable words which it is not lawful for man to utter; and while ready to render a reason for all things, even for the things which are above reason, he presumes against both reason and faith. What can be more contrary to reason than to undertake to transcend reason? and what more contrary to faith than to be willing to believe what we cannot by reason attain?"

If it had been as simple as this, the matter would not have been important. The gravest sin of Abélard was that he was removing the mystery of God and announcing the end of God's reign by giving primacy to man; if all objective phenomena were to be tested by reason, where was the sacrament —the *sacrae rei signum*, in which men found their peace? In a treatise called *Against the Error of Abélard* Bernard wrote:

At the very beginning of his theology, or should I say silly-ology (*stultilogia*), Abélard defines faith as opinion, as an estimate of the truth. As if one were at liberty to think and to say whatever one pleases concerning matters of faith: as if the sacraments of our faith were suspended uncertainly, on vague and various human opinions, and were not established on certain truth. If faith wavers, is not salvation empty? Then were our martyrs foolish, sustaining torture for things uncertain, running to their anguished deaths for a doubtful reward! . . . Where then becomes the miraculous Virgin birth of Christ, the blood of the Redeemer and the splendor of His resurrection . . . How can one dare to say that faith is opinion, unless it be that he has not received the spirit, or ignores the gospels, or thinks them fables? . . . Faith is the substance of things hoped for, not the fantasy of empty imaginings. Faith is not an estimate of the truth; faith is certitude.

For Bernard, such a quiet rejoinder suggested that he felt a curious affection for Abélard. There are no *anathemas*. He had humbled kings to the dust, but he had no desire to humble a scholar. Abélard was living near by. Bernard sought an interview with him, and seems to have believed that all danger was over when he returned to Clairvaux. But on June 4, 1141, at the Cathedral at Sens, not far from Fontainebleau—Sens being then the archiepiscopal city of a vast province—the Church held a great synod attended by the bishops of Troyes, Orléans, Chartres, Auxerre, Nevers, Meaux, and Paris. The King was to be present. There was to be a vast concourse of priests and nobles. Suddenly Abélard wrote to the Archbishop of Sens, claiming the privilege of appearing before the synod to vindicate his belief. The Archbishop consented. Bernard was informed that he would once more have to sit in judgment. He had no liking for the task. With unaccustomed humility he said: "I am but a boy beside him, and he a warrior from his youth." For some reason he seems to have been nervous when he entered the Cathedral, his head bowed, invisible beneath the white woolen cowl, and he kept repeating under his breath: "The Lord is my helper, I shall not fear what men can do to me."[2] Shortly afterward Abélard entered, surrounded by his disciples, "with head erect and proud mien, startling those who looked on his worn and scornful face." Then Bernard quietly began reading seventeen heretical passages from Abélard's writings. The Cathedral was deathly silent, and suddenly, to the surprise of everyone, Abélard strode into the middle of the aisle and shouted: "I will not be judged like a criminal. I appeal to Rome!" Bernard reminded him that no one could or would harm him. For a moment Abélard stood there, irresolute, an old man with white hair and the face of a wounded eagle; then he ran out of the church, followed by his disciples.

Bernard's triumph was complete. There was, however, little satisfaction to be gained from it, for less than a year later

[2] There was, perhaps, something ominous in Bernard's use of the phrase. Abélard had called his oratory in the wilderness the Paraclete, meaning "the helper," and it was well known that this phrase was particularly dear to Abélard.

Abélard died at the priory of St. Marcel near Châlons-sur-Saône, having traveled only a little way to Rome.

Bernard's greater triumphs were to come later, but henceforth they were never to be quite so simple as they had been in the past, nor so final. The virtue seemed to be seeping away from him. More and more he dreamed of Hugh of Burgundy, the great prince whose body lay at Citeaux. For years he had slept beside a copy of the Song of Solomon; he thought in terms of its oriental imagery, the splendor of its prophecy. The Latin kingdom in Palestine was in danger. The time had come, Bernard thought, observing how the people tended to love their comforts rather than Christ, for a new hardening of the spirit, a new adventure in the East. Louis VII was determined to lead the Crusade; the Pope blessed it; it needed only the spark of Bernard's sanctity to bring it about. Bernard saw his opportunity. He traveled everywhere, attended all the councils which were brought about to speed the venture, and at Vezelay, on Easter Day, 1146, he spoke to immense crowds of the need to safeguard the Holy Land with such fervor that a fever spread through the multitude, and they would have marched in the direction of Palestine then and there if Bernard had not prevented them. There was no church large enough to house them. He addressed the people from a high platform in the open air. The King and Queen, together with half the nobility of France, were there; and when the cry of "Crosses! Crosses!" was heard, clothes were ripped apart to form waving crosses nailed to branches.

All through Bernard's life there had been the fever for heroism. Small and shrunken, with deep-set glowing eyes, he was still a power in the world. In all but name Bernard was head of the Church. Almost all France was prepared to follow him, and he could say with a touch of his old pride that wherever he went "castles and towns were emptied of their inhabitants, and one man could hardly be found among seven women, while the women were being everywhere widowed while their husbands were still alive." The Crusades enforced chastity, which pleased him, but he was full of sorrow that Conrad, Emperor of Germany, had so far refused to join the Crusade. At Christmas, Bernard bearded the Emperor at Spires and preached to him, saying: "What is there, O man, I should have done for thee and have not done?" Everywhere Bernard had gone in Germany there had been miracles, and now the Emperor wondered whether he could disobey a man who so evidently spoke with the authority of the greatest of saints. The Emperor said: "I am ready to serve Him, seeing I am admonished by Him." He joined the crusade.

It had been hoped that Bernard would himself lead the crusaders to the Holy Land. He refused, afraid perhaps that his pride would reach unknown heights if he set himself at the head of the two Emperors. "You may be sure," he wrote to the Pope, "that it is not of my counsel or will, and has no possibility in it. I beseech you, by the love which you owe me, that you shall not deliver me over to these human desires." Bernard returned to Citeaux, to the unshaven monks, the kitchen gardens, the long brooding hours spent with the Song of Solomon on his knees as he sat in the gardens, waiting for the moment when his Templars would send a messenger saying that Palestine had been retrieved for Christ. Instead the crusaders were cut to pieces.

When the defeated remnants returned to France, he said: "Better that I be blamed than God." But he blamed the people for their irreligion, and when he wrote his *De Consideratione* he took care to show exactly where the blame lay.

The *De Consideratione* is a violent book written at a violent time. Bernard addressed himself to Pope Eugenius III, who had once been his inferior in the monastery, and with all the resources at his command he urged the Pope to change his conduct, to mend his ways entirely, and to model himself on Gregory the Great, who went on quietly working at his *Homilies of the Prophet Ezekiel* when Rome was being besieged. With the failure of the Second Crusade a kind of panic had overtaken the papacy. Eugenius was flying in all directions at once, giving orders, countermanding them, wholly at a loss to deal with the situation; and quietly, tartly, sometimes cunningly and always rashly, Bernard reminds him to take care of his own body, to put the government of the papacy in order, to remember the cardinal virtues (in which Eugenius was almost entirely lacking), and above all to remember the words of the Psalmist: "Be still, and know that I am God."

Bernard wrote the *De Consideratione* during the last three years of his life: he had hardly finished it when he died. In a sense it was his testament, and in another sense he was not talking to Eugenius so much as to the world at large. By "consideration" he meant "contemplation," and it was this that he found lacking in the world. "Consideration," he wrote, "purifies the fountain of the mind, governs the affections, directs actions, corrects excesses, softens manners, adorns our lives and bestows upon us the knowledge of human and divine things. Consideration puts order in all things, weighs all truths, exposes all fallacies. In prosperity consideration has knowledge of adversity: in adversity it is as though it had no feeling." The world without contemplation is without God, and Bernard hints that God has departed from the papacy, which is more concerned with money and power than with the souls of men. "The Church," declared Bernard, "is full of ambitious men. The time has gone by for being shocked at the enterprising efforts of ambition: we think no more of it than a robber's cave thinks of the spoils of the wayfarers."

Though he rebukes Eugenius, Bernard rebukes himself. More than anyone else he had been responsible for the Second Crusade; and he quotes against himself the ancient texts: "He craftily led them out that he might slay them in the desert," but defends himself by remembering how rebellious the army had been. They had thought of Egypt, not Jerusalem: so they were scattered and confounded. Though he takes some of the blame, he refuses to take all. It was God's word. He had spoken. Bernard was merely the messenger of God. He is not very convincing; nor is he very convincing when he makes a distinction between contemplation and consideration, saying that one involves the unerring apprehension of the truth and the other is merely the mind working toward truth. Distinctions do appear, but they vanish and then recur: and it is not when Bernard is splitting theological hairs so much as when he is exhorting or plumbing the curious depths of the soul that we feel he is on safe ground. He was not a theologian, but a mystic who wrote passionately about divine love, and like many mystics he would be cruel and intolerant as he urged others to fight wars. Again and again, hardly troubling to veil his language, Bernard summons the Pope to a third Crusade:

Go out, I say, into the world: for the field is the world, and given into your charge. Go out, not as the lordly owner, but as the steward, so that you may see and attend whereof you must give an account. . . . Do you lift up as it were the eyes of your consideration and see the earth, if it was not rather dry for burning than white for harvest. So it will happen many times that what you take for the fruits of the earth will prove to be briars; nay, not briars, but old and rotten trees, and not fruit-trees either; the trees here bear only fruit fit for swine, acorns and husks. Should you go out and clearly see them, will you not be ashamed that your ax is idle? (Bernard, *De Consideratione*, II, 12.)

The picture of the earth dry for burning is terrifying, but Bernard has not finished with it. He reminds Eugenius that the prophets and apostles were brave warriors, not idle voluptuaries, not robed in silk. "Be clad with wisdom, and saintly fortitude: then the inheritance will be yours. The whole ancestral estate is yours by right." Then, with extraordinary invective, Bernard denounces the "painted pomp" of the papacy and reminds his former pupil that he is a man, nothing more, a helpless babe in need of consideration and advice:

So tear away the covering of leaves which conceal your shame, but do not cure your wound. Strip off those disguises of temporal honor, the tinsel of false glory, and gaze at your nakedness, for naked you came from your mother's womb. Did you then wear the fillet? Did you shine with jewels? Were you robed in flowery silk? Did the plumes wave over your head? Were you decked with gold and silver embroidery? If you put away all these things from your mind, as the morning mists scatter and altogether melt away, if you blow them from before the face of your consideration, you will behold yourself as you are—poor, naked, wretched, pitiable, grieving over your birth, ashamed of your nakedness, weeping to be born; a man born to labor, not to honor; born of a woman, and therefore damned; living only a little while, and therefore full of fear; full of miseries and forever bathed in tears. (Bernard, *De Consideratione*, II, 18.)

As though the portrait of the human condition was not enough, Bernard goes on to remind the Pope of how his predecessors had fared, hinting that there was little enough difference between the rule of Eugenius and the rule of the terrible Popes of the tenth century. At this point, for no particular reason except that his sense of mystery demands it, Bernard launches out into a discussion on length, breadth, height, and depth. These he will interpret in his own manner at intervals through the work. When he talks of the evil within the Pope's breast, then length means "going beyond all bounds," breadth means "a rent in the fabric," height means "a falling down," and depth means the abyss. In something of the same manner the ancient Chinese interpreted the trigrams. Bernard, like them, changes the interpretations at will, quite arbitrarily, and yet he is curiously revealing. It is not nonsense. He is talking about real things, about good and evil, about the flaming edges of things, where words are of hardly any avail. Later the mist clears, and when he says that God is fourfold, containing length, breadth, height, and depth, he becomes more intelligible. What is length? he asks. It is eternity. What is breadth? It is love. The answers seem simple enough, but suddenly the mist thickens again, and he says in almost the same words that Pascal was to use after him: "So God is immeasurable, Who hath made all things by measure: and although He is immeasurable, His very immensity must be measured." It is a disturbing phrase, flashing like a shower of meteors across the skies only to vanish, leaving no trail in the upper air, for immediately afterwards Bernard is once more back again at the game of checkers. What is height? he asks. It is divine power. What is depth? It is divine wisdom. So length, breadth, height, and depth correspond to eternity, love, majesty, and wisdom; and it is still not the end, for fear corresponds to height and depth, love to breadth and length, and at the very end of *De Consideratione* Bernard discovers that in human terms length corresponds to meditation upon the divine rewards, breadth corresponds to the remembrance of benefits, height corresponds to the contemplation of God's majesty, and depth to the consideration of God's judgments.

It is easy to dismiss such arguments as childish; it is also dangerous. He must be judged by the fruits of these strange arguments written in hot haste. Out of them come poetry. Bernard is trying to say something, he is not quite sure what, and suddenly all the odd fragments crystallize into a passionate and revealing statement of faith; and having twisted length, breadth, height, and depth into the oddest shapes, like a conjuror playing with an immense number of different colored ribbons, he suddenly reveals the one eternal ribbon in all its purity:

Most wonderful is the height of His Majesty, most fearful the abyss of His judgments. Divine love demands your zeal, the eternity of God portrays your constant endurance. Who wonders, but he who contemplates the glory of God? Who fears, but he who searches the depths of His wisdom? Who glows with zeal, but he who meditates on the love of God? Who endures and perseveres in love, but he who aspires to copy eternal love? In truth perseverance is a sort of likeness here to eternity hereafter. In fact it is perseverance alone on which eternity is bestowed; or rather it is perseverance which bestows man on eternity; as the Lord says: "He that shall persevere unto the end, the same shall be saved." (Bernard, *De Consideratione*, V, 31.)

There at last, faintly concealed as though with a thin covering of ice, the tremendous concepts of height, depth, breadth, and length take their proper place in his poetry.

But poetry is rare in the *De Consideratione*. Bernard assumes all postures. He taunts, raves, thumps the table, whispers the most sinister suggestions, swears by the living God that the papacy is mortally wounded, and by the same God proves that the star of Bethlehem still shines over it. He cajoles, threatens, rebukes, and sneers. He reminds Eugenius of the parable of Nathan concerning the man who, having a hundred sheep, coveted the one belonging to a poor man. He reminds the Pope that the bishops are attended by beautiful boys who wear silks and curl their hair. There must be an end to it. The Pope is plagued by appeals to his court. Why does he allow these appeals to be heard? Presumption, avarice, pride, and the corruption of the Papal court—these are the things that Bernard finds himself fighting against, and all his arguments end in this: Unless the papacy is pure, faith is corrupted at its source; *therefore beware!*

Toward the end of the book Bernard gathers momentum, and dives deeper. He is concerned that Eugenius should understand the nature of God and the nature of the corruption around him, these above all. He defines God in a hundred ways, but all the ways are mystical: the dove slips from his hand, flies into the air, is nowhere in sight, and lo! it is still in his hand, and he must attempt to grasp it all over again. As for the corruption around him, there is no end to it, and all of it comes from the presumptuous desire to oppose the will of God. The evil must be punished. It is as simple as that. With relish he quotes the text of Jeremiah: "Break them with a double breach, O Lord our God." Between the evil and the holy there is eternal war, and one of them will be injured: it will certainly not be God. To the evil God says: "It is hard for thee to kick against the pricks." "It is not hard for the pricks," Bernard observes, "but it is infinitely hard for him who kicks." And then quite suddenly there flies into his mind

the text: "Everyone that doeth evil hateth the light," and at
this point, in what are perhaps the last words Bernard ever
wrote, there occurs the most beautiful, as it is the most majes-
tical of all his writings: a brief, fierce dissertation on the
nature of evil and the second death:

God shines in darkness, and the darkness comprehends Him
not. The light sees the darkness, for with it seeing and shining
are the same thing; but it is not seen by the darkness, because the
darkness comprehends it not. They, then, are seen that they may
be confounded, and they do not see that they may be consoled.
Nor are they seen only by the light: they are also seen in the
light. Who, then, sees them? They are seen by all who can see,
so that the greater the number of beholders the greater may be
their confusion. Out of the whole multitude of the spectators
there is no eye more troublesome to a man than his own. There
is no glance, whether in heaven or earth, which an evil conscience
would rather escape, or is less capable of escaping. The darkness
is not hidden even from itself: though it sees nothing else, it sees
itself. The works of darkness follow after, and there is no hiding
place for darkness, not even in the darkness. This is "the worm
that dieth not"—the memory of the past. Once it gets within,
or rather is born within through sin, there it stays, and never by
any means can it be plucked out. It never ceases to gnaw at the
conscience, feeding on conscience as on food that can never be
consumed, and so prolonging the life of misery. I tremble to contemplate the biting worm, the never-dying death. I tremble at
the thought of being the victim of the living death and the dying
life: for this is the second death, which never kills, but is always
killing. None shall grant them the power to die once and for all,
but they must die eternally. So they say to the mountains, Fall
on us, and to the hills, Cover us, and they desire to put an end to
death by death's mercy, or escape from it. They call upon death,
but death comes not, and they die not. (Bernard, *De Consideratione*, V, 25, 26.)

It is like the roll of drums at the Last Judgment: this slow
gathering of dark arguments upon death. It was a subject he
knew well, for in a sense his whole life had been concerned

only with three things: the utmost life, the utmost God, and the utmost death.

When Bernard was writing the *De Consideratione* in the last years of his life, he was living in a small wattle hut in the monastery grounds, "a hut so small," they said, "you might have taken it for a leper's shack." He was living alone except for a servant who came to see that he was fed occasionally. He rarely ate, and he could not distinguish the difference in taste between butter and raw blood. He loved the taste of water, hardly anything else. Guillaume de St. Thierry, who visited him in the hut, said: "I found him dwelling in his own solitude, yet he was not alone, since God was with him, and he had the guardianship and comfort of the holy angels." His red beard turned white, his face became like parchment, almost transparent, and his eyes blazed with some inner light. Honors came thick upon him. The deacons of Milan begged him to follow Ambrose in the archbishopric; Rheims offered him the archiepiscopal throne. Ten or twelve other bishoprics were offered him; he refused them all. In any event he was too frail to move: his eyes were bloodshot, he could not remember when he had last slept, and his legs and arms were atrociously swollen.[3] At last he was carried back into the monastery to die. When the monks thought he was recovering and urged him to take food, he said: "Why do you detain a miserable man? You are the stronger and prevail against me. Spare me! Spare me, I beseech you, and permit me to depart." They insisted again that he should remain among them. He said, weeping: "I am torn between the two. I do not know whether to stay with you or to go to Christ, and so I leave it to the will of God."

He died at nine o'clock in the morning of August 20, 1153. He was sixty-two.

He belonged to that great order of the saints who combine,

---

[3] The swelling of Bernard's ankles was noticed very early in his life. He seems to have suffered from some form of heart disease.

by some miracle, a relentlessly active life with a relentlessly contemplative one. He seems never to have been still. Even in his contemplations, we are conscious of the waters boiling beneath. But sometimes, and usually these moments occur when he is traveling, there are moments of profound peace. Jacques de Vitry tells the story of Bernard riding abroad on a spring morning. Bernard saw some boys keeping their flocks in the fields, and then he said to his companions: "Turn, I pray you, and bless these boys, that they may bless us: so, armed with the prayers of the innocent, we may ride on with an easy mind."

X. ✠ FRANCIS: THE LOVER

AS HE GAZES OUT OF THE MAGNIFICENT PORTRAIT
by Cimabue, sorrowful and silent, standing alone
and a little apart from the Virgin as though he
dared not draw near to her, a small, dark-skinned
man wearing a brown habit folded loosely, with a low forehead, eyes like black olives, a long nose, a puckered mouth, and
a scrubby beard, with wrists as thin as chicken bones and no
flesh on him, we are hardly aware that he belongs to the great
order of the Fathers of the Church; and indeed he does not
appear among the lists of the Fathers, and he contended with
no theological problems and attained to no scholarship. He
laid down the law, but it was the simplest law of all, exactly
the same law that Augustine announced at the end of *The
City of God*: Have mercy on every living thing; do unto
others as ye would be done by; praise God. That was all, and
for Francis who called himself "ignorant and an idiot," *igno-
rans et ydiota*, it was enough. The statement, of course, contained a pardonable exaggeration. What was learning? If learning meant knowing the songs of the peasants and loving them,
Francis was learned: when he sang, with that soft, eager,
heavy voice, the peasants stopped work and ran to listen.
"What am I?" Francis asked once, and then told of a dream
in which he had seen himself as a little black hen. "Look at
me well," he laughed. "I am that hen, small of stature and
black."

It is right that Francis should be included among the
Fathers, for he puts them to shame. He came at the end of the

long process of discovery. With him, the wheel has turned full circle: we are back again in the gold-illuminated days of the apostles and of the early catacombs, the days when to be a Christian was to be carefree, before the heretics had arisen and the disputatious theologians had assumed the role of law-givers. Francis threw learning away and the world sighed with relief, for learning was already weighing heavily in the cloisters, and the librarians, as usual, were wondering whether they would be able to keep count of the books. "What have I to do with books?" Francis said. "O my brethren, all we need to do is pray."

One feels a very real respect for Ambrose; one likes and admires Gregory; it is singularly easy to feel kinship with Augustine; and there is no great difficulty in penetrating the damp cell in Bethlehem to find ourselves watching Jerome, big-boned and long-bearded, scribbling industriously and taking those immense breaths whose length is reflected in his majestic periods. They are giants, fit to be drawn by Michel-angelo, but we would not take them down a country road and we would not sing songs to them. But it is dangerously easy to love Francis even to lunacy.

Perhaps it is because he threw the books out of the win-dow with such a clatter and a bang that it can be heard down the ages. Almost he detested books. He was never known to read any book except the Bible, and even that he seems not to have read very extensively: a few passages were enough. One day a doctor of divinity approached him and asked for elucidation of the text of Ezekiel: *If thou speakest not to warn the wicked from his wicked ways, his blood will I require at thine hand.* The doctor of divinity explained that he knew some wicked people, and thought it time they should be warned. Francis said he was a fool. The doctor of divinity insisted that he had heard many learned men comment upon the passage, and the sense of it was clearly that unless you warned the wicked, all kinds of evils would be visited upon you by God. "No," said Francis, "I take the sense to be this.

The servant of God should so burn with holiness that he becomes an example to others. His splendor and the perfume of his name should be enough to warn the wicked of their iniquities." According to *The Mirror of Perfection*, the doctor of divinity went slowly on his way, muttering something about Francis's theology being "like to the flying eagle" while the learning of the theologians "crawled with its belly on the earth."

The Mirror of Perfection is not an impeccable witness to the truth, yet "His splendor and the perfume of his name" is the kind of phrase Francis would use. Jerome would have grappled with the text, held it to his breast, choked some wayward sense out of it, and erected upon the small foundations an edifice of theory demonstrating the perfect necessity of retribution. Francis was not concerned with retribution. He hardly ever mentions Hell. If he went there, he would have addressed the sinners as brothers and sisters, and unable to bear their torments he would have blown out the flames.

All the Church Fathers had thorns in their flesh, but it was Francis who received the stigmata. Thomas was obese, Jerome was tortured by the vision of the pit, Augustine was tortured with lust, Ambrose and Gregory with pride. Unlike them, Francis felt no need to suffer remorse for his gay past or to struggle with demons. As a youth he had a great deal of money and he liked to wear colored coats, the left side red and the right side yellow. He sang love songs as a youth, and he was still singing love songs when he was old. He even sang a love song when the learned doctors were drawing a red-hot poker along the whole length of his face from the chin to the temple in a futile effort to save his sight; and he blessed the doctors, who went on to cut the nerve near his eyes, and he prayed very humbly to the red-hot poker. When Francis was almost screaming with pain, a brother observed that "God is laying His hand more heavily on thee than is right."

"What a simple-minded little fool you are," Francis observed. "If I didn't know you better, I think I would have shunned your company for talking such nonsense. It's God's will that I should suffer, and there's an end to it."

In such simple ways did Francis speak of the problems which occupied the voluminous attention of the Church Fathers. He sang as sweetly and clearly as the cranes which Dante heard as they swept low over the marshes of Ravenna, and he saw no reason to do otherwise even when he was in pain.

As we read of the Church Fathers, we are made aware of immense strains, heroic efforts, terrible responsibilities. The Fathers of the fourth and fifth centuries were shoring up the ruins of Rome with their naked shoulders. They fought prodigiously, with superlative cunning, against the barbarians and the Emperors and all the tribes of wanton and evil people in the world. All is urgency, the smoke of camp fires, the trumpets on the towers. Slowly, almost imperceptibly, they drew away from life and found themselves devoted to concepts: righteousness, virginity, the hypostasis, the heresies. It was as though in their exhaustion they had come to believe the battle maps had more validity than the soldiers. Francis was inherently incapable of playing with concepts. He must see real people, dance with them, talk with them, play with them, suffer with them. The disputes of the theologians did not concern the humble farmers of Tuscany. He must make them dance and laugh: it is the simplest way: and if he had no fiddle, he would, says Thomas of Celano, "draw a stick across his arm and sing in French the praises of the Lord." Indeed, with his sweetness and gentleness he was more French than Italian, and there must be some truth in the story that his mother was French, for otherwise it is unlikely that he would have been called Francesco when he was born Giovanni.

If Francis was gay, there were yet moments when he could be terrible. The terrifying part of Francis is only hinted at in the records, though it is indisputably there: at such moments the face becomes skull-like, the little puckered mouth becomes a slit, and there is a horror shining behind the eyes. He said once:

Lift up a dead body and place it wherever you wish. You will see that it does not murmur at being moved, does not complain of the place where it is put, does not cry out at being left there. Placed on a high throne, it looks not up but down. Clad in purple, it becomes doubly pale. Well then, here is a truly obedient man, who does not ask why he is moved, does not care where he is put, does not beg to be placed elsewhere. Such a man, set in a place of authority, preserves his accustomed humility, and the more he is honored, the more unworthy to himself he becomes.

It is, of course, the monastic tradition which was to flower later into the Jesuit retreat, when the candidate during a retreat assumes in himself the postures of the dying and the dead Christ. But there is an unexpected chill in the phrase: "Clad in purple, it looks doubly pale." He said at another time that he never felt comfortable unless he was reviled. Once, when he saw in a dream an empty throne in heaven, he was told that the throne had belonged once to one of the fallen angels but was now reserved for Francis, and when he spoke of this to a saintly friend, he said: "I think I am myself the chief of sinners." Asked why he should think so, he answered: "If any man, howsoever guilty, had received such mercy from Christ as I, I verily think he would have been far more acceptable to God than I." There is a hint of terrible pride here, but it is no more than a hint: the words are too ambiguous to be understood clearly. There was a similar pride in his answer to Ugolino when he was urged to draw up a rule which followed the conventional practices of the past. Francis replied:

God has himself shown me the way of simplicity and humility, both for myself and for those who wish to believe and to follow me. Do not speak to me of the rules of St. Benedict, St. Augustine and St. Bernard, or any other. For me the only rule is the form of life which God in His mercy has shown to me and bestowed on me. *God made known to me that I was to behave with a mad-*

*ness that the world knew nothing of, and that such madness was
to be all the learning that we were to have. May God confound
your learning and your wisdom.* May He send evil spirits to
punish you, and you shall return to your own place, whether you
will or no, and curses shall be upon you.

There was some excuse for the outburst. Francis had returned
to Assisi to discover that the brothers, assembling together
for a chapter of the order, had built a large building for the
convenience of the more distinguished members. To Francis
the action was a kind of adultery against his Lady Poverty. He
climbed on the roof, and in his rage he began to hurl the tiles
down on the brothers below; and he would have stripped the
roof if the Commune of Assisi had not pointed out that the
building, erected within the city, belonged to the Commune.
Glowering with rage, Francis came off the roof. Shortly afterward, sick of distinctions of rank and sick of learning, he
wandered off to Egypt and, making his way through the
battlelines with astonishing audacity, bearded the Sultan in
his den, took a silent part in the bloody battle for Damietta,
and then wandered barefoot over Palestine. It was as though
in these perilous wanderings he was attempting to remove
from himself that *terribiltà*, the explosive prideful wrath
which came to so many men of his time.

Francis' fear of learning was real and undisguised, as the
chapter at Assisi showed, yet it was strangely modified. The
rule of his order did include, when finally composed, much
that was similar to the rule of St. Benedict. Curiously, Francis
omitted in his speech any reference to the Dominicans, an
order founded ten years before his own. The doctor of divinity who questioned the interpretation of a passage of Ezekiel
was a Dominican. But it was not so much Dominicans Francis
disliked as all those who talked too much and worked too little.
Such people he called "Brother Fly." He must have detested
flies as much as he detested laziness, for he talked about flies
with deliberate malice. When some of his friars had collected
more money than they needed, he said: "So you have got

some flies." It was part of his greatness and his newness that he invented words or changed their meaning. "Money" became "flies." It was also called "asses' dung." Such words were not important. What is important is the extraordinary depth and reverberation he gave to the words "brother" and "sister." There is no indication that anybody at any time before had talked of "Brother Wolf" or "Sister Lark," or "our brother the Sun." He was determined that words should possess familiar meanings. He shocked many by calling the Christ-child "Bambino." Contrary to the established rule, he accented the first syllable of "Bethlehem," saying that in this way he could call to mind the bleating of the lamb Jesus. He attempted to create a language of the affections where there was none before; and it was because they spoke in a language which was not affectionate that he half despised the scholars.

One day a novice came to see him to ask whether he could have approval to compile a collection of the Lives of the Saints. It was a subject on which Francis possessed strong views. He saw no reason to grant the request. He said: "Charlemagne and his paladins performed mighty deeds of valor against the infidels and they died in battle, martyrs for Christ's sake. Then came the poets who made epics from their great deeds and received money for reciting them in the streets and courtyards. It is the same with us. The saints accomplished great deeds, and now there are brothers who desire fame in recounting them." There he left the matter. A few days later, the novice returned to Francis and begged that in this case an exception should be made. He pointed out how the examples of the saints would improve the lives of the brothers. "Will they?" asked Francis. "After the legends of the saints you will want prayer-books, and then you will climb up into a chair like a bishop and say to your brother in God: 'Go, fetch me my prayer-book.' You see—" At this point Francis broke off, scooped up some ashes from the hearth, and placed them on his head. "There's your prayer-book!" he exclaimed. Francis had been in a rage. He grew calmer, and in a quiet voice went on: "It is given to you to know the mystery of God: for others there is book-learning. So many resort to book-learning that he is blessed who is ignorant and a witness for the love of God." For the second time the novice went away, but he returned to the charge some months later. Francis was ashamed of his burst of anger, and said: "Well, then, do as your confessor says." Then he added quickly and softly, as though he was talking about something else altogether, though in truth he was still talking about the legends of the saints: "He who would join the brotherhood shall possess only the cloak, the girdle and the pair of breeches, and if he really needs them he may add sandals to the list."

The appeal to poverty gave Francis authority for his relentless attack on the scholars. "The letter killeth," he said repeatedly. In the Rule of 1221 he wrote: "The clergy may have only such books as are necessary for their office, and the laymen who can read may be allowed to possess a psalter." Two years later, in another Rule, Francis wrote: "He who does not know his letters need not trouble to learn them." The order was ten years old before any book beside the New Testament was permitted to the monks, and even this they did not keep, but gave to the poor. Yet in this, as in other things, Francis was far from being consistent. In his youth he had read the *Song of Roland*, and the heroic strains of the French epic are echoed in some of his sermons: they formed, as it were, the groundswell of his heroic life. He was relentlessly opposed to anyone else's reading them. All evil was in them: surely it was enough that men should contemplate the glory of God. And if he was inconsistent in this, he was inconsistent in his attitude toward the habits of scholarship, for though he detested all books, he ordered that his sermons and conversations should be written down for the benefit of those who came after him, and he was especially careful that he should be reported accurately. Almost there was a scholastic in him. Augustine said once, thinking more of the pagan philosophers than of Christian scholars: "I accuse not words.

I accuse the wine of error that drunken doctors pour out for us in these fair goblets." Gregory, too, though he wrote interminably, came at moments to fear those words which so inadequately expressed his visions. The wine of error! For most of the Fathers scholarship was a heady wine which made them drunk with the glory of words. Francis believed it was of greater moment to be drunk with the glory of God, without words, even without the word of God.

But it was not the lives of the saints, the legends, and the Scriptures that Francis feared so much as the commentaries. When he lay dying, having composed his Testament, he begged that it should be read without subtle interpretations, for was not the meaning clear? When he spoke of poverty, he meant poverty; and when he spoke of eternal glory he meant simply that. To him it was easy, since he saw with his innocent eye everything bathed in clarity, but it was not so easy for his successors. Words change their meanings. There is a place for commentaries. In the years after his death inevitably the commentaries arose; there were even commentaries on his Testament, the most subtle disquisitions on the meaning of every phrase; it could hardly be helped. Yet the Testament was simple enough, for in it he announced only that the priests should possess a single habit, a girdle, and a pair of breeches; they must work; they must never enter houses as hosts but always as guests; they must never transgress against Holy Poverty; they must salute each other with the word of peace. He wrote:

We loved to live in poor and abandoned churches, and we were ignorant and submissive to all. I worked with my hands and would continue to do so, and it is my desire that all other friars work at some honorable trade. Let those who have none learn one, not for the purpose of receiving the price of toil, but for their good example and to flee idleness. And when they do not give us the price of the work, let us resort to the table of the Lord, begging our bread from door to door. The Lord revealed to me the salutation we ought to give: "God give you peace."

But what exactly was meant by peace? Was it simply the same greeting Francis had heard among the Mohammedans: *"Salaam aleikum"*? Or did it mean, as it seemed to mean, the peace of the first day of creation? or was it the peace Francis himself possessed in his heart through all his days?

With Francis a complete break is made with the past. The symphony becomes song again. He did not speak in that over-rich medieval Latin, which rings like metal and reverberates like echoes and seems to have been fashioned for the usage of Emperors. With Francis grandiloquence vanished. He would talk as ordinary people talk, or not at all. He refused to invent problems. The Church Fathers discoursed at length on the nature of man. Francis answered briefly: "Whatsoever a man is in the face of God, that is he, and no more." Sometimes, too, he spoke in a child's language, with a child's logic and a child's bad temper. When he had received the stigmata, he had no desire to show his wounds, and when one of the brothers saw the wound on his hand and asked him the cause, he answered bluntly enough: "Mind your own business!" At another time a brother observed some bloodstains on his clothes and asked the reason. In answer Francis put a finger to his eye and said: "Why don't you ask me what this is?" But that childishness, that clarity and good humor were to have unfathomable consequences: one of them was that he became as he lay dying the first Italian to write a great religious poem in the vernacular, and therefore he became the herald of all the songs that came after.

During the last days of his life, shortly before the doctors cauterized his ears and cheeks and temples in the hope of saving his eyesight from the trachoma which was fast eating into his eyes, Francis lived in a small straw hut beside the monastery wall. He was ill and feverish. The rats came through the straw and climbed on him, and though he loved

animals, he made an exception of rats, and was terrified.
Their creeping kept him from sleep. They rustled in the
straw and gathered the few crumbs on his table. He was in
delirium. But one morning, to everyone's astonishment, he
was found leaning against a tree outside the hut with his cowl
drawn over his face. He had never drawn his cowl down like
this before, and now he resembled the ancient Romans who
veiled their faces when they approached the gods. At such
times the Romans spoke with bated breath, haltingly and
ponderously; but the brethren who came out into the garden
to hear Francis as he spoke beneath the tree were surprised
once again by the singular sweetness of his voice. As so many
times before, he told a morning parable. He said: "If the Emperor gives to one of his servants an entire Kingdom, ought
not that servant to be grateful? If the Emperor gives to one
of his servants the entire Empire, should he not be even more
grateful? So ought I to be grateful for my sufferings, and
give grace to God, for while I am still in the flesh, He has
given me the certainty that I shall enter His Kingdom. Therefore, in praise of Him, and for the consolation and edification
of the world, I will make a new song of praise for all the creatures of the Lord whom we make use of every day, and without whom we cannot live, though we are not grateful enough
to Him for his help, and often offend Him." For a while he
was thoughtful, withdrawn in the darkness of his cowl. Then
they heard him singing:

Most high omnipotent good Lord:
To Thee be the praise, the glory, the honor and all blessing:
Only to Thee do they belong:
And no man is worthy to name Thee.

Praised be my Lord God with all his creatures, especially our
brother the Sun,
Who brings us the day and enlightens us with it:
Fair is he, and shining with great splendor:
O Lord, he bears Thy similitude.

Praised be my Lord for Sister Moon and for the stars:
For Thou hast formed them clear and beautiful in the heavens.

Praised by my Lord for Brother Wind and for the air and clouds
and calms and all weathers:
By which Thou givest sustenance to all Thy creatures.

Praised be my Lord for Sister Water:
Who is most useful, humble, precious and chaste.
Praised be my Lord for Mother Earth:
Who doth sustain and keep us, and bringeth forth various fruits
and colored flowers and grass.

Praised be my Lord for Brother Fire,
Through whom Thou givest light in darkness:
And he is bright and pleasant and very mighty and strong.

Praise ye and bless the Lord,
And give thanks unto Him and serve Him with humility.

This is the "song of the creatures" as we know it, but it was not the end. Other verses were to come later, dedicated to those who endure in peace the infirmities of the body; finally, there was a song about death:

Praised be my Lord for those who offer pardon for Thy love's
sake,
Who bear infirmity and tribulation:
Blessed are they who shall endure in peace:
For Thou, O most High, shalt give unto them a crown.

Praised be my Lord for Sister Death,
From whom no living man escapeth.
Woe to him who dieth in mortal sin!
Blessed are they who find themselves within Thy most holy will,
For the second death shall do no harm to them.

In these verses nearly all theology was contained. So artless that they come with the breath, so rude and vigorous that they might have been sung by a gifted peasant, they spoke directly of the things which Thomas Aquinas was to speak about at great length, and with the utmost difficulty. So it was nearly always with Francis, who reverenced fire, air, earth, and water like the Greeks, but with a Christian tongue. At times he seems to emerge from some long-distant past, from a prehistoric age when miracles abounded and a sense of wonder still informed people, a time when the most casual things assumed a profound significance, and men, animals, and trees were brothers. "Sister Rat," he said once in a long agony before his death, "I am tired and would like to sleep," and it was characteristic of him that he should address the rats gently, though horrified by them.

The last letter he wrote was addressed to Lady Giacoma dei Settesoli asking for a piece of gray cloth to patch his clothes and some of the sweet almond cakes they had once eaten together: the homespun and the sweetness were there from the beginning. For the rest there was song, which is itself no small part of theology, and he was still singing when he died on Saturday, October 4, 1226.

If Francis was the most wonderful of the saints, it was because he was the simplest, the most human, the most recognizable; and if we call him a Father of the Church, it is because his learning was prodigious: he knew God, and by knowing God he changed the atmosphere of his times. There was a directness about him which came in the end to be a part of the western tradition: he has left his mark on us all, and we can no more escape him than we can escape the knowledge of Jesus. And as though the continuing tradition of the Church was to be maintained even chronologically, there was born in the year before he died another Father of the Church, who was the antithesis of Francis in nearly everything. Between the humble Francis and the imperious Thomas Aquinas the field of the Church is enclosed.

XI. ❧ THOMAS AQUINAS: THE ANGELIC DOCTOR

N O ONE WILL EVER KNOW HOW THOMAS AQUINAS found time to write his monumental studies. He was called "the dumb ox," and though he was prodigiously fat, suffered from dropsy, and had one enormous oxlike eye which seemed to look out upon the world while the smaller eye looked inward, no one ever resembled a dumb ox less. He could be, and often was, moved to fury. Like Socrates, he could stand for hours, completely unconscious of the world around him, as he thought out in an odd, colorless, and flexible Latin he had invented for the purpose, all the permutations and combinations of God in man. He was the pure Christian and at the same time the pure Aristotelian. He had the scientist's temper. The causes *for* and the causes *against* were marked out in separate columns. He would weigh one against the other, and calculate nicely the differences between them. Everything was to be weighed, valued, interpreted, and placed in a proper order. All books were to be read, all sources analyzed, every manifestation of the spirit placed in the balance. In all this he was almost the exact contrary of his school friend Bonaventura. There is a story that when Thomas Aquinas paid a visit to Bonaventura, he asked to see his friend's library. Bonaventura pointed to the crucifix hanging on the wall. "There," he said, "is where I have learned everything I know."

The story is probably true. Thomas's passionless, excited mind thought more in terms of concepts than emotions. For him the world was finite, obeying heavenly laws as strict and calculable as the laws of the mathematicians. Bonaventura found no library greater than the one he found in his own soul as he contemplated God. For him everything was immediate and infinite, touched by the Godhead, remote and perfect. He detested the scholars who put their faith in Aristotle, calling them "followers of darkness," and he roared against "the accursed heathen Aristotle" as Luther was to do later, and perhaps for the same reasons. When Luther said of Thomas Aquinas that he was "the dregs of all heresies, errors, and destruction of the Gospel," he was only repeating the hint made by Bonaventura. Yet Thomas and Bonaventura were friends. They studied together in Paris, took their licentiate together, taught in the same schools, and held one another in high honor, though they differed in everything. "*Credo ut intelligam,*" wrote Augustine. "I believe in order to understand." With Bonaventura a simple *Credo* was enough. With Thomas Aquinas *credere* and *intelligere* seem to have become synonymous: an incredible intelligence lay behind those aristocratic brows.

Accustomed to remember him as the author of the great *Summa Theologica*, that vast inquiry into the nature of the universe which he intended characteristically as a mere introduction for the use of beginners, we forget the living man. He seems not to breathe. He is pure logic. There are even moments when he has the appearance of a terrifying theological precision machine, reducing everything to straight lines, a man who has killed the marionette in himself and exists only to solve conundrums, as unfabulous a creature as anyone could imagine, and as insensitive. In fact there was a great deal of the fabulous about him, and there were many moments in his life when his senses spoke out aloud.

He was born high up on the hills beyond Monte Cassino, in the dark desolate regions where the eagles had their eyries, in one of those immense castles which had grown out of small mountain fortresses. His father was a nephew of Frederick Barbarossa, and bore the name of Landulf, Count of Aquino,

Lord of Loreto, Acerra, and Belcastro. He was a Lombard noble, while his wife came from Norman stock and could trace her descent back to the Anglo-Saxon kings. Before her marriage she was Theodora Carraciola, Countess of Teano. Through one or the other of his parents Thomas could claim kinship with two Emperors and with the kings of Aragon, Castile, and France; Honorius III, the Pope who had confirmed the Order of Preachers, was his godfather; his grandfather was the Captain-General of all the imperial forces. He believed that the name Thomas meant "abyss," and it pleased him that he could interpret his name in the sense of a text from Habakkuk: "The abyss put forth its voice." He knew danger early. When he was three, in the summer of 1228, lightning struck the tower where he was sleeping beside his nurse. He was unharmed, but his sister lay dead and charred, and all the horses in the stables beneath the tower were killed. It is unlikely that the story was invented. On those mountains summer storms rage with a ferocious intensity, and for the rest of his life he had a dread of storms and continually referred to this incident in his childhood, wondering why he was spared.

At the age of six and a half he was sent to the Benedictine monastery at Monte Cassino. In the previous year the monastery had been looted by Frederick Barbarossa and the Aquinos had done nothing to defend it; but it was remembered that they fought against Roger, King of Sicily, when he had swept down the valley, and the boy was placed in a special school for those of noble birth and was given various privileges. He was attended by his own private tutor. It was observed that he was almost unbearably refined and sensitive in his manner, clung to his books, and spent long hours in the seclusion of the church. When he was eleven or twelve, he quietly disappeared from Monte Cassino and went to study at Naples University, where he learned mathematics, astronomy, and music, made some study of dialectics, and read Caesar, Cicero, and Seneca. At moments when he was concentrating or when he was praying, men said they saw a faint gold shimmering halo around his head.

In Naples Thomas possessed his own residence, his own retinue, a host of servants. He took to riding on horseback, with plumes and flowing silks, around the bay. He visited the blue grotto at Capri. He had a taste for beauty and liked to repeat Augustine's saying: "If the work of His hands be so lovely, O how much more beautiful must be He who made them." He learned lucidity as much from the clear outlines of the bay as from the venerable old Irishman who taught him. And then quite suddenly, saying nothing to his parents, he embraced the Dominican Order of Preachers, put on their white and black habit, and announced that his titles were henceforth in abeyance. He seemed hardly aware of the furore that would inevitably arise from his action. His mother complained to the Pope and the Archbishop of Naples. He had been a prince and was now vowed to mendicancy as a wandering friar, and he did not care. The Pope offered to make him Lord Abbot of Monte Cassino with the privilege of wearing his Dominican habit. He refused and wandered alone to Rome. His mind was made up. Years afterwards, when he came to write the *Summa Theologica*, he wrote beneath the question: "Whether duties toward parents are to be set aside for the sake of religion?" the simple answer: "Whoever loves father or mother more than Me is not worthy to follow Me," and he quoted from Jerome's famous letter to Heliodorus: "Though your father fling himself down on the doorstep, trample him underfoot, go your way and fly with dry eyes to the standard of the Cross."

If Thomas had hoped it would be easy to disappear from his family, he was mistaken. While the Countess was deluging Rome with complaints, Thomas hurried north in the direction of Paris. He was resting with two friars beside a spring between Siena and Lake Bolsena when he suddenly heard the clang of bridles, followed by the shouts of his two brothers

Landulf and Reynaldo. They tore off his white and black habit and bore him back to the castle on Rocca Secca. Later he was shut up in a castle on Monte San Giovanni, some miles away. His sisters Marietta and Theodora were sent to implore him to change his mind. He refused. Other weapons were employed. One night an entrancing young woman was sent into his prison. Thomas picked up a burning faggot from the hearth, drove her from his cell, then traced the sign of the Cross on the wall with the brand, leaving a scorched mark which could be seen there for years afterwards. When he went to sleep again he dreamed that two angels were placing a white girdle around him. They said: "We come to thee from God, to bestow upon thee the grace of perpetual virginity." They girded him so tightly that he awoke with a loud cry of pain. For the rest of his life, according to his chronicler and confessor, Reginald of Piperno, he wore the white girdle secretly under his habit.

Thomas was not entirely alone in the cell. Not only his sisters but his brothers came to visit him. The Dominican friar, John of St. Julien, contrived to enter his cell secretly and supply him with a new habit. The old Count Landulf heard of this and ordered that Thomas should be taken to another cell underground, with only bread and water; but he was already relenting. Somehow Thomas received books, parts of the Bible, Aristotle's *Metaphysics*, the *Sentences* of Peter Lombard. The Dominicans lodged complaints with the Pope and the Emperor against the unjust privation of liberty; both issued stringent orders for his release. The old Count still refused. As the son of the Captain-General of the imperial forces, he regarded himself as equal to the Pope or the Emperor, but his other sons contrived to let Thomas escape one night from a window. For eighteen months Thomas had been imprisoned. Now, though his health was broken and he was as white as a ghost, he prepared to enter the order afresh. There were still complaints against him from his family. He presented himself

to the Pope, and either during this audience or shortly afterwards he composed the greatest, as it is the simplest, of his
prayers:

Lord Jesus Christ, I pray that the fiery and honey-sweet power
of Thy love may detach my soul from everything under heaven,
so that I may die from love of Thy love, Who out of love for my
people didst die upon the tree of the Cross. Amen.

It is perhaps worth remembering when we read the dry logic
of the *Summa* that he was perpetually conscious of a "fiery
and honey-sweet power."

"The fiery and honey-sweet power" remained with him
through his life. He was poet as well as metaphysician, and
wrote, to the meter of an old Roman marching song, some of
the greatest of medieval hymns, including the hymns for the
Office of Corpus Christi and the famous *Pange, lingua, glori-
osi corporis mysterium*, though this was based on another
hymn by Fortunatus. When he was at his devotions, it was
observed that he was shaken to the depths, weeping and sighing, throwing out his arms, remaining sometimes all night on
the steps of the altar. The calm of his prose is delusory, concealing furious emotions. When his brother Reynaldo was
killed, taking up arms against the Emperor, and his mother
was exiled from the castle on Rocca Secca, he showed the
same implicit calm, but once again it was the calm of banked
fires.

With John of Wildeshausen, Master-General of the Order
of Preachers, Thomas walked to Paris in the autumn and
winter of 1245. They went on their way slowly, carrying
nothing except their staffs, their breviaries, and their wallets
with their food. They plodded across the rainy plains of
Lombardy in November, crossed the Alpine passes in December, and followed along the Valley of the Rhone in January. They paused briefly in Paris at the Priory of St. Jacques,
and then for some reason decided to march on to Cologne,
where the "Universal Doctor," Albertus Magnus, another
aristocrat from Bavaria, was teaching. Here in Cologne

Thomas for the first time received the name of "the dumb Sicilian ox": Sicilian, because his mother's family came from Sicily; dumb ox, because he leaned quickly out of a window when a student said there was a winged ox flying over the convent. When the other students roared with laughter, Thomas replied: "I was not so simple as to believe an ox could fly, but I never imagined a religious man could stoop to falsehood." He was not usually so sententious, but the name stuck to him, even after Albertus Magnus said that if he was an ox, at least he could bellow doctrine louder than anyone else in Christendom. He was a good pupil, his mind moving easily within the complex dialectics of the time: the retorts, the axioms transgressed, the subdivisions of subdistinctions. Albertus admired him, and when he was invited to lecture in Paris, he took Thomas with him.

It was in Paris that Thomas first came under the influence of St. Augustine. For the rest of his life he was concerned to recast the wild outpourings of Augustine into the terse and accurate speech of Scholasticism, weighing every sentence Augustine wrote and putting order into Augustine's wild disorder. Thomas spent two years in Paris. A huge man, with dewlaps and a heavy fat face, he would be seen walking in the priory garden lost in thought, completely unaware of his surroundings. Once, returning from St. Denis with his students, he was so oblivious of his surroundings that he failed to see the shape of Paris rising before him. One of the students said: "Master, do you not see how beautiful Paris is?" Thomas snorted: "Oh yes, quite beautiful." "Master," said the student, "I would to God the city was yours!" Thomas turned to him slowly: "What do you think I could possibly do with it?" "You could sell it to the King of France," the student laughed, "and with the money build convents for the Order of Preachers." Thomas thought for a moment. "There is only one thing I want now—the homilies written by St. Chrysostom on the Gospel according to St. Matthew." Then, ponderously, he walked on toward Paris.

There are other stories told about him: all of them reveal the flavor of the man. Once he found his friend Bonaventura engaged in his cell on the composition of a life of St. Francis. Thomas had important matters to discuss, but Bonaventura was in one of his rapt studies, and Thomas tiptoed out of the room, whispering: "Let us leave a saint to write about a saint." An even more revealing story is told of the time when he was summoned to dine with St. Louis, the King of France. He forgot where he was, lost in some debate with himself on the nature of good and evil, and while the others were in the midst of conversation he suddenly struck the table with his huge hand, saying: "Ah, there's an argument which will destroy the Manichees." There was consternation round the table; the prior jerked his shoulders, and whispered hotly that he must ask humble pardon of the King, who observed kindly: "Our friar has been thinking. Summon the secretary to take down the thought before it escapes."

It was a request which Thomas entirely approved of. Like Jerome, he liked to have three or four secretaries around him. In his short life he wrote thirty books, many of them voluminous. He found himself as a writer only after he had returned to Cologne, having passed two years in Paris. Inevitably he began with studies on the three books he had read in his prison cell at Monte San Giovanni. His first work was a treatise called *On Being and Essence*, being an examination of some ideas in Aristotle's *Metaphysics*. He went on to write a *Commentary on the Sentences of Peter Lombard*, and having passed through Brabant on his way to Cologne and met Adelaide Duchess of Brabant, he compiled for her a treatise *On the Government of the Jews*.

There followed unruly years in France. "The dumb ox," usually regarded as passive, quiescent, and determined only to seek God by the study of God's laws, hurled himself into the fray. The University of Paris has never been a quiet place. Some students were murdered. Orders came from the chancellor that all lectures must cease until the culprits were punished. The Dominicans continued to teach, Thomas among them. There were doctrinal disputes, waged bitterly. While Thomas was preaching on Palm Sunday at St. Jacques', a University proctor marched into the church and read out a letter from William of St. Amour and other doctors, full of bitterness against the mendicant orders. The letter demanded the curtailment of the influence of the mendicants. Thomas went calmly on with his sermon. But the issue was now joined. The matter engaged the attention of the Pope, who had to decide whether the Dominicans and Franciscans were to be allowed to teach in the schools. Both parties were summoned to appear in Rome. Finally the mendicant friars won the dispute, and Thomas returned to Paris to receive the cap and ring, the outward signs of his doctorate. He lectured, he became a member of the King's Privy Council, and there began in those years the immense correspondence which he carried on till his death. He also began to write the *Summa contra Gentiles* at the invitation of Raymund de Pennafort, who had resigned from the order to become a preacher in Spain. It was the first of the long works, written in the calmest professorial tones, an "unhurried hunt" after his quarry. There is no flashing of wings. He was following the precept of his favorite St. Chrysostom, who wrote in one of his homilies on St. Matthew: "The full measure of philosophy is to be simple with prudence: such is an angelic life." But simplicity and prudence were abandoned when he wrote on the margins of his manuscript, in a crabbed medieval handwriting: "I pray to Thee, O Lord, or else I am lost." The margins were peppered with the words: "*Ave Maria.*"

In 1261 Thomas was summoned to Italy by Urban IV. For the next eleven years he was always traveling. He taught for short periods in Rome, Pisa, and Bologna, and when the General Chapter of the order met in London at Pentecost in the year 1263, he accompanied them, staying in the priory at Holborn, receiving a new white and black habit from King Henry III, and taking part in the election of Albertus Magnus as the new Vicar-General. He returned to Rome by way of Paris and Milan, and composed the Office of Corpus Christi, in which there was so great a marriage of doctrine and song that Urban IV presented him with a large silver dove containing the sacred species. Shortly afterwards, amid a host of other occupations, he began to compose the *Summa Theologica*.

He was now at the height of his powers, and every kind of position was offered him. He refused them all, content, as he said, "to remain a humble religious." His appearance grew more commanding. They said that his skin was "the color of new wheat," his nose aquiline and strong, his mouth firm, the lips sucked in a little: only his eyes were still a little frightening, the larger one seeming to have more life than the other and to be concerned with separate things.[1] His habits were formed. The long hours spent on the steps of the altar at night were continued sometimes all day; he could fall into a kind of meditative trance whenever he desired. Sometimes he would dictate to three secretaries at once, and when he was dictating he would be completely oblivious of the world around him. Once, so that his secretaries could see the parchment they were writing on, he held the candle, and until he smelled the burning flesh he did not know it had burned down to his hand. He saw visions. The apostle Paul came quietly into his room to explain a problem of interpretation. Once he entered his cell to see Christ standing among his tumbled manuscripts written on odd scraps of paper. Toward the end of his life he spoke frequently of seeing the Virgin in a corner of his cell. He wrote prayers to her, though none was as fine as the prayer on "the fiery and honey-sweet power." Inevitably, when he described her, he saw her in terms of pure light, saying she was "the brightest of bright mirrors, more

---

[1] There was a tradition in the Middle Ages, at least as old as Gregory the Great, that the right eye represented the contemplative life, the left, the active life. (*Dexter namque vita contemplativa est sinister activa. —Moralia,* VI, 57.) Accordingly, commentators have always referred to Thomas's large *right* eye, though the portraits show the left eye as being greater.

polished and purer than the Seraphim, of such purity that nothing purer can be imagined except it were God." He had called God once "intelligible light," and like the perpetual opening of windows the words for "light" and "shining" flow through his work.

To the very end he remained the aristocrat, never smiling overmuch, inflexibly resolved to seek God. He said he could never understand how anyone conscious of mortal sin could laugh or be merry. When his sister Theodora inquired how to become a saint, he replied with one word: *Velle* (Resolve). When he gave sermons, he threw back his head, closed his eyes, and gripped the handrail so tightly that the knuckles shone white; and this strange posture gave him the appearance of a general about to order an attack. His favorite ejaculation was: *Tu Rex gloriae, Christe: Tu Patris sempiternus es Filius*, and perhaps it was characteristic of the man who was related to half the kings of Europe that he should have praised the King of Glory and omitted the Holy Ghost.

He spent the last years of his life at Naples, suffering from toothache and malaria, seeing visions and talking to the dead. He once saw the devil as a Negro. Once he saw Father Romanus, to whom he had vacated his chair at the University of Paris. Thomas asked: "How do I stand with God, and are my works pleasing to Him?" He had asked the same question of his dead sister, and now received the same reply: "Thou art in good state and thy works are pleasing to God." Thomas then asked: "How do the Blessed see God, and do our acquired habits abide with us in Heaven?" Romanus answered: "It is enough if I tell you that I see God: ask me no more: as we have heard, so have we seen, in the city of the Lord of Hosts." He vanished, and shortly afterwards Thomas wrote down in his notebook: "Therefore it is by specular vision that the Blessed see God."

What he meant by this no one has ever been able to discover. Not all his visions appear to have been valid, but toward the end of his life they came in increasing numbers. On the feast of St. Nicholas, in December 1273, he had a long ecstasy while celebrating Mass. He never explained what was revealed to him, but from that hour, in the words of William de Tocco, his biographer, "he suspended his writing instruments." His secretary Reginald of Piperno urged him to resume his task. He answered: "I cannot; such things have been revealed to me that what I have written seems but straw." Just before Christmas he spent a week with his sister, Marietta Countess of Severino, but all he could speak of was the joys of life everlasting.

He was ill when he returned to Naples. He had hoped to stay there, but Pope Gregory summoned him to attend the Council of Lyons, and toward the end of January, with two friars, he set out on his last journey. Years before he had marched across the Alps without difficulty. Now, though he was only forty-eight, his body had been weakened by fastings and mortifications: he was in no shape to make an arduous journey. On a mountain road near Terracina he stumbled and fell against a fallen tree. While he was recovering, his secretary begged him to continue the journey on the grounds that he would receive the Cardinal's hat, like Bonaventura, as soon as they reached Lyons. "What is that to me?" Thomas answered. "Rest assured I shall never be anything but a simple religious all my life."

Italy was dotted with castles belonging to his relatives. His strength failing, he was taken on muleback to the castle of his niece, Countess Francesca Ceccano, at Maienza. It was Lent. The doctor asked whether there was any food he would cherish. Thomas sighed. "I have several times eaten herring in France, but I believe it is rare and dear in these parts." By luck herring were found at the bottom of a fisherman's creel of sardines. "Where do they come from?" Thomas asked, when Reginald had prepared them. "From God," Reginald answered. Thomas was too weak to eat them, or perhaps he regarded them as a delicacy, which therefore should not be eaten in Lent. A few days later, having said Mass twice in the castle, his strength a little greater, he went on his way toward Lyons, but he fell ill again a few miles further on, in sight of the Cistercian Abbey of Fossa Nuova. It was February 10, 1274. He knew he was dying. As he was carried through the cloisters he repeated the words of the Psalmist: "This is my rest forever: here I shall dwell, for I have chosen it." They laid him down in the abbot's cell, heaped small fires of faggots around him, and were silent when he complained: "Why should holy men carry wood for my fire?"

At his request they read to him as he lay dying the Song of Solomon. He dictated a rambling commentary on some of the verses, and then at the words: "Come, my beloved, let us go forth into the fields," he fainted. The Viaticum was brought to him. Lying in the arms of his secretary, he said: "I receive Thee, ransom of my soul. For love of Thee have I studied and kept vigil, toiled, preached and taught. Never have I said word against Thee." He said a little later: "If I have received more graces and lights than other doctors who have lived a long while, it is because the Lord wished to shorten the days of my exile, and to take me the sooner to be a sharer in His glory, out of a pure act of mercy. If you love me sincerely, be content and comforted, for my own consolation is perfect." He died in the early morning of March 7, at the age of forty-eight or forty-nine.

In one of the few letters of Thomas which have come down to us, he wrote to a novice who had asked for advice:

I exhort you to be chary of speech, and to enter the conversation room rarely. Embrace purity of conscience, pray unceasingly, love to remain in your cell if you would be led to the mystic wine cellar. Be loving to all. Do not bother yourself unduly about the doings of others, nor be familiar, since too great familiarity breeds contempt and easily leads away from study. Do not join in the doings and conversations of the worldly. Do not roam outside the monastery walls. Give an account to yourself of your every word and action: see that you understand what you hear:

never leave a doubt unsolved: lay up all you can in the storehouse of memory. Seek not the things which are beyond thee.

Almost it is a self-portrait, but the trap is sprung in the last sentence, for Thomas had deliberately attempted to seek out the nature of God and, though he was humble, he was also proud. He made efforts to drown his pride, but was not wholly successful; and the *Summa Theologica*, that extraordinary document in which the nature of all things is examined under 512 questions and 2,658 articles, is a monument both of his humility and of his pride.

This strange work in which God is schematized resembles Gregory's *Moralia* in that it combines the most amazing insights with the most desultory and cursory examinations. He could not always be brilliant, but he was brilliant a sufficient number of times to make the *Summa* an intensely exciting work of art. To read it is to share the same emotions one experiences when listening to a Bach fugue. Everything is in its appointed place, precise, perfect, logical. The first part (*God in Himself and as Creator*) deals in rigid analyses with demonstrations of the proof of God's existence, His attributes, the nature of the Trinity, the six days of Creation, the Angels, and lastly Man. All this is set forth in 119 questions subdivided into 584 articles. The second part (*God as the End of All Things*) is further subdivided into two books known as *The First of the Second* and *The Second of the Second*. They deal with man's advance toward the Vision of God, with morality, the passions, sin, the theological and moral virtues, God's Law, and His Grace. Altogether they comprise 303 questions subdivided into 1,535 articles. The third part (*God as Redeemer*) treats of Christ, the Redemption, Incarnation, Baptism, Confirmation, the Eucharist, and Penance—in the middle of the discussion on Penance it abruptly breaks off, and at this point the Oxford manuscript says: "Here Thomas died. O death, thou art accursed!" This third part comprises 90 questions subdivided into 539 articles. The first part was written in Rome over a period of two years, the second part in Bologna and Paris over a period of five years, and the uncompleted third part was written in Naples.

It is necessary to speak of the *Summa* mathematically, because it is a profoundly mathematical book. There are great flashes and coruscations of excitement in it, moments when mathematical symbols seem to hold their breath and await a revelation, but for the most part it is closely logical, and it is at least conceivable that a translation into mathematical symbols would make easier reading. Thomas had no gift for irony: when he quoted in the introduction of the text: "As unto little ones in Christ, I gave you milk to drink, and not meat," he seems to have been at least *tending* toward irony. One might well ask, if the *Summa* is milk, what in God's name does the meat look like?

To understand the *Summa* it is best to bear in mind all that commanding generals mean by strategy, tactics, logistics. Though the arguments are presented for both sides, these arguments have nothing in common with lawyers' briefs. The war is fought with strength and skill, with invisible reserves which can be brought up whenever desired, and when the enemy territory is occupied, it is not destroyed but made to serve the purpose of the commander.

Yet in its essentials the *Summa*, like war, is simple enough. Certain essential weapons are sharpened and employed for a large number of different purposes. Thomas relies implicitly on Aristotelian dialectic, but his arguments are presented in a form which Aristotle would never have recognized. First he states the objections, then the truth as he knows it and as it is revealed by the Fathers and by Scriptures, and then he offers replies to the objections. First he subtracts the negative figures, then he gives the total sum, then he adds the positive figures. There is an element of illogicality in the arrangement, and the explanation seems to lie in the privileged place of the middle position in medieval minds, for it is in the middle of the argument that he places the final truth as he knows it.

Let us reproduce his analysis of the question: "Whether

the essence of God can be seen with the bodily eye." He answers:

Objection I. The essence of God can be seen by the bodily eye, for it is written: *In my flesh I shall see God* (Job xix, 26), and *With the hearing of the ear I have heard Thee, but now my eye seeth Thee* (Job xlii, 5).

Objection II. Further, Augustine says: *The eyes of the glorified have a greater power of sight . . . and see even incorporeal things.* Therefore the eyes of the glorified can see God.

Objection III. God can be seen in vision, for it is written: *I saw the Lord sitting upon a throne* (Isaiah vi, 1). But such visions originate from the senses, and therefore God can be seen in a vision of the senses.

I answer that it is impossible for God to be seen by the corporeal eyes, or by any sense of power of the sensitive part of the soul, for such powers derive from corporeal organs. The act is proportioned to the being whose act it is, and since no power of the senses may go beyond corporeal things, God, who is incorporeal, cannot be perceived by the senses, but only by the intellect.

Reply to Objection I. The words, *In my flesh I shall see God* do not mean that God can be seen with the eye of the flesh, but man existing in the flesh after the resurrection will see God, and so with the words: *Now my eye seeth Thee*, which are to be understood as referring to the eye of the mind.

Reply to Objection II. Augustine himself comments on the words: *The eyes of the glorified have a greater power of sight . . . and see even incorporeal things.* He says: *We shall see the new heaven and the new earth, not as we now perceive intellectually the invisible things of God, but as we see the men among whom we live, and we do not need to believe they live, for we see them living.* So it follows that the glorified see God as now our eyes see the lives of others.

Reply to Objection III. The essence of God is not seen in a vision of the imagination, but the imagination receives an image of God; and so, in the same way, the divine Scriptures metaphorically describe divine things by means of sensible objects. (Thomas Aquinas, *Summa Theologica*, I, Q. 12, Art. 3.)

As it stands, the argument has the appearance of a deliberate weighing of issues rather than of a logical process: and in fact all Thomas's arguments are of this kind. The logic goes by default: what remains is an attempt to grope with the human understanding. He calls Augustine to his aid, and he is forever calling other Fathers to his aid; and it is significant that he quotes most often from Dionysius, the bewildering genius who wrote *The Divine Names*, a strangely convincing account of all the majestic attributes of God and the angels. Just as Gregory used his daily sermons on the Book of Job as an excuse for commenting on all the conjunctions of God and man, so Thomas employs the strict form of his argument to say those things which are closest to his mind. The *Summa* is many things. It is an attempt to put some kind of order into men's minds, an attempt to explain God and the universe, an attempt to introduce a Christian logic into a theme which defies logic: it is also the commentary of Thomas's own life, the daybook of his passing thoughts. When he talks of love, he is also talking about *his* love. When he talks of angels, he is talking about the angels he knows or has faith in. What is logical in his method is supremely dangerous. He was the first, or among the first, to talk of "the will which wills itself," so founding a whole school of philosophy which believed in the disembodied will. "In a certain sense," said Descartes, "the disembodied will may be regarded as infinite." Honest John Locke replied: "There is no such thing as the disembodied will, there is only the human will, and none other." John Locke had not solved the problem, for he avoided inquiring into the nature of the will of God. Yet there were always dangers in the theories of the disembodied will, in the will which moved by its own accord—where? whence? how? "The will," said Thomas, "moves itself to will the means." On these Himalayas the will is sometimes lost in the snow-mists.

When Thomas employs the *Summa* simply to state his most intimate thoughts, he can be extraordinarily exciting. An anthology derived from Thomas could be as exciting as an anthology derived from Augustine. There are moments when he is the pure humanist. "Man," he says, "is bound by a kind of natural debt to live with others merrily [*ut aliis delectabiliter convivat*]." He notes in passing that even in the state of innocence there would be enjoyment of sex. He offers no fundamental objection to sexual pleasure; and he says of the blessed innocents that their pleasures would be all the greater. "Some say they would have less pleasure; I answer that the purer the nature, the greater the pleasure." He is superb when he talks of *caritas*, the holy love which St. Paul discussed at great length:

He who wills to enjoy the gift of loving is perfect when he loves as much as he is able. For then the whole heart of a man is borne toward God, and this is the perfection of the love of heaven (*caritas patriae*), unattainable here by reason of life's infirmities which do not allow us to meditate upon God all the time. So too, by loving, a man may strive to keep himself free for God and things divine, putting other matters aside, save as life's needs require, and this is the perfection of love, possible in this life, yet not for all who love. Then there is the way of loving which consists in habitually setting one's heart on God, so that one thinks and wills nothing contrary to divine love: and this grace is common to all who love. (Thomas Aquinas, *Summa Theologica*, II, ii, Q. XXIV, Art. 8.)

This is not quite as Thomas wrote it. I have stripped from it the terrible little phrases that Thomas constantly employs: *In the first place, in the second place, in the third place*. They add nothing; they conceal the poetry; and words like *So too* and *Then* serve the purpose equally well.

He is always finding trinities and triplets. He will divide God's beauty into its three attributes for no better reason than that he likes the number three, until one could almost cry out against the pervasive influence of the number which haunted Thomas all his life. He is in love with God, and sometimes he will forget that God is a trinity: sometimes God is simply perfect beauty, the most beautiful of beings, "with whom is no variableness nor shadow of turning," permanent, beautiful in Himself, perfect word and perfect art. Baudelaire speaks somewhere of "the immortal instinct for the beautiful which makes us consider the world and all its pageants as a glimpse of, a correspondence with, Heaven," and Thomas is almost content to prove the existence of God by appealing to the incredible beauty of the universe.

As one reads through the daybook, there is heard a familiar tone: the voice of the Psalms coming from a long way off. He does not quote the Psalms often, but occasionally and for no apparent reason the familiar cadences appear, breaking across the formal precision of the schoolman who proposes to solve every question by dividing it into three parts. It is hardly possible to say where these cadences begin or where they end: only we know they are there. And then sometimes, just as muted, there come vibrant passages which seem to speak with the authoritative voice of the Gospels, as when in his sermon *On the Body of Our Lord* he declaims: "He gave us men for the refreshment of our souls the bread of angels. . . . On the breaking of the bread Thou art not broken, nor art Thou divided: Thou art eaten: and like the Burning Bush Thou art not consumed." It is characteristic of him that he quoted from St. Hilary in his *Catena Aurea*: "The Lord, having taken upon Him all the infirmities of our body, is then covered with the scarlet-colored blood of all the martyrs." Though too often he hypostatized abstractions, he could write when it suited him vividly, with a sense of color and drama; and even when he spoke of the angels and was concerned with the problem of their effective will, he wrote poetically:

Angels grieve neither over the sins nor the punishment of men. For, as says Augustine, punishment and grief arise only from what contravenes the will. But nothing happens in the world contrary to the will of the angels and the blessed. Their will is entirely fixed upon divine justice, and nothing takes place in the world save what takes place according to their command. And so, in brief, nothing takes place in the world contrary to the will of the blessed. (Thomas Aquinas, *Summa Theologica*, I, Q. CXIII, Art. 7.)

He could write just as poetically concerning the nature of man's ultimate felicity:

The ultimate felicity of man lies in the contemplation of the truth, for this is the sole action of man which is proper to man alone. This alone is directed to nothing else, as an end, since the contemplation of truth is sought for its own sake. But for perfection of contemplation soundness of body is needed, to which all the arts of living are directed. Then too there is required quiet from the disturbance of the passions, to which one comes through the moral virtues and prudence; and quiet also from tumults, to which end all rules of civil life are ordained; and so, if rightly conceived, all human affairs seem to serve the contemplation of truth. (Thomas Aquinas, *Summa Philosophia Contra Gentiles*, III, 37.)

Finally, the great doctor was not always wholly serious, and he could joke wryly about his own dreams. He relates how a man hardly dreams at all when he falls into a dead slumber, but inconsequential dreams do appear when the sleeper sleeps less heavily, and when he sleeps very lightly, "if he is a sober man and one gifted with a strong imagination," then he may enjoy consecutive dreams, especially toward the end of sleep. Sometimes a man dreams in terms of logical arguments. Unfortunately, "if he syllogizes when asleep, when he wakes up, he usually finds a flaw in the argument." Thomas's article which includes his dissertation on heavy sleepers occurs in the *Summa Theologica*: the title of the article is "Whether the judgment of the intellect is hindered through suspension of the sensitive powers."

The glory of Thomas was that he took the whole universe into his purlieu. He had said at the beginning of the *Summa*: "In the sacred science everything is contemplated from the standpoint of God, and the content of this science is in part God Himself and in part other beings in as far as they are ordained unto God as unto their beginning and end," but by this phrase he had meant no more than that theology was concerned with all events as they occurred between the topmost height of Heaven and the bottommost pit of Hell. Later, but not much later, Dante would perform the same service in the *Divine Comedy*. In the *Divine Comedy* Dante introduced himself as the protagonist. Thomas desired to efface himself. He did not succeed, but his efforts were heroic. From the very beginning he seems to be saying: "It is not I, but the order, the harmony, the beauty of the universe which is speaking." It was a heroic performance. No one followed him. By the time he was dead theology was becoming as intricate as the sciences of our own time, so voluminous that no one could write about its totality because no one could possibly read all the books or spare the time to study all the problems involved. In this sense he was the last of the Fathers, and since the first was Paul, we see how the wild sapling grew into a forest.

Francis had denied the books, but the books remained. It was as though Thomas were saying: "There may be a burning of the books, therefore I have placed all that is known into my *Summa*."

Like all the other Fathers of the Church, Thomas stands out at a time of crisis. He placed his stamp on his age, but there was a desperate tranquillity within him: a man does not write a *Summa Theologica* except as a bastion and with the consciousness that desperate measures are needed. He was shoring up the faith, and he could not do otherwise: his enemies were heresy and all the subtle reasonings of the scholastics who refused to believe implicitly in the mercy of Christ. It is doubtful, however, whether he valued the *Summa* highly. It attempted perfection, and perfection is dangerous, if only because it is never attained except in Heaven. "Dear brother Leo, God's little beast," said St. Francis, "if a minor friar were to speak the language of the angels and raise to life a man already four days dead, write it well that even in so doing perfect joy is not to be found." The only joy, the only perfection lay in God; and Thomas was content that it should be so; and there is a sense in which all his work was simply a toying with the name of Jesus.

So it was, perhaps, with all the Fathers. They came as close as men dare to understanding the workings of God, but always there is a moment of retreat, and sometimes they tell us more when retreating than when leading the assault. They gave strength to the West, but it should not be forgotten that they derived their roots from the East. Augustine sharpened his mind against a Persian heresy; the historian who forgets Jerome's stay in Jerusalem and Gregory's in Constantinople would be in error. The flood came from the coasts of Syria and Asia Minor. All our Christian habits of thoughts partake of the East; our hymns derive from Egypt as well as from the chants of the Babylonian priests; our forms of prayer and even our doctrines are derived from shadowy sources which emerged long before the emergence of Christ. Christ crystallized them. Then afterwards, as the religion moved toward the West, they were crystallized afresh, not only by the Fathers but by the martyrs and by all the worshipers in their own way: but the Fathers left the greater impress. So it is that Christianity remains a marriage between the active principle of the West, believing that all things are real and tangible, or can be made so, and the passive principle of the East that regards the world as illusion, puts meditation and withdrawal and detachment above material success, and considers eternal life more important than human.

But it was the merit of the Fathers that they went further than performing a marriage. They went hunting after absolutes; they gave shape and distinction to western civilization; they fought the barbarians; they gave grace and meaning to the word "man." Again and again in the Fathers we come upon their reverence for "man," not as some abstract thing, but as the very real possessor of an immortal soul. Man in the words of St. Bernard is *celsa creatura in capacitate maiestatis*: every man was touched with majesty: every man's dignity must be upheld: he was part of the breath of God, and he was infinitely beloved by God. Spinoza invented a harsher law when he declared: "He who loves God cannot expect God to love him in return." To the Fathers, God's love was something to be expected by the mere fact that a man was a man.

At a time of distress and crisis we look in vain to the Fathers for any easy solutions to our doubts. They were not men who trafficked in ready answers. They raged against the evils of their times and they hoped there was time enough to erect in the world a city which would be pleasing to God, and often they failed, and all were human. It is their spiritual dignity, their sense of adventure, and their sense of the brotherhood of man under God which should commend them to us now. Today, as in the time of the Fathers, "we wrestle not against flesh and blood, but against principalities, against powers, against the rulers of the darkness of this world. The weapons of our warfare are not carnal, but mighty through God to the pulling down of strongholds."

❧ CHRONOLOGICAL TABLE

A.D.	
c. 30	Death of Christ.
c. 54-64	Work of St. Paul.
70	Fall of Jerusalem.
c. 92-101	Clement, Bishop of Rome.
c. 100	Death of St. John the Evangelist.
c. 110	Martyrdom of Ignatius.
c. 160	Birth of Tertullian.
c. 155	Martyrdom of Polycarp.
c. 165	Martyrdom of Justin.
177	Marcus Aurelius orders persecution of Christians.
c. 202	Death of Irenaeus.
c. 193	Conversion of Tertullian.
c. 210	Birth of Cyprian.
249	Cyprian, Bishop of Carthage.
250-251	Decian persecution.
257-258	Persecution of Christians by Valerian.
258	Martyrdom of Cyprian.
	Army of Valerian destroyed by Shapur I.
261	Gallienus issues edict of toleration.
303	Persecution of Christians by Diocletian.
c. 309	Saint Antony founds monachism in Egypt.
311	Edict of toleration by Galerius.
330	Founding of Constantinople.
337	Death of Constantine.
c. 339	Birth of Ambrose at Treves.
c. 342	Birth of Jerome at Strido.
354	Birth of Augustine at Thagaste.
359	Birth of Gratian.
361	Gregory ordained presbyter.
363	Death of Julian.
364	Valentinian I elected Emperor of the West, with Valens Emperor of the East.
366	Damasus I becomes Pope.
367	Gratian elected Emperor at Amiens.
370	Ambrose appointed Governor of Aemilia-Liguria.
374	Death of Auxentius, Bishop of Milan. Baptism of Ambrose, and his consecration as Bishop of Milan.

375	Death of Satyrus and Valentinian I. Valentinian II proclaimed Emperor. Goths cross the Danube.
383	Gratian murdered at Lyons.
384	Death of Pope Damasus I. Augustine goes to Milan as professor of rhetoric.
385	First executions for heresy.
386	Invention and translation of SS. Gervasius and Protasius. Jerome settles in Bethlehem.
387	Baptism of Augustine, death of Monnica. Invasion of Italy by Maximus.
390	Massacre at Thessalonica. Penance of Theodosius.
392	Murder of Valentinian II by Arbogast at Vienne.
393	Honorius created Emperor. Invention of relics of SS. Agricola and Vitalis.
394	Battle of the Frigidus. Suicide of Argobast.
395	Death of Theodosius the Great.
397	Death of Ambrose.
404	Death of Paula.
408	Execution of Stilicho.
410	Alaric the Visigoth captures Rome. Death of Alaric.
413	Murder of Count Marcellinus.
420	Death of Jerome.
c. 420	Anglo-Saxons begin invasion of Britain.
428	Count Boniface summons the Vandals to Africa.
430	Death of Augustine.
439	Vandals take Carthage.
450	St. Patrick converts Ireland.
c. 480	Birth of Benedict.
481	Schism between Rome and Constantinople.
493–526	Reign of Theodoric in Italy.
518	End of schism between Rome and Constantinople.
523	Execution of Boethius.
527–565	Reign of Justinian.
529	Closing of the Schools at Athens. Founding of monastery of Monte Cassino.
533	Belisarius conquers North Africa.
537	Rededication of Santa Sophia.
c. 540	Birth of Gregory the Great.
543	Totila lays siege to Rome. Death of Benedict.
546	Rome taken by the Goths.
547	Rome recovered by Belisarius.
554	Narses appointed Viceroy of Italy.
568	Lombards invade Italy.
570	Birth of Mohammed.
573	Gregory appointed Prefect of Rome. Death of Narses.
578	Gregory ordained "Seventh Deacon."
582	Death of Emperor Tiberius.
586	Gregory returns to Rome from Constantinople.
597	St. Augustine, the Benedictine monk, lands in Kent.
602	Fall of Emperor Maurice and coronation of Phocas.
604	Death of Pope Gregory the Great.

622	Mohammed's flight from Mecca to Medina.
628	Heraclius defeats Persians.
632	Death of Mohammed.
638-650	Arabs conquer Mesopotamia, Egypt, and Persia.
673	Arabs attack Constantinople.
713-34	Arabs conquer all Spain except Asturias.
717-18	Siege of Constantinople.
720	Arabs in Narbonne.
732	Arabs defeated by Charles Martel.
764-71	Persecution of image-worshipers.
772-804	Saxon wars.
778	Roncesvalles.
789-809	Harun al-Rashid.
789	Irene restores images.
800	Coronation of Charlemagne at Rome.
843	Treaty of Verdun, dividing the dominions of Charlemagne.
871-901	Reign of Alfred the Great.
918	Henry the Fowler King over the German duchies.
962	Otto the Great crowned Emperor at Rome.
987	Hugh Capet in Paris.
1061-1091	Normans settle in Sicily.
1066	William the Norman in England.
1079	Birth of Abélard.
1091	Birth of Bernard.
1095	Council of Clermont.
1096-1099	First Crusade.
1098	Founding of Cistercian Order.
1100-1200	Emergence of cities as center of freedom: slavery disappearing.
1128	Council of Troyes. Founding of Order of Templars.
1142	Death of Abélard.
1147-1149	Second Crusade.
1152	Frederick Barbarossa becomes Emperor.
1153	Death of St. Bernard.
1154	National unity of England under Henry II.
1182	Birth of Francis.
1189-1192	Third Crusade.
1215	Magna Charta.
1224-1243	Mongol-Tartar invasion of Russia.
c. 1225	Birth of Thomas Aquinas
1226	Death of Francis.
1245	Thomas Aquinas arrives in Paris.
1263	Thomas Aquinas attends Chapter-General in London.
1265	Birth of Dante.
1274	Death of Thomas Aquinas.

❧ INDEX